TAILOR'S PROGRESS

BENJAMIN STOLBERG

Tailor's Progress

THE STORY OF A FAMOUS UNION AND
THE MEN WHO MADE IT

An American Mercury Book

DOUBLEDAY, DORAN AND COMPANY, INC.
GARDEN CITY   1944   NEW YORK

THIS BOOK IS
STANDARD LENGTH.
COMPLETE AND UNABRIDGED,
MANUFACTURED UNDER WARTIME CONDITIONS
IN CONFORMITY WITH ALL GOVERNMENT
REGULATIONS CONTROLLING THE USE
OF PAPER AND OTHER MATERIALS

In Acknowledgment

THIS BOOK owes a great deal to a great many people. I want to thank those leaders of the International Ladies' Garment Workers' Union who appear in these pages for the generosity with which they have contributed of their time and their intimate knowledge. Other officers of the Union and many rank and file members, too many to mention, have been equally patient and helpful.

To Frederick F. Umhey, executive secretary of the International, to Simeon L. Hamburger, its general auditor, to Dr. Lazare Teper and Nathan Weinberg of the Research Department, and to Hannah Haskel, secretary to President David Dubinsky, my obligation is very great. They have met my constant quest for factual information with a keen understanding of what I wanted, which sometimes they knew better than I did.

Mark Starr, Fannia M. Cohn and Louis Schaffer of the Educational Department were ever ready to help. And I must also pay tribute to the editorial aid I received from my friend Clara G. Stillman and to the secretarial intelligence of Nettie Minkes.

But my greatest debt is to President Dubinsky, to Max Danish, the editor of *Justice*, and to Will Herberg, research director of the New York Dress Joint Board.

Dubinsky's knowledge of his own union and of American labor in general is immense. And intellectually (if not politically) his attitude toward it is utterly objective.

Max Danish, whose intimacy with the history of the International of the last quarter of a century is encyclopedic, gave me of his experience and knowledge with the comradely readiness of one journalist to another.

Finally, Will Herberg's research assistance, given unstintingly outside his working hours, amounted to real collaboration. By training a mathematician, by trade a student of labor and by avocation an eclectic savant, whose interests range from the Early Christian Fathers to the history of tap dancing and from prehistoric rock paintings to the latest infantry tactics, Will's outlandish catholicity of learning provided the recreational touch so essential to the dismal task of fact-gathering.

And here is the place for all good authors to state that not a soul in the world, dead or alive, is responsible for any opinions, interpretations or facts that can be found in their work. This is true for this book in the simple sense that no one but myself is responsible for my decisions as to what facts to choose, what interpretation to put on them, what opinions to derive from them and what prejudices to cherish. But it would be rank ingratitude for the historian of a living institution to claim that none of the hundreds of people whom he has pumped for all they are worth—and who gave him gladly of their wisdom and folly—have failed to contribute to his understanding of that institution. On the contrary, I hope that this book reflects not only my own responsibility but also the influence of the men and women who have helped to build a great American union.

BENJAMIN STOLBERG

March 1944
New York City

Contents

Prologue to an Industry

THE WORLD'S oldest trade is tailoring. As soon as Eve ate of the apple and sensed the possibilities of modesty she began to worry about clothes. For once social science and sacred writ see eye to eye: dress originated in the game of sexual coyness and attraction. In the balmy air of Paradise Eve was not afraid of catching cold. The fig-leaf apron is the symbol and the source of style.

In His anger at Eve's provocative demureness, so sketchily suggested, the good Lord Himself became the first cloakmaker. "Unto Adam also, and to his wife, did the Lord God make coats of skins, and clothed them." Then He deported them from Eden for having lost their innocence, a loss which with Freudian astuteness He identified with the beginning of knowledge—and of trouble. Ever since then mankind has had to clothe itself for seasonal protection as well as for allure, for utility as well as style. And men have had to make their garments in the sweat of their brow. The problems of style, of season and of laboring conditions —or, more fundamentally, the problems of vanity, of man's struggle with nature and his struggle in society—are still the major problems of the needle trades.

That is why in literature, from the Bible to *Sartor Resartus*, the tailoring trade appears as the most absurdly human of all crafts. It is really more than a craft. When the plumber fixes the kitchen sink, that's that. But when the tailor fits a garment he must fit not only the figure of his customer but also the hidden man—his romantic illusions and his secret anxieties about his appearance to the world. The tailor has always been privy to the follies and self-deceptions of the race. Professor Diogenes Teufelsdröckh, Carlyle's philosopher of the needle trades, was pretty shrewd when he decided to study the story of mankind in the cut of its clothes and the nature of man with the eyes of a tailor. For the wisdom of the tailor, he thought, reveals the sorry farce of "our dislocated, hoodwinked, and indeed delirious condition of society."

THE TAILOR IN THE NEW WORLD

From prehistoric times until the first decades of the nineteenth century, when the Industrial Revolution finally caught up with the garment trades, tailoring was predominantly a household craft. In our own colonial period and during the early days of the Republic almost every family made their own clothes. Of course the well-to-do and modish patronized the custom tailor and the dressmaker, or imported their finery from abroad. But most people could not afford such luxuries. "It is computed in a number of districts," wrote Alexander Hamilton in 1791 in his *Report on Manufactures,* "that two-thirds or three-fourths or even four-fifths of the clothing of the inhabitants are made by themselves." It was not until the spread of Jacksonian democracy that the Common Man blossomed forth in "store clothes," the proud uniform of middle-class leveling.

The Jacksonian Era, from the late 1820s almost to the Civil War, saw the rise (and decline) of merchant capitalism, an economy characterized by small individual enterprise with a comparatively simple technology. In this country the rise of this economy was intimately bound up with the conquest of the frontier. It was a period of great venture, motility, expansion. A new society was in the making, proliferating armies of small businessmen and manufacturers, middlemen and clerks, artisans and homesteaders. Hordes of emigrants were moving West. Our rapidly spreading Merchant Marine absorbed thousands of young men. All these people on the move needed outfits, and the stores began to stock up with finished garments. The California Gold

Rush in 1849, and later the tremendous need for uniforms during the Civil War, finally established the men's clothing industry.

During this whole period, however, women's garments were still made at home for the most part, though in the big cities there was a busy luxury trade in custom-made apparel. But the commercial ladies' tailor had not yet become a manufacturer. Before the invention of the sewing machine by Elias Howe in 1846 the women's clothing industry hardly existed; in fact it hardly existed before the Civil War. It was the child of the Reconstruction period, which lasted from the end of the Civil War almost to the end of the century. The Civil War was the revolution which transformed our mercantile capitalism into industrial capitalism, into the highly competitive economy of Big Business, with an ever more complex technology. The economic leaders of the Reconstruction were the industrial titans who built the railroads and the oil and steel trusts. They were daring, able, unscrupulous, and wasteful. And they set the tone of ruthlessness in deadly competition and labor exploitation.

Into this strenuous and dynamic building of an industrial continent came the early women's garment manufacturers. There was nothing of the Rockefellers or Hills or Harrimans about them. Like their brothers in the men's clothing industry, they followed the old-style merchant capitalism of the Jacksonian Era. They had to. At base the two industries were very similar. The clothing store could grow into a factory but not into a trust. Both the men's and the women's clothing manufacturers were individual entrepreneurs, supplying a local market and catering to the demands for variety and novelty in style.

This incongruity between the mercantile habits of the clothing trades and the new industrial drives of the Reconstruction period fixed the manufacturers in a curious pattern of their own, which has lasted until very recently. They were always up to date in matters of style and in the tricks of merchandising. But they were always behind the times in productive efficiency. Their industrial methods were petty and haphazard, and they cared only for immediate profits. The industry became infested with hordes of contractors, subcontractors, jobbers—commercial parasites who kept the trade in a state of demoralization. And though the manufacturers inevitably introduced mechanical improvements, they never rationalized these improvements until the late 1930s. In short, for over half a century they remained peddlers in a highly industrial society. The only thing they imbibed from large-scale capitalism was a spirit of economic callousness toward labor. And even in this they lacked the impersonality of big industry. They fought and squabbled with their workers with all the informality of a family brawl. In the course of time the uninhibited exchange of recrimination and suspicion between boss and workers has developed into an art indigenous to the trade—boisterous, colorful and inimitably funny.

Most of the early manufacturers were German Jews who had come to this country in the wake of the liberal and revolutionary refugees of 1848. But they themselves were not inspired by the libertarian dreams of such forty-eighters as Carl Schurz, any more than they were influenced by the revolutionary capitalism of the Rockefellers. In Germany the Jews had been for many generations the principal dealers in both new and secondhand attire. When they came over they usually began as peddlers or retail merchants and gradually expanded into manufacturing. They were typical German *Kleinbürger*—industrious, conformist, steady, men of conventional commercial honesty, narrow outlook and petty good will.

Gradually between 1860 and 1880 they built up their businesses. Until 1860 the industry was too insignificant to be listed in the census, and in that year it reported only 188 plants, which employed 5,739 workers and produced a little over $7,000,000 worth of goods. But in the next twenty years the industry grew rapidly. By 1880 the number of shops had increased to 562, with 25,000 workers and an annual output of more than $32,000,000 worth of garments. During the first phase of the women's garment industry the tendency was toward comparatively large plants employing a hundred workers or more. Later these plants became known as "inside" shops because they farmed out none of their work. They made the whole garment, from cutting the cloth to the last finishing touches. And they marketed their own product through wholesale departments. But in time even the largest "inside" plants found it profitable to have some of their work done outside.

About 90 per cent of the workers were women and girls. The majority were English-speaking, native or Americanized. During the 1880s, however, the women in the industry were being rapidly edged out by men. The reasons were technological. At first the cutting was done by shears and the sewing by a treadle machine whose pedals worked up and down. Both operations could be easily managed by women, who formed the cheaper labor market. But in 1880 the cutting knife was invented. It could cut from six to eight thicknesses of cloth, and the operation required considerable strength. The women cutters were displaced by men, mostly Americans of Irish or German descent. A little later the so-called Shaver sewing machine came into use. In the Shaver machine the pedals worked forward and backward like those of a bicycle, and women were apt to catch their long skirts in the treadle. Women operators were now largely displaced by East European Jews, mostly from Russia and Poland, who had recently been coming over by the thousands.

The impact of the East European Jew on the garment industry was tremendous. He transformed it almost completely, in both its manufacturing and its labor aspects. The Russian Jews were very different from their German brethren—in their history, their outlook and, for that matter, in racial composition. For throughout known history the Jews have, of course, intermixed with the peoples among whom they lived, the racial purists among them to the contrary notwithstanding. The German Jews were a more or less homogeneous group. The Russian Jews, on the other hand, were a highly differentiated lot, bringing over the cultural, religious and politically sectarian divisions of their homeland. Czarist Russia in the eighties was already a Babel of dissident and revolutionary movements, all of which were reflected in this new immigration.

A significant and highly articulate minority among them were the revolutionary intellectuals and semi-intellectuals. Many of these arrived with full-fledged factional creeds which they proposed to apply without delay to the American Leviathan. Among them were orthodox socialists of the Marxist school, followers of Bakunin's violent anarcho-syndicalism or of Kropotkin's philosophical anarchism. Others drew their inspiration from Fourier's plan of segregating the human race into "phalanxes"—1600 people in each utopian beehive. Still others were disciples of the Comte de Saint-Simon, who advocated a social order run by industrialists and scientists working in a literally Christian spirit for the benefit of the poor. The calmer spirits among this new immigrant intelligentsia were members of ethical culture societies, or believers in Comte's positivism, an insipid rationalism quite in vogue in those days.

A few of these intellectuals—such as Morris Hillquit or Abraham Cahan, both of whom were to achieve distinction in our national life—came over with the basis of a sound formal education. But a good many of them were half-baked and semi-educated, vehemently misinformed and vociferously muddled. More often than not their early training had been of the orthodox Jewish variety, which in those days in Eastern Europe was really nothing but a mumbo jumbo of vulgar scholasticism. With this background, against which they had rebelled, it was no wonder that their radicalism often turned into a new orthodoxy, an equally hairsplitting body of prejudice to be defended with more heat than light. Today, as one looks back with the perspicacity of hindsight, it becomes clear that all these varieties of left-wing doctrine fundamentally reflected the Byzantine socialism, the mongrel mixture of Western Marxism and Eastern nihilism, which has characterized the Russian Revolution from Bakunin to Stalin.

All this may sound invidious; it is not meant to be. Generally speaking, these radical intellectuals were young enthusiasts, intoxicated by new ideas as old as the history of social misery. They threw themselves into the movement "to uplift the masses" and became the early agitators, the ferment which set these masses in motion. In this respect they played an essential and valuable role in the early movement of the garment workers. By the turn of the century the virulence of their bolshevistic prepossessions had become diluted by our free political atmosphere, and most of them turned to the democratic socialism of Eugene V. Debs and Morris Hillquit or to the benevolent anarchism of the co-operative movement.

Another group which rose from the new immigration, an equally if not more important group, were the self-educated workers who developed as trade union leaders. They were the practical officials who protected the infant labor movement in the garment trades against the furies of utopia. Having to rise out of the very processes of trade union organization, they of course appeared on the scene later than the agitators—in the nineties and in the first decade of this century. They were such men as Joseph Barondess, John Dyche, Abraham Rosenberg, Abraham Bisno, Benjamin Schlesinger, all of whom we shall meet in their role of union leaders, engaged in the daily ordeal of trial and error. This type of early bureaucrat also began as a socialist or anarchist or later as an IWW. But he was first and foremost a trade unionist, whose business tended to wean him from doctrinaire obsessions. Usually he stayed on in his political church, voted the Socialist ticket, or sympathized with the philosophy of anarchism. But he was no partisan; in fact, what he hated most was the "party line." It introduced civil war into his union and interfered with collective bargaining.

The third group among the new immigrants consisted of a sprinkling of skilled craftsmen. Most of them were Hungarians who had learned the tailoring trade in the old country. They were the aristocrats of the garment trades, commanding high wages in the better shops. And they looked down on the horde of semiskilled cloak operators who crowded the sweatshops. They called them "Columbus tailors," because they had just discovered America and the art of tailoring. To the skilled craftsmen these "Columbus tailors" were practically scabs, debasing the quality of workmanship and the conditions in the shop, and permitting themselves to be shamefully exploited.

The rest were the "masses." They came from the town ghettos

or from the Tobacco Road hamlets of Galicia, Poland and the Russian pale. As their subsequent history in this country shows, they had great vitality and endurance, and were to furnish their quota of ability to our national life. They were to contribute and to receive a great deal by their struggles in American labor. But we must guard against the sentimental humbug of the professional immigrant lovers and folklore cultists who have presented the early East Side as teeming with suppressed genius and poignant idealism. The American ghettos of the eighties and the nineties were picturesque because poverty and ignorance, if steeped in tradition, are always rich in human drama. But on the whole these masses were dark, illiterate and superstitious, like all the children of centuries of oppression. In the words of Morris Hillquit, who did as much as anyone to galvanize them, "they were dull, apathetic, and unintelligent." Many of them were in the grip of a semibarbarous and reactionary priesthood and of a bigoted racial isolationism. In the old country they had lived in that classless limbo of the ghetto, part ragged proletarian, part ragged bourgeois—hawkers, hucksters, cobblers, shoestring middlemen—all preying on each other's poverty.

Naturally they found it difficult to adjust themselves to the new American environment. The American enigma of political liberty infected by corruption, and of economic freedom degraded by labor exploitation—the characteristic complex of the Reconstruction period—had them baffled. In self-defense they crowded into new ghettos of their own making, in New York and Baltimore, in Philadelphia, Boston and Chicago. And they hardly dared leave their familiar warrens. (Indeed, most foreign-language groups have spent their first decades in this country in similar voluntary segregation.)

To venture beyond [writes Dr. Lewis Lorwin, the distinguished labor historian], and to seek work in the factories where "American girls" were employed, where English was spoken, where work was done on Saturday, was too difficult. It was much easier to work for someone who could be spoken to simply and who could initiate a "green hand" into the mysteries of the trade. In New York there grew up a sort of labor exchange in the district around Essex and

Hester Streets which became known as the "Pig Market." Many a newly arrived immigrant would come to this market and wait for a contractor in need of "hands" to come around and offer him a job.

What made the organization of the garment workers possible was the continuity of immigration, which went on without letup from the Russian pogroms of 1881 and 1882 until the outbreak of the first World War in 1914. And each new wave of immigrants found a more conscious labor movement than the preceding one. It all took time, because the East European Jew had little or no notion of modern industry and even less of organized labor. And he had not come to the Promised Land of wealth and freedom to become a laborer. To remain a worker after he got here frustrated his hopes and made him feel a failure. If he had to work in a shop, he at least tried to keep his children out of it. Those who had sufficient background attempted to enter the professions, and a good many of the intellectuals who started as workers in the shops sooner or later were lost to the labor movement in professional careers. Many more succeeded in becoming contractors or even manufacturers. It was not until 1914, when immigration practically ceased, that this progression from the working to the middle class came to an end, and enough garment workers accepted their status to stabilize their own trade union movement.

On the garment industry as a whole the effect of the new immigration was far-reaching. One result was industrial: the sweatshop. The other result was social: the beginning of a labor movement in the women's needle trades, which derived its militancy and its staying powers from the unconscionable exploitation of the sweatshop system.

THE SWEATSHOP

Between 1880 and 1890 the women's garment industry grew rapidly in volume and in diversity of finished goods. The total value of the output jumped from $32,000,000 in 1880 to $68,000,000 ten years later. The number of workers increased

from 25,192 in 562 establishments to 39,149 in 1224 shops.
Almost all the new workers were men, and three quarters of
them were in New York, always the center of the trade. Most
of them were cloakmakers, employed as sewing machine operators in the cloak and suit trade.

Even before 1880 the system of contracting had infected the
industry. During the eighties it spread like a fungus and by the
following decade it was a universal blight. The contract or "outside" shop arose when the large manufacturer, the owner of the
"inside" shop, farmed out the garments cut in his plant to be
made up elsewhere. The "outside" manufacturer, or contractor,
agreed to do each lot at so much per garment. There was no
standardization of prices or wages or shop conditions. It was an
industrial jungle.

The contractor might be a *Landsman* who came from the
same region or even the same village as his workers. He was
really one of them, almost as poverty-stricken as themselves.
Their relation was very similar to that of the tenant farmer and
his sharecroppers in the South today. Nine times out of ten the
boss had worked in another sweatshop long enough to save up
fifty dollars or less, which was enough to set him up in "business."
All he needed was to get a few sewing machines on credit—later
the workers had to supply their own machines—install them in
his own home, or in a near-by loft or cellar, and exploit himself,
his family and as many workers as he could use. They all worked
from sunup to late at night and lived in filth and wretchedness
all the year round. Dr. William M. Leiserson, in an unpublished
monograph written in 1908, has an excellent description of one
way in which the system operated. He points out that very few
skilled tailors got caught in the sweatshop racket; most of them
worked in the higher-priced inside shops. The sweatshop victims
were the green and semiskilled "Columbus tailors." In many
shops they worked under the so-called task system.

There would be [writes Dr. Leiserson], a team or "set" composed
of a Baster, Half Baster, Operator, Helper, Finisher, Half Finisher,
Trimmer, Bushelman and Presser. All these were paid by the week,
but the team had to turn out a certain amount of work every day.

The contractor took advantage of the absence of a union and constantly added to the day's task. Originally it had been nine coats a day. It rose to ten and fourteen, then up to eighteen and twenty. Men often came to work at 4 A.M. Ten o'clock at night would usually see the day's task done. But if not, the team would work till midnight or until their powers were exhausted. Sometimes they would have to finish in the morning the previous day's work, which might take till noon. Thus a man who had worked six days of fifteen to eighteen hours might get at the end of the week three and a half to four days' pay.

Weekly wages for the best operators were $18.00. But working according to the task system they would get $12.00. Other members of a team who should have earned $8.00 or $10.00 were paid $5.00 at the end of the week. In 1886 weekly wages for men were supposed to be about $15.00 and for women $8.00; but after working sixteen to eighteen hours a day for a full week, they could only finish about four days' tasks and they received pay for only four days.

As the system spread the competition among the contractors became more frenzied. Indeed in time the manufacturer no longer accepted competitive bids. He just set his own price, for he could always find some contractor to snap it up. Naturally the contractor passed on each cut in prices to his workers by forcing down their wages. There seemed to be no bottom to this process of economic degradation. Even where the task system did not prevail, wages and conditions were just as miserable. Boston cloakmakers, mostly women and girls, had to slave to earn an average of six dollars a week the year round. Many of them were piece workers and were paid, according to the report of the Massachusetts Bureau of Labor for 1884, "fifteen cents for an entire cloak, raised, however, on protest, to twenty-five cents." It took three and a half hours to make a cloak.

In Baltimore, during the same period, women cloakmakers earned as little as three and a half dollars a week, working indefinite hours. In New York City wages for men fell from fifteen dollars a week in 1883 to six and seven dollars a week in 1885, and women earned from three to six dollars. In 1882 a Chicago cloakmaker could earn about fifteen dollars a week during the busy season, but by 1886 he was lucky to make twelve, and women earned only half as much. In 1893 the fastest cloak-maker could barely earn ten dollars a week, while the women earned between three and five.

A system of extortionate fines might reduce wages still further. "For instance," says the 1890 report of the New York Bureau of Labor Statistics, "before new spools of silk were given out, the old empty spools had to be returned; if they were lost, a fine of 50 cents had to be paid for each, the real value being nothing; for the loss of a 'number' ticket the fine was 25 cents; if an employee lost a 'trimmings' ticket before he had received the trimmings, he had to pay the full value of the trimmings, which were valued from $1.00 to $10.00. It was as though he had lost the trimmings and not the ticket." In most shops workers had to supply their own sewing machines or else "rent" them from the boss. When the machines were electrified, they had to pay for the power. Some shops forbade the workers to bring their lunches or to send out for beer, a universal custom in those days. Shop discipline began and ended in the spirit of petty persecution. Workers might be fired for any reason or none whatever, for arriving five minutes late or quitting five minutes early or going to the washroom.

Hours of work were completely unregulated. Even during the slack season fourteen or fifteen hours was considered a fair day. In the busy season people simply worked to exhaustion. Men and women would snatch a few hours' rest after midnight, sleeping on their "bundles" in the shop. There were, of course, humane contractors, many of them socialists or anarchists who kibitzed with their workers about the beauties of the "co-operative commonwealth." But these lovable Shlemiels always had to fold up and go back to the machine.

The sweatshops were located in the slum areas of the big cities where the people lived. They were veritable cesspools which infected the whole community—hygienically, morally, socially. During the sweatshop era it was estimated that one out of every three persons in New York's lower East Side slept in a room without a window or other ventilation. At dawn these crowded rooms were often turned into workshops. The already fetid air became heavy with the fumes of gasoline from the pressing irons, with the smell of damp wool, the sweat of the half-suffocated workers and the odors from the cookstove.

In one Chicago shop the factory inspector found twenty-nine people crammed with their machines into a room twenty by twenty-eight feet. In another, the shop of one Peter Darwut, the same inspector discovered four men and three women working in a room fourteen feet square in a low, dark, filthy basement. "Room contained four machines, stove with fire in it . . . air was intolerably bad; folding doors were open between this shop room and the living-room in which Darwut and wife sleep and eat and cook and keep boarders; the boarders (two) slept in low room off shop, unlighted and unventilated."

One New York cloakmaker turned one of his four rooms into a shop, and supposedly kept the other three as a home for his wife and seven children. But the shop was all over the place. "In the room adjoining the shop, used as a kitchen," the factory inspector reported, "there was a red-hot stove, two tables, a clothes-rack, and several piles of goods. A woman was making bread upon a table upon which there was a baby's stocking, scraps of cloth, several old tin cans, and a small pile of unfinished garments. In the next room was an old woman with a diseased face walking the floor with a crying child in her arms." Such conditions were not unusual. They were typical in all the garment centers of the country.

Inevitably these districts became social Gehennas. In Jeremiah's day Gehenna was a valley near Jerusalem where children were sacrificed to Baal and Moloch. The sweatshop system sacrificed the children of the poor to the same old gods of greed and vice. Disease and delinquency, crime and prostitution were familiar aspects of neighborhood existence. Little Augie and Lepke and Gurrah, the notorious industrial gangsters of a later day, were all brought up in the alleys of the East Side. Brothels were in the same tenement buildings with sweatshops and the homes of decent families. Daily some middle-aged woman would rush into the police station on Mulberry Street, frantic because her daughter had disappeared, which meant only one thing. In those days New York was wide open, and the corrupt Tammany machine worked with white slave rings, who in turn used the criminal elements among the sweatshop bosses as recruiting agents. Hundreds of young girls vanished in this way.

Health conditions were scandalous, even by the standards of that day. Aside from the ailments caused by overcrowding, ignorance and poverty, the sweatshop bred its own occupational diseases. Garment workers were notoriously subject to tuberculosis and other pulmonary disorders, to rheumatism and to skin diseases of all sorts, contracted from poisonous dyes in the cloth. The trade life of the garment workers was the shortest of any industrial group. Physicians diagnosed the infirmities of men in their thirties or forties as due to galloping "old age."

The contracting system had a devastating effect on the industry itself. It lost ground technologically, the standards of workmanship deteriorated, and the productive process became demoralized. The inside manufacturer disclaimed all responsibility for the evils of the sweatshop, insisting that he was not the employer of the workers in the contract shops. His cutters, he pointed out, were well paid. The contractor, the immediate employer, insisted with considerably more justice that he was completely at the mercy of the big manufacturer, who was forever forcing down prices. The public did not know and did not care. And the day of factory legislation was not to come for another generation. Some social amelioration was attempted by the pioneers of the settlement movement which, let us remember, began in the sweatshop sections of Chicago and New York. Jane Addams and Ellen Gates Starr opened Hull House on the South Side of Chicago where the garment workers lived, and Lillian Wald founded the Henry Street Settlement on the East Side of New York.

But real reform could come only from the united action of the workers themselves, from labor organization which could change conditions inside the industry, the center of infection. The early organization of the garment workers was, of course, a move-

ment for economic betterment. But it was and had to be a moral
crusade as well. It had to purge the social ravages of the sweatshop before trade unionism could take hold. At bottom this was
the reason why early trade unionism among the garment workers could appear in the guise of socialism or anarchism, as a
struggle for the good life not less than a movement for collective
bargaining.

FOUR BASIC CRAFTS: A CONTRAST IN TEMPERAMENTS

More than half a century has passed since the women's garment workers of the eighties and nineties made one attempt after
another—painfully, fumblingly and furiously—to organize.
Today the International Ladies' Garment Workers' Union is
one of the richest and most powerful unions in the country. And
it is organizationally by far the most complex. Its growth has
been accretive and empirical. It has been shaped by a rich
variety of political, social and racial backgrounds, all of which
are reflected in the structure of the union. But of course the main
reason for its intricate setup lies in the evolutionary complexity
of the industry itself, which is continually branching out into new
styles and lines, created by changes in public tastes and habits.
Each major innovation, such as slacks and sportswear, has required either a readjustment in existing crafts or the creation of
a new local union. Hence the International seems like a medley
of trades and jurisdictions. There are cloakmakers, dressmakers
and patternmakers, cutters, pressers and finishers, workers in
underwear, knit goods, embroidery, brassières, plastics—and
heaven knows how many more.

Even a union member can easily get lost in this labyrinth. The
outsider is utterly confused. It is therefore well to keep clearly
in mind that there are four basic crafts which form the backbone
of the union, have determined its course and structure and have
shaped its policies and outlook. These four basic crafts are the
cloakmakers, the cutters, the pressers and the dressmakers.

The Philosophers

The cloakmakers, more than any other group, laid the foundation for unionism among the immigrant garment workers during the last two decades of the nineteenth century. Traditionally they represent in the International its immigrant past—the folklore of the Jewish worker in America. Many of the radicals who stirred up the East Side tailors and started organizing them began as cloakmakers themselves.

The early cloakmakers' unions were always torn by doctrinal disputations and eschatological refinements. They forever debated and fought about how many ideological angels could stand on the point of a cloakmaker's needle. Unlike the cutter or presser, the cloakmaker is a philosopher. The average cutter or presser is a trade unionist, "pure and simple," without any theoretical undertows or utopian overtones. But the cloakmaker is the eternal Sartor Resartus, trying to fit society into new patterns.

He is highly oral, racy and curious, a born kibitzer and folk commentator, full of yarns and stories to illustrate his point. In the early days he was way on the left: it was the cloakmakers who formed the bulk of the militant rank and file of the socialist and anarchist movements. But time has mellowed him: today he is usually a devout New Dealer. Yet for all his beliefs in some sort of collectivism, he is an incurable individualist. Authority does not impress him, and he knows no sacred cows. You've got to tell him the reason why—and then he has a better reason. He believes not only in free speech but in free vituperation, which doesn't make for a docile rank and file. In the course of their history the cloakmakers have followed some leaders through thick and thin. But even their fanaticism was voluntary and democratic; it was never of that mystical sort which is bred by demagogy and terror.

The cloakmaker's influence on the union cannot be exaggerated. The International is undoubtedly the most democratic of our large American trade unions. No leader of the International could be a dictator like John L. Lewis of the United Mine Workers or Sidney Hillman of the Amalgamated Clothing Workers.

President David Dubinsky has to win the support of the top leadership before he can have his way on important issues. And in the long run he has to popularize his policies with the rank and file as well. Of course no modern union could exist without bureaucratic domination, for reasons which it would take another volume to explain. But in the International at least the appearance of democracy is sincerely and scrupulously observed. And this is largely due to the tradition created by the cloakmakers.

The Realists

The cutter is a very different animal. He has always been among the most highly paid and skilled of the workers in this industry. In the early days a good many of the cutters were native-born, of Scotch-Irish or Irish or German stock. Uriah Stephens, founder of the Noble Order of the Knights of Labor, the dominant labor movement of the seventies, was a cutter; in fact Assembly No. 1 of the Knights was a cutters' local established in Philadelphia in 1869. As a group the cutters were little affected by the storms of doctrine which agitated the immigrant cloakmakers. They tended to be more conservative and realistic, and they looked down on the semiskilled "Columbus tailors" as the Holy Rollers of trade unionism. They believed in cutting the coat to fit the cloth.

Psychologically the cutters are a good deal like the skilled workers in other seasoned AFL unions, such as the cigar makers or printers. They are middle-class in outlook, like to live well, are good dressers and good poker players. On the whole they escaped the degradation of the sweatshop, for they usually worked in the big "inside" shops. After the turn of the century many immigrant Jews became cutters, but they too were highly skilled, made good wages, and though many of them were socialists they did not carry their socialism into union affairs. In effect they were pure and simple trade unionists. And they were apt to become quickly Americanized, not only in their habits and standards of living, but in the sense that psychologically they were living here. The "idealism" of the cloakmakers left them cold, and more of them were with Tammany Hall than with the Socialist party. The influence of the cutter on the International has been one of skeptical and sober realism, of sound opportunism based on the practical capacity to rise above principle for the good of the organization.

The Balagulas

The third important group are the pressers. In the days before the International they were recruited from the most ignorant of the immigrant community. They had to be physically quite powerful to handle the heavy irons, and they often acted as the strong-arm boys during strikes, protecting the girls on the picket line. A great many of them had been hucksters or teamsters or common laborers in the old country, where they were known in the Jewish communities as *Balagulas,* which connotes a husky, heavy, inarticulate and good-natured soul. They are still the real proletarians of the industry, workers without middle-class habits or ambitions. You will seldom find a clothing manufacturer who began his career as a presser.

They are now among the best-paid workers in the industry, because they work at piece rates, and modern machinery and the simple lines of today's garments make pressing a speedy operation. But in spite of his prosperity the average presser lives like a laborer. And all he demands of his leaders are practical benefits. He is not much interested in the educational or uplift-ing activities of the union. It is the presser who gives the International the proletarian and horny-handed touch which every union must have to keep in character.

The Romantics

The fourth great basic trade are "the girls"—the dressmakers. The girls appeared on the scene rather late, during the great shirtwaist makers' strike in 1909, which with characteristic romanticism they called the Uprising of the Twenty Thousand. Many of them were young Jewish women who had left Russia during the period of the first Russian Revolution in 1905—the dress rehearsal for the revolutions of 1917. Their radicalism was very different from that of the other garment workers, which stemmed from the theoretical and utopian socialisms of the eighties and nineties and which by this time had become Americanized into the industrial democracy of Debs and Hillquit. Their leaders were definitely revolutionary in outlook, deeply class-conscious, idealistic firebrands. It is well to remember that the Russian Revolution of 1905, half forgotten today, created a great wave of sympathy and enthusiasm among American liberals and progressives. This helps explain the public support of the strike of 1909 which established the dressmakers' union.

Besides, in industrial struggles the Poor Working Girl, our favorite national Cinderella, always has had the edge on her brothers in the sympathies of the public. When a cop on the picket line begins shoving a girl around, especially if she is halfway good-looking, she becomes a martyr then and there. In the strike of 1909 the dressmakers had the help of the suffragettes, of broad-minded clergymen, of social workers, of honest or publicity-hungry liberals, of most of the newspapers. Great society ladies like Mrs. O. H. P. Belmont and Anne Morgan came to their aid and college girls discovered that the shirtwaist makers were sisters under the skin. Naturally this Joan of Arc appeal was wanting in the pressers or the cloakmakers, who had to fight the cops without co-operation from society matrons and Wellesley brigades.

This subtle art of fusing social exaltation with the technique of sound public relations—the gift for combining the best features of Karl Marx and Edward L. Bernays—is still characteristic of the dressmakers. Whenever the union is down and out, as during the struggle with the Communists in the 1920s, the old red militancy blazes up again. But now that the International is powerful and prosperous, the revolutionary fervor of the dressmakers has become sublimated into a more generic idealism. They are always interested in progressive and humanitarian causes. They place a high value on educational activities, on culture with a capital C, and "the finer things in life." They have an exaggerated respect for intellectuals. They insist that the union must be more than a "mere" economic organization. They stress the need for sacrificial service to the union and exalt "the masses." And they demand from their leaders a demonstrative devotion to the ideals of labor to a degree that seems sentimental to the average man in the union.

All this does not mean that the dressmakers feel more deeply about their union than the cloakmakers or pressers or cutters. To the men the union is a marriage for life; to many of the girls it is only an affair of the heart. After all, they are less interested in the union than in marriage and a home, and the turnover among them is high. This is one of the reasons why they have developed few top leaders, though probably a more important reason is the general prejudice against women in high office, a prejudice just as strong among the feminine rank and file as among the male bureaucracy.

The influence of the dressmakers on the International has been especially important in its public relations. Such triumphs of the stage as *Pins and Needles,* or the superb pageants of working-class life produced by the union—indeed, all the cultural activities which have made the Ladies' Garment Workers famous —have been largely inspired by the dressmakers. These activities are the best kind of institutional advertising. But even more important has been the influence of this high-minded view of labor upon the public character of the International leaders. The International has been the one labor union to take a public stand in the American Federation of Labor against graft and racketeering. The romantic idealism of tens of thousands of young women was bound to play a part in bringing out a leadership which, whatever its faults, is neither cynical nor corrupt nor cheap.

These four crafts have complemented one another in shaping the International Ladies' Garment Workers' Union as an institution. And the union has had the good fortune to be guided at each critical phase of its development by a leader from that craft whose peculiar virtues it particularly needed.

Benjamin Schlesinger, who was president of the International from 1914–23, represented whatever was permanent and valuable in the immigrant past of the union, at a time when immigration was cut off and the social and racial composition of the union was changing rapidly. Today no more than a third of the members are Jews, and quite a few of these are native-born. Schlesinger personified the historic residues of the formative days of the union—its struggles with socialist and utopian programs, and its efforts to adjust to American life. Though these programs are now obsolete, they are nonetheless part and parcel of the spiritual heritage of the American ladies' tailor. Needless to say, Schlesinger was a socialist, an individualist, an opportunist—a cloakmaker.

In the 1920s the International almost went under in the "civil war" between the democratic trade unionists and the Communists. Morris Sigman, who was president from 1923–28, led the field against the Communists. He was tough, though not hard-boiled, utterly honest and fanatically logical, unbending, and proletarian both in his habits and his outlook. Sigman was a presser.

The New Deal enabled the union to recover from the civil war and enter a reconstruction period. The last decade has been one of growth, prosperity and power. It has required a sophisticated and up-to-date leadership, able to deal with new and confusing forces. Since 1932 David Dubinsky has been president. He is shrewd, alert and knowledgeable, and always realistic. By trade he is, of course, a cutter.

Nothing illustrates more characteristically and amusingly the contrast in the temperaments of these three men than their methods of dealing with the grafter who is bound to show up in any large organization. For years the police had to be bribed during strikes. Ordinary cops on the picket line rated anywhere from five to twenty dollars, while superior officers came higher. Such "expenses," of course, could not be itemized for the record. Therefore members of a strike committee, especially of the finance committee in an important strike, had to be absolutely reliable. But inevitably some chiselers managed to be elected to one of these committees.

Once, while Schlesinger was president, such a committee consisted of three union officials. One of these handed in as his day's unitemizable expenses ten dollars; the second reported fifteen dollars; the third member claimed to have dispensed four hundred dollars. The first two men went to Schlesinger and accused their colleague, whom they knew only too well, of corruption. Above all things Schlesinger hated a mess. He said quietly: "Let him have the money, get him off the committee—and *never* trust him again."

While Sigman was president a business agent handling strike funds presented him with an unitemized statement for twelve hundred dollars.

"Can't you make it cheaper, Charlie?" Sigman asked.

"All right, let's make it a thousand," said the union official.

"Oh, come on," Sigman urged. "Make it cheaper."

"Eight hundred."

Whereupon Sigman seized a brass inkstand and brought it down on the man's head. "Why, you lousy son of a bitch," he yelled. "How can you afford to lose four hundred dollars out of your own pocket?"

When Sigman was through with him, the man had to have five stitches taken in his head.

Dubinsky handles such problems very differently. Whenever there is the least question of a man's honesty, he thoroughly investigates. And if he is satisfied that the man cannot be trusted, he calls him into his office and hands him a prepared letter of resignation. "I'll have your resignation now," he says. And so far no one has had sufficient grounds to refuse.

The Conquest of Chaos

THE International Ladies' Garment Workers' Union was founded in 1900 after confused and desperate struggles which had extended over two decades. Its roots lead back to the immigration of the eighties and nineties. Even today the needle trades are referred to as "immigrant unions," especially by themselves. And indeed about 70 per cent of the members of the International are Italians and Jews, foreign-born or of the first American generation.

ALIEN INTO NATIVE

The term "immigrant" has many inherited connotations which are obsolescent and misleading. Immigration is a vanishing problem in American life, of interest mainly to those twin racketeers, the professional alien baiter and the professional immigrant lover, who batten on perpetuating the cultural divisions in our society. The fact is that unofficially since the outbreak of the first World War in 1914 and officially since the quota laws went into effect in the early 1920s, we have had no immigration to worry a country of our size. Of the foreign-born members of the International over 95 per cent have been here for a generation or more. They present no problem in Americanization. They are what they are—part of our national society: their ideas, their ways of doing things, their industrial problems are quite inconceivable elsewhere. Like the rest of us they are regional animals with an occupational stamp. They form a powerful section of a distinct American type: the urban, socially conscious trade unionist. For good or bad, this type of worker, with his European background, has exercised a deep influence on the development of the New Deal. And yet the New Deal is in many ways as characteristically American as were its milder forerunners—Populism, Bryanism, the Bull Moose movement and Woodrow Wilson's New Freedom.

So much then for the American woman's tailor as a type. The historian may, of course, find significance in the fact that Jewish and Italian workers came here later than the Pennsylvania Dutch or Scotch-Irish. Many of the garment workers still cling to the cultural remnants of their past. Many speak a jargon of English and Yiddish or Italian or Spanish and still read the foreign-language press. What is, however, historically completely false is the idea that the *unions* of these workers are in any sense alien. They are among the oldest in the AFL, indeed older than the AFL itself. They have participated notably in the various social and labor movements which have agitated American life since Reconstruction days. In other words, while many of the garment workers still retain their Old World habits and ways, in their trade union thinking they follow the American pattern.

There is another thing to remember. In relation to pre-Civil War labor our whole modern trade union movement is "immigrant." The Civil War was a revolution which not only changed the nature of American industry but broke the continuity of organized labor. Between the Civil War and the first World War over 30,000,000 people entered the United States, as many as were here when Lincoln took office. The vast majority of them were, of course, workers. They came in successive waves—from the British Isles and possessions, from Scandinavia and Germany, from Eastern and Southern Europe. These newcomers formed the basic labor market of our expanding industrial capitalism and they had little historic connection with the sporadic and primitive associations of the "mechanics" of pre-Civil War days. Naturally these immigrants reflected the cultures from which they came. Yet the labor movement they created was American because they built it from scratch in the American environment. And though this new movement had little connection with antebellum trade unionism, it nonetheless was profoundly influenced by native radical forces, such as Jeffersonian and Jacksonian democracy, Know-Nothingism and the various expressions of Populism.

The comparative recency of our whole trade union movement and the European influences in its earlier phases are not sufficiently appreciated.

Some time ago I wrote an article on William Green, who is certainly representative of American labor. But in studying his background, which is that of the United Mine Workers, it was startling to realize how British were the formative influences upon the miners' union. Almost all the founders, and the majority of the original rank and file, were either natives of the British Isles or first-generation British-Americans. And they represented in its purest form the tradition of the early labor movement among the Scottish, Welsh and English coal diggers. Green's father was English, his mother Welsh, both came from old mining families. They were pious almost in the fundamentalist sense and at the same time devout believers in the Christian socialism of Keir Hardie, founder of the British Labor party. Throughout the nineties William Green and his father and many of the old-time miners formed a socialist opposition within the AFL. Without this British socialist background the whole development of the United Mine Workers—its organization as an industrial union for instance—is incomprehensible. William Green and other old miners have this Fabian Christian socialism in their bones, no matter how much later influences have modified their outlook, just as the old cloakmakers have somewhere in their make-up an East European variety of Marxism.

Another great American union, the teamsters, has a radical Irish Catholic tradition, lower middle-class rather than proletarian. Their early background is deeply tinged by the Irish struggle for independence; and they have always been more wage- than class-conscious. Dan Tobin, president of the teamsters and one of the half-dozen most powerful labor leaders in the country, still has about him an unmistakable Fenian touch. To understand the history of the teamsters it is well to know something of the Irish revolution and of its alliance with the nationalist wing of the Catholic Church.

And of course the very symbol of American labor, as indigenous as the cigar-store Indian, was the cigar maker Sam Gompers, founder of the AFL and totem of "pure and simple" trade unionism. Yet his rich and fascinating personality had no old-American roots. He was born in London, a Dutch Jew of Spanish descent, went through a brief socialist phase in his youth, was a philosophical anarchist the rest of his life, and in his daily practice an inveterate campaigner for bread-and-butter unionism. Had he been as nativist as the leaders of the Knights of Labor or of the Greenback movement, he would have been far less effective in his day and age—and to that degree less American. For our trade union movement grew out of a conflict between Old and New World ideas which was finally resolved in terms of our national conditions and culture.

THE BATTLE OF THE ISMS

One of our favorite notions is that typically American movements—as against "imported" ones—have been free of theories and isms. The very word "ideology" sounds a bit alien to us. We pride ourselves on being practical and hardheaded and we flatter ourselves that we function on a trial-and-error basis, untempted by abstract principles and utopian programs. This notion is, of course, pure fantasy. No movement can arise without a basic theory to give it meaning and direction. The fact is that in America we have suffered from more isms, from transcendentalism to behaviorism, than any other great society.

For half a century after the Civil War the ideological drive behind our labor movement was anarcho-syndicalist. Labor was syndicalist in the simple sense that it believed that the workers should organize only in the economic sphere, and it was anarchist in its distrust of all government. Anarcho-syndicalism was indeed the traditional American attitude, the conception underlying both Jeffersonian democracy and Hamiltonian business enterprise; this national attitude animated capital no less than labor. Big business too demanded the right to build its syndicates—trusts—without "government interference" of any kind. Anarcho-syndicalism might range from the revolutionary anarchism of the IWW to the reactionary anarchism of the United States Steel Corporation under Judge Gary, but it was essentially the same social philosophy.

In this sense the two most indigenous labor organizations in our history were the Knights of Labor, who were the first to organize the women's garment workers, and the IWW, who a generation later exerted a considerable influence on these same workers. Both the Knights and the Wobblies were for One Big Union of all labor, against political action and against the state. The Knights began as radical, and wound up as conservative, anarcho-syndicalists; while the IWW throughout their career remained on the wildest left.

The great rival of the Knights, the American Federation of Labor, which rose in the eighties, was also an anarcho-syndicalist movement, only of a more conservative cast. Gompers proudly called himself a philosophical anarchist, an enemy of the busy and bureaucratic state. He too believed in the purely economic organization of the workers and in non-interference by the state in the struggles between capital and labor. He was opposed to the very idea of a Labor party. For years he fought all labor legislation, no matter how benevolent, even workmen's compensation. The main difference in theory between the Knights and the AFL was that the Knights believed in One Big Union of all workers, while the AFL believed in strictly autonomous unions for each craft. The main difference in practice was that Gompers was a shrewd, tough and flexible statesman, while the Knights petered out in militant and romantic futility.

THE SYNDICALISTS

The Noble Order of the Knights of Labor was founded in 1869 by Uriah S. Stephens, a garment cutter of Philadelphia. It grew rapidly and by 1873 the Order had over thirty "Assemblies" (local chapters) of carpenters, shoemakers, machinists and clothing workers.

The Knights, like all anarcho-syndicalist movements, appealed to the lower middle-class instincts in the worker rather than to the proletarian in him. The Noble Order was essentially a laborite version of the Know-Nothing movement. It was a secret society with an elaborate ritual and a penchant for fomenting unrest and disorder, which it was incapable of exploiting by sustained organizational effort.

In spite of their non-political attitude the Knights played with all sorts of political vemoments whose radicalism, like their own, stemmed from lower middle-class unrest. They supported various monetary reform cults, they co-operated with the free-land agitators, they played their part in the Single Tax, the Greenback and almost every other Populist movement of the time. And they were deeply involved with the socialist movement, whose most powerful support came from the garment workers. The reason we think of the Knights as so indigenous is that the America of the Reconstruction era was a land of wide-open economic frontiers, which is a natural breeding ground of anarcho-syndicalist rebelliousness. In Europe anarcho-syndicalism also flourished in industrially undeveloped countries—in Italy and Spain, and under various socialist disguises such as Bolshevism, in czarist Russia. In industrially developed countries like England or Germany working-class opposition was never anarcho-syndicalist but always more or less socialist.

When the industrial frontier in America began to close and the highly competitive trusts gradually gave way to monopolies, our labor movement began to throw off its anarcho-syndicalism, the classic radicalism of guerrilla warfare in an industrially immature society. It moved in an "un-American" socialist direction: it tried more and more to influence the state in its favor. Today's alliance of organized labor with the New Deal is the culmination of this historic trend. In this development the women's garment workers have played a more significant role than any other American union. And the reason is that among the Jewish immigrant workers of the eighties and nineties there were a great many social radicals of all schools, who fought out those issues in the microcosm of the East Side.

The Knights died because they could not adjust themselves to this transition. And the IWW, who a generation later represented the last spasm of militant anarcho-syndicalism in American labor, died in a paroxysm of violent frustration when the industrial frontier was closed once and for all after the first World War. Only the AFL survived. And the AFL survived because it could, and did, adjust itself to the evolution of American labor from purely economic action to political and social action as well. For all his "pure and simple" trade unionism, Gompers was shrewd enough to let the affiliated unions in the AFL mix in partisan and social politics. The AFL permitted socialist opposition within its own ranks, and the socialist trade unions played in the Federation the same role that Bryanism played in the Democratic party or the Progressives in the Republican party. The Gompers machine fought the socialists tooth and nail, but it adopted many of their planks. In every convention of the AFL His Majesty's Opposition were the socialist unions, some sections of the miners, the bakers, the machinists, the brewers, the milliners and especially the women's garment workers. The AFL was successful because it assimilated the conflicts of a long historical transition. And in no section of organized labor can we study these conflicts and their effects as clearly as in the history of the garment workers.

THE SOCIALISTS

The modern socialist movement in this country—as distinct from the utopian socialist colonies of pre-Civil War days—began with small groups of Marxists in New York, Chicago and San Francisco in the late sixties. They were made up almost entirely of German socialists, intellectuals and self-educated workers, many of them forty-eighters, refugees from the unsuccessful German revolution of 1848. In 1869 these various groups got together and joined the International Workingmen's Association, founded and dominated by Marx and Engels, and known to his-

tory as the First International. Within the next three years
French, Bohemian, Irish and native American "sections" were
organized, and in 1872 the American socialists held a national
convention and formed the North American Federation of the
First International. This Federation became very active in politics and in the trade unions. It supported strikes, nominated candidates for local office and endorsed many of the radical ideas
and movements of the moment.

In the meantime the historic contest between Marx and
Bakunin for the control of the First International in Europe had
come to a head. Michael Bakunin, the Russian aristocrat, was the
founder of modern terrorist anarcho-syndicalism, the spiritual
forerunner of Bolshevism. He almost succeeded in capturing the
First International, whereupon Marx decided to save it by the
simple device of transferring its headquarters from London to
New York. This was done in 1872 and the new secretary of the
First International was Friedrich A. Sorge, a forty-eighter and a
devoted Marxian disciple. The transfer was really intended to
kill the organization and the maneuver succeeded. The First
International died in a suicide convention in Philadelphia in
1876, and with it died its affiliate, the North American Federation.

But the young American socialist movement went marching
on—in all directions. It split and fissured for the next three decades, involving the trade union movement in its factional agonies.
Yet all through the years there was a steady socialist core which
survived and grew and profoundly influenced our labor movement. In 1876 the surviving socialist "sections" regrouped into
the Workingmen's Party of the United States, which a year later
changed its name to the Socialist Labor party. This was the first
real Socialist party in the country and lasted out the century. It
was an urban phenomenon, in fact largely concentrated in New
York City. And much of its support came from the rank and
file of the garment workers.

From its very beginning the Socialist Labor party was torn by
incredibly bitter factional feuds. During the 1880s the American
followers of Ferdinand Lassalle, the great German popular social-

ist leader, who believed in capturing the state and ignoring the trade unions, fought bitterly with the orthodox Marxists, who believed in using the trade unions as agencies for conquering the state. Then there were the various schools of anarchists and syndicalists who piled into the party in order to destroy it. But whatever their theories, the various factions fought each other for control both of the Knights of Labor and of the AFL. And just to complicate the picture the AFL and the Knights were engaged in mortal combat with each other. By the early nineties, the AFL got the upper hand and most of the scattered garment workers' unions went into the winning Federation, bringing with them their assorted ideologies.

DANIEL DE LEON

In 1890 the Socialist Labor party came under the influence of a single outstanding personality. Daniel De Leon was born in Curaçao in the Dutch West Indies in 1852. He claimed descent from Ponce de Leon, the seeker of the Fountain of Youth. Gompers supplied him with a less romantic genealogy. "De Leon," he told me, "came of a Venezuelan family of Spanish and Dutch Jewish descent with a strain of colored blood. That makes him a first-class son of a bitch."

De Leon was educated in a German *Gymnasium* and the University of Leyden, graduated with high honors from the Columbia Law School and became a lecturer in Latin-American diplomacy at Columbia. He was deeply influenced by Edward Bellamy's *Looking Backward,* and in 1886 he was active in the New York mayoralty campaign of Henry George, the inventor of the Single Tax. After that De Leon moved rapidly toward the left and in 1889 he joined the Socialist Labor party, of which he assumed leadership almost immediately.

De Leon was one of the great scholars of his day—jurist, historian, linguist and economist. Lenin considered him one of the first and greatest of all Bolsheviks. "De Leon was the only one," he said, "who added anything to socialist thought since Marx." Like Lenin, De Leon was an intellectual fanatic. But unlike

Lenin, he lacked all flexibility as a practical politician. In fact he lacked all common sense.

In its attempt to capture the trade unions the Socialist Labor party under De Leon's dictatorship used three successive strategies. (A generation later the communists repeated this pattern in their efforts to dominate the labor movement. And both attempts almost wrecked the women's garment workers.)

The first strategy, which lasted until 1895, was to "bore from within" the Knights of Labor and the AFL. De Leon himself joined the Knights and developed a large following, mostly among the garment workers. At one time he might have seized control of the Knights, had it not been for his inflexibility and personal vindictiveness. His main lieutenants worked within the AFL and almost succeeded in wrecking it. In 1894 they were able to unhorse Gompers from the presidency and to elect the miner John McBride by combining with the radicals in the United Mine Workers. (The next year Gompers was back in the saddle.)

De Leon's humorless and slanderous fanaticism made the strategy of boring from within impossible. He was incapable of working with anybody. And so he shifted to his second strategy, the policy of dual unionism. In 1895 he launched the Socialist Trade and Labor Alliance for the purpose of organizing rival unions under the totalitarian domination of the Socialist Labor party. This disruptive policy in time so alienated the more sensible socialists, especially the leaders of the garment workers, that they began to crystallize into a right wing. The Socialist Trade and Labor Alliance remained a paper organization. In short, the dual-union policy broke up not the trade union movement but De Leon's own party. A decade later De Leon and his simon-pure disciples made a third attempt to control American labor. They helped to found the IWW and for a brief time the Wobblies were able to capture some of the local unions of the women's garment workers in New York.

De Leon's bigotry and heresy hunts kept the Socialist Labor party in a constant state of upheaval and prevented it from growing. Even at its height it had no more than 6000 members, about half of whom were in the garment trades. But De Leon persisted in his policy of rival unionism and gradually the right-wingers in the party broke with him. Abraham Cahan, Morris Hillquit and Meyer London made contacts with several Midwestern socialist groups led by Victor Berger and Eugene V. Debs. Berger, who later became the first Socialist congressman, was all his life a moderate Marxist, while Debs, a man of great spiritual nobility and equally great intellectual confusion, developed in the course of years into a benign socialist rebel, the glorified Jimmy Higgins of the movement.

In 1897 the anti-De Leon leaders in New York opened negotiations for a merger with the Debs-Berger group. And after considerable maneuvering in which both sides sloughed off their more utopian contingents, the Socialist Party of America was founded in Indianapolis in 1901.

UNIONS AND FACTIONS

Unorganized workers cannot be organized without radical agitation, without a social program which would change society for their betterment. Hence we almost always find one or more radical ideologies behind initial drives to organize the workers. Missionary schools of thought—socialism, anarchism, syndicalism, communism or militant "pure and simple" trade unionism —send their votaries as agitators among the masses to organize, to dominate, to control. This agitational impetus can be found in the formative stages of every trade union. In 1936 John L. Lewis called in his worst enemies, the communists, to help him organize the CIO. But after a union is formed, it develops antibodies to resist extremist infections. The union becomes interested in bread-and-butter gains, it calls strikes not for utopian but for immediate ends, it develops leaders who are less interested in the co-operative commonwealth than in collective bargaining. Very soon these leaders find it necessary to fight off the radical partisans, who endanger their position and divide the membership. Such is the origin and mechanism of factionalism in the labor movement.

The women's garment workers followed this pattern with

unusual fidelity. Their outstanding trade union official during the nineties was Joseph Barondess, and his career was one long struggle to throw off outside partisan influences. John Dyche, secretary of the International and its most important leader from 1904–14, was a pure and simple trade unionist who fought all isms. Benjamin Schlesinger, president of the International from 1914–23, was an exception: he was a lifelong socialist who disapproved of "mere" trade unionism, though in practice even he was forced to resist undue pressure from the Socialist party. Morris Sigman, who followed Schlesinger, led the "civil war" against the communists in the 1920s. Not until David Dubinsky became president in 1932 did the union have inner peace.

THE EIGHTIES

When in the early eighties the women's garment workers were groping for some form of protection against the sweatshop, they accepted the first aid that offered—that of the Knights of Labor. The first union among them was an assembly of the Knights, organized in New York City either in 1879 or 1880. We do not know what branch of the trade was involved, we do not know the name of this shadowy body, how many members it had or how long it lasted. In 1882 the Knights organized another assembly, and this time we know that it was a local of cloakmakers. Soon it too disappeared. A year later the Knights made a third attempt. This local, the Dress and Cloak Makers Union, sprang up during a strike of 750 workers in a number of the larger shops, and evaporated soon after. The Knights were also active among the dress and cloakmakers in Toledo, Baltimore and one or two other centers. But all these unions were short-lived. They were known as "seasonal unions." At the beginning of a busy season the workers would strike for a raise and when they got it they would go back to their machines. They had no experience, and hence no discipline, as trade unionists.

The cutters, who were more highly skilled, and who as individuals had a longer industrial experience, were much easier to organize. In 1884 the Knights unionized the cutters in both the men's and women's trades into the Gotham Knife Cutters Association of New York and Vicinity. Two years later a separate charter was granted to the cutters in the women's cloak and suit shops, who now called themselves the United Cloak and Suit Cutters Association. This local is the ancestor of the present powerful cutters' union of New York, Local 10 of the International.

The Knights were a secret order who took their symbols and ceremonials very seriously. They "met silently and secretly," wrote a contemporary, William M. Davis of the Ohio Miners Union, and their order was "hedged about with the impenetrable veil of ritual, sign grip and password," so that "no spy of the boss can find his way in the Lodge room to betray his fellows." The Jewish immigrant workers, who didn't understand the language, let alone the heavy symbolism, were at first bewildered and then amused by the initiation rites with which they were inducted into the ranks of American labor. Abraham Rosenberg, who later became president of the International, gives a vivid picture of such an ordeal in his *Memoirs of a Cloakmaker:*

The district master-workman (like the grand master of an order today) with several deputies, all Irish, came to install us. Since we were for the most part immigrants, we of course did not understand a word they said to us. We merely looked on while one of the deputies took a piece of chalk and drew a large circle on the floor. He bade us all stand in the circle. After that one of the deputies laid a small sword on the table and hung a globe on the meeting hall door.

Many of us, on seeing the sword, thought that we were all going to be slaughtered, or else drafted into the army. Most of us bade life farewell. Afterwards some of those who had understood a little more of what had gone on explained that the meaning of the ceremony was as follows: if one of us should break the oath which he had taken to remain true to the workers' interests, this sword would pursue him, for the Knights of Labor were mighty the world over.

The sporadic organization of the cloakmakers by the Knights went on while the country at large was entering a period of turmoil. The two years from 1884–86 are known as the Great Upheaval. The industrialization of the country had been rushing ahead at breakneck speed and the inevitable depression set in. The expanding factory system had sucked in millions of unskilled and semiskilled workers, mostly immigrants, and wholly unorganized. America had become a battlefield of industrial giants and the victorious trusts were developing into monopolies. It was then that the American people first turned against Big Business and against the "sinister influence" of Wall Street. Unrest spread everywhere, farmers organized into Wheels and Alliances, small businessmen and professional people made common cause with the various anti-monopolistic movements. Above all, labor became deeply apprehensive and a perfect epidemic of strikes broke out.

In the women's clothing industry this unrest lasted until the end of the decade. In 1887 there were over thirty strikes of cloakmakers in New York alone, and innumerable walkouts in the other garment centers, in Boston, Baltimore, Chicago. They were all seasonal strikes, some of them mere stoppages of a few hours. These petty walkouts were pathetic in the humility of their demands and the homely informality of their settlements. Again we quote from Rosenberg's memoirs:

> They were all conducted in the same way; when the workers in an outside shop were dissatisfied with the prices, they would gather near their shop in the morning or at noon and one of them would make a motion—today they would not work. The others seconded the motion and all of them immediately proceeded to the Market Street dock, which was the headquarters for the striking cloakmakers, or took a trip to Cindele (Central) Park.

> When the boss came to the shop and discovered his workers were absent, he knew just where to find them, and after long negotiations settled the argument. Usually the boss would raise prices five cents on the garment and roll out a barrel of beer. Thus ended almost every strike.

THE NINETIES

During the 1890s the organizational drive continued in an intensified form, though in the same hit-or-miss fashion. Strike followed strike like a string of firecrackers all over the country.

And a deeper residue of union consciousness was left after each struggle. Some of these strikes were no longer settled casually with a five-cent raise and a barrel of beer, but by genuine collective bargaining agreements which fixed hours and wages and sometimes even included a crude setup for mediation. The business prosperity which began in 1889 produced the usual wave of strikes, for good business always suggested the idea of a raise. But now the cloakmakers in the various centers were getting at least a glimmering of their common interests.

One of the reasons for this greater awareness was that the radicals, who in the eighties had been largely utopian, had gained enough experience in the labor movement to get a more general picture of the situation. To be sure, this only intensified their rivalry for the control of the workers and made the nineties a welter of factional struggles. But at least these rivalries were no longer wholly doctrinaire; they were to some degree concerned with the daily problems of the unions. The socialists especially began a campaign to educate the workers along trade union lines. In 1888 they founded the United Hebrew Trades in New York, which was a society for stimulating union organization among the Jewish workers. It was modeled after the United German Trades, with which Morris Hillquit, Abraham Cahan and other leaders in the Jewish socialist and labor world had been closely associated.

In the first year of its existence the United Hebrew Trades set up a Cloak Makers Society, a sort of educational club which in 1889 was reorganized as the Dress and Cloak Makers Union of New York. The anarchists of Philadelphia established the Jewish Federation of Labor, which included a cloakmakers' union. And in Chicago Abraham Bisno, who later became an important leader of the New York cloakmakers, founded a Workers Education Society, which also paid especial attention to the garment workers.

During this period the Knights of Labor were rapidly losing ground in the garment trades. The AFL was clearly winning against the Knights throughout the country, and the more realistic socialist leaders were quietly siding with the AFL. To be sure, Daniel De Leon was as bitter as ever against "that faker

Gompers" and his pure and simple trade unionism. But in spite of De Leon's stranglehold on the official Socialist party, the garment workers began to orient themselves toward the more effective unionism of the AFL.

In January 1890 over 3000 New York cloakmakers went out on strike. The sweatshop system was at its worst; nine dollars was considered a fair wage for a ninety-hour week. But this time, instead of relying on the usual spontaneous leadership, the strikers asked the United Hebrew Trades to direct them. The United Hebrew Trades sent three representatives to strike headquarters at 92 Hester Street, and one of them, Joseph Barondess, became the chairman of the strike committee. It demanded union recognition and the right to pass on the business responsibility of the contractors employed by the inside manufacturers. Most of the large firms accepted these terms, and even Meyer Jonasson, the largest cloak manufacturer in New York, came to the Hester Street basement to sign up. The union which emerged from this short and victorious struggle began with a membership of 2800 and called itself the Operators and Cloakmakers Union No. 1. By the end of the year it claimed 7000 members.

On a smaller scale similar organizations were founded in other cities, where the picture was very much the same. Early in 1890 Abraham Bisno led in the formation of the Chicago Cloak Makers Union. A decrepit local of cloakmakers was reorganized in Philadelphia as the Cloak Makers Local Union No. 1. At the same time the Boston Cloak Makers Protective Union and the Baltimore Cloak Makers Union were formed. All these bodies outside New York were small and miserably poor. But at least they were no longer seasonal. They were tied up with the local labor movements and were conscious of the need for permanent organization. The employers recognized the new challenge. The moment these unions arose they had to fight for their very existence. In Boston, Philadelphia and Chicago strikes broke out; they were brief, bitter and unsuccessful. But in New York the cloakmakers determined to consolidate the victory of their January strike, and struck again on May 19, 1890, staying out for nine weeks. The employers retaliated with a lockout, which drove the cutters and even the contractors to join forces with the cloak-makers against the Cloak Manufacturers Association. They formed a "triple alliance" and elected a joint strike committee to direct the fight. It was at this juncture that the AFL made its first contact with the women's garment workers. Samuel Gompers spoke at one of their mass meetings and the Federation watched the struggle with close interest. As for the Knights, they hovered ineffectually in the background.

The strike began with tremendous enthusiasm, with parades, demonstrations and mass meetings. The press and public sided with the workers. Churches, clubs, benevolent societies of all kinds furnished speakers and collected money for strike benefits. One of the most active sympathizers was a Professor T. H. Garside, of whom little was known except that he had anarchist leanings and had been a lecturer for the Knights of Labor. Daily he would arrive at strike headquarters with "sacks full of money," which he said he had collected from friends and well-wishers. He was an effective speaker, extremely radical in his talk, and became very popular with the rank and file. On his own initiative he became the intermediary between the manufacturers and the strikers and worked out an agreement which called for union recognition, without, however, providing for the reinstatement of all the strikers.

The cutters accepted the proposed agreement; they were too highly skilled to suffer discrimination in getting their jobs back. The contractors too were glad to settle. But the cloakmakers rejected the olive branch on the advice of Cahan, Hillquit and Barondess. They suspected Garside of being a questionable character, possibly in the pay of the employers. To this day his part in the whole affair remains a mystery. Chances are that he was no worse and no better than other self-appointed busybodies so frequently encountered in the history of American labor struggles, a type of ambitious meddler of which the late Lincoln Steffens was a notorious example.

Barondess now began new negotiations with the employers and within a week they accepted his terms. The agreement provided for the union shop, for some reforms in the contracting system, for a minimum of fifteen dollars a week for operators and fourteen for pressers, for the settlement of grievances through peaceful negotiation and for the reinstatement of all strikers. It is a highly significant commentary on the times that Barondess agreed that none of these provisions should apply to women workers. But even so, it was an important and far-reaching victory, foreshadowing the arbitral machinery which was to distinguish this industry. And it established the leadership of Barondess among the cloakmakers, which was to last through thick and thin for many years.

JOSEPH BARONDESS

Joseph Barondess was a Russian Jew who had come to this country in 1888. He had spent some years in England, where he had been active in trade union affairs. On landing here he got a job as a knee-pants operator, and at once became immersed in the socialist and labor movements.

Barondess came of a family of rabbis and had an orthodox Jewish education. He was a magnificent orator, still remembered for his golden voice and almost hypnotic powers over an audience. And he had an uncanny feeling for the temper and mood of the workers. In a meeting of cloakmakers he was the mellow philosopher, full of wit and parables, quoting the Bible in the manner of a cultivated freethinker, which delighted his audience. But in a meeting of pressers, who notoriously couldn't grasp the ABC of parliamentary procedure, he was quite capable of leaving the chair and slapping some *Balagula* into line. And the pressers loved it. "I was slapped by Barondess today," was a proud boast among them.

The strikes of 1890 brought Barondess into the limelight, and in a minor way he became a national figure, the stormy petrel of the women's garment workers. He was the first bona fide trade union leader among them. Above all, he could inspire fanatical loyalty and fanatical antagonism—a Bryanesque figure in his eloquence, his gift for controversy and his unpredictability. He died in 1928, having spent the last decade of his life as an insurance agent, selling policies to the workers in the needle trades, who kept him going in affectionate remembrance of his early services to their movement.

At the very start of his career as a union leader Barondess became involved in a bitter feud with the socialists, especially with Abraham Cahan, the most colorful personality in the Jewish labor world. Cahan, who is now in his eighties and still going strong as editor and autocrat of the *Jewish Daily Forward,* has always felt that the socialist movement was the natural mentor of the trade unions, and especially of such "socialist" unions as the needle trades. Barondess, though nominally a socialist, resented all outside interference. It was the Barondess-Cahan feud, full of fire and brimstone, which touched off the virulent struggle in the needle trades between the trade unionists and outside agitators. Through the nineties the women's garment workers, especially the cloakmakers, were torn by a veritable civil war between the "Barondessists" and the "anti-Barondessists."

Barondess' hold on the workers was so secure that he weathered a crisis serious enough to have wrecked the career of most leaders. In March 1891 he went with ten other union men to a small scab shop run by a man named Greenbaum in Jamaica, Long Island. Greenbaum was a "runaway" contractor who had left New York City to escape the union. When Barondess and his men tried to pull out the workers, they resisted and there was a fight. In the rumpus a lighted stove overturned and one of the Greenbaum children was slightly burned.

The next day the New York papers ran lurid tales of the disturbance. One paper had it that a union delegate "seized little Willie by the ankles, and holding his head downward in the air, poured almost a pint of vitriol over the little fellow's body." Barondess and his companions were arrested, charged with arson and assault, and placed under $10,000 bail each. The union could raise bail only for Barondess. One man, Frank Reingold, was found guilty of burglary and sentenced to five years and nine months in the penitentiary. The charges against the others were dismissed, after some of them had stayed in jail for months. Excitement ran high and New York labor as a whole felt that the "Jamaica affair" was an effort to wreck the union and to discredit its leaders, especially Barondess.

The next attack on Barondess, which came on the heels of the Jamaica case, was an obvious frame-up. A contractor named Papkin paid a fine of $100 to the union with a check made out to Barondess personally. Barondess was promptly arrested on a charge of extortion. The whole organized labor movement of the country, from Gompers down, rushed to his defense, and even Abraham Cahan took up the cudgels for him. They all knew that the charge was preposterous, for his integrity was beyond question. But while out on bail Barondess lost his head completely and fled to Canada, intending to go back to England. Friends followed him and persuaded him to return. His appeal was denied, and he spent a few weeks in prison in the spring of 1892. Finally he was pardoned by Governor Flower, who had received a nationwide petition with over 60,000 signatures.

These troubles practically wrecked the New York cloakmakers' union. The legal fees and court expenses amounted to over $15,000, and what was worse, the Papkin frame-up exacerbated the factional conflicts. By the end of 1892 the union was a mere shadow of the growing and confident organization it had been the year before. It didn't have a nickel in the treasury, it had lost over half its members, and every meeting was a free-for-all.

TOWARD A NATIONAL UNION

While the Papkin affair was still in full blast the various cloakmakers' unions throughout the country made tentative efforts toward national unification. Barondess, who was then out on bail, issued a call early in 1892 for "a convention of all cloakmakers of the United States and Canada to meet in New York on May first." Twenty delegates from five cities, representing about 1500 members, responded, and formed the International Cloak Makers Union of America. (Unions which claim jurisdiction in Canada as well as in the United States usually call themselves "International.")

THE CONQUEST OF CHAOS   43

The first national organization of cloakmakers claimed a membership of 1000 in New York, nearly 200 in Chicago, and 100 each in Boston, Philadelphia and Baltimore. The convention recommended affiliation with the United Garment Workers, the AFL union of men's tailors. Each member was to pay one dollar initiation fee and ten cents a week in dues. The officers were to consist of a general secretary at a salary of $20 a year and an executive committee of seven workers from the shops. Since Barondess was in danger of going to prison the convention elected two New York cloakmakers, Louis Koppenheim and Morris Kunz, general secretary and chairman of the executive committee. But within three months the Boston and Chicago locals pulled out and in a year the whole "International" was no more.

This initial effort toward national unity collapsed because of factional disruption. No sooner was the weak little International formed than it became the focus of partisan conflicts. The Knights were fighting a desperate rear-guard action against the AFL. Daniel De Leon sided with the Knights, whom he was trying to capture with his usual complicated maneuvers. The United Hebrew Trades, under the leadership of Hillquit and Cahan, and officially tied up with De Leon, were flirting with the AFL. And all socialists, right and left, were in conflict with the anarchists, who sided with Barondess; in their aversion to all political parties, especially the socialists, the anarchists in the labor movement invariably tended to make common cause with the strict trade unionists. The polemical crossfire confused everybody, even the gunners, while the rank and file rushed from one sector of the fray to another in wild disorder.

Fierce journalistic battles raged between the right-wing socialist *Arbeiter Zeitung* and the anarchist *Freie Arbeiter Stimme,* which opened its columns to Barondess, while De Leon's *Weekly People* kept up its doctrinaire fire on all and sundry. In those days journalism in general was far more personal and vitriolic than nowadays. The new yellow journalism of Hearst and Pulitzer set the tone of colorful slander and irresponsibility. The radical press, especially its foreign-language section, could let itself go even more, for it functioned in a world of its own in which the general public was not interested. Moreover, character assassination was quite safe since no one within the "movement" would dream of suing for libel in the "capitalist courts." In this journalistic war for the control of the cloakmakers, defamation became as ugly as communist smearing is today. Epithets such as "international scab," "boodle politician," "crook," "faker" studded the pages of the various journals. And hitting below the belt became the favorite sport. The socialists, for instance, who had been very active in agitating for Barondess' pardon in the Papkin case, now turned on him and accused him of cowardice. "His petition to Governor Flower shows how low this braggart can stoop," screamed the *Arbeiter Zeitung*.

DUAL UNIONISM

The hatreds engendered by all this factionalism made union solidarity impossible. Rival unionism was the inevitable result. And in August 1893 the simon-pure followers of Daniel De Leon organized the International Cloak Makers Union in opposition to the Barondess union. The moving spirit and secretary of the dual outfit was Joseph Schlossberg, in those days a fire-eating Bolshevik, who later became the Caspar Milquetoast and secretary-treasurer of the Amalgamated Clothing Workers under Sidney Hillman, and is today a venerable member of the Board of Higher Education of New York City. For a year the Barondess-ists and the Schlossbergites led a bitter competitive existence. Finally Barondess decided, for the sake of unity, to step out of the picture. And the rival unions merged.

But Schlossberg could not control the merged union, because the rank and file insisted on staying with the AFL and were sick and tired of De Leon's obsession against Gompers and the Federation. A month after the merger the cloakmakers went out on a sympathy strike with the men's tailors in the AFL, and Barondess was called back to leadership. Unfortunately the men's clothing workers, to whose defense the cloakmakers had so romantically rallied, settled their own strike after a brief two weeks, and left the cloakmakers holding the bag. The employers refused to settle with them and their strike fizzled out miserably after months of futile sacrifice. Once more the union fell apart. Whereupon the De Leonites resuscitated their dual union and took it into the Knights of Labor, but within eight months it died. The Barondess union dragged along until the spring of 1896. Then the discouraged members voted to sell the office furniture and donate the money to the Cuban revolutionists in their struggle against Spain.

Meanwhile, in December 1895, De Leon had set up his Socialist Trade and Labor Alliance as a rival federation to both the AFL and the Knights of Labor, neither of which he had been able to "capture." But he got nowhere with his paper federation; and the new local of cloakmakers which Schlossberg organized under the S.T. and L.A. was a miserable abortion.

Barondess, however, succeeded in reviving his old union under the name of the United Brotherhood of Cloak Makers Union No. 1. It set out in September 1896 with 28 members and within three years had a membership of 10,000. The reason for this astonishing growth was that the period of dual unionism was over. De Leonism was on its last legs. The right-wing socialists, who dominated the United Hebrew Trades, were through with Comrade De Leon and all his works. They soon walked out of the Socialist Labor party and joined hands with the Social Democracy of America founded by Debs and Berger. In 1897 they founded the *Jewish Daily Forward,* which was immediately successful in rallying the workers against all dual unionism and in helping to organize them as a socialist opposition within the AFL.

(The Socialist Labor party survives to this day, a small group of Marxist puritans, venerating the memory of Daniel De Leon. They still publish the *Weekly People,* which—believe it or not—reprints in every issue a long editorial from the pen of their one and only prophet, written in the 1890s.)

Outside of New York the story of the cloakmakers during the nineties was very much the same, only on a lesser scale. The Chicago Cloak Makers Union under Abraham Bisno was broken up in 1895 in a quixotic sympathy strike with Gene Debs's

American Railway Union. Benjamin Schlesinger, a young man then beginning his career as a labor leader, reorganized the local under the Socialist Trade and Labor Alliance, but another strike in 1899 finished it off. The Philadelphia cloakmakers led a precarious existence, were reorganized several times, moving from the Knights to the AFL and back again, until in 1899 they became a "Barondess union" and affiliated with the AFL. In Baltimore a feeble cloakmakers' union languished as a local of the United Garment Workers. In Newark, Cleveland, Cincinnati and San Francisco small local unions of cloakmakers bobbed up and down throughout the decade. Yet everywhere the idea of unionism was taking hold.

During this period other branches of the women's garment trades began to organize. A crop of unions appeared among the shirtwaist, skirt and wrapper makers, among the workers in children's apparel, embroidery, lingerie and petticoats. In all these branches the workers were mostly women and girls and their unions were short-lived. Their organizations suffered less from factional fights than from neglect by the established leaders, who showed slight interest in the women of the industry.

In retrospect it might seem as though the garment workers before the turn of the century were doing their best to disorganize themselves rather than to gather into effective agencies of collective bargaining. But the undercurrent of trade union organization was growing stronger all the time. All the factional confusions—the bolshevism of De Leon, the syndicalism of the Knights of Labor, the utopianism of the anarchists, the orthodox Marxism of the right-wing socialists, the native ferments of the various Populist movements—all these had to be burned through and absorbed before the women's garment workers could create an organization sufficiently united to survive every gust of doctrine and every shift of leadership.

III

Birth of a Union

THE ATTEMPT of the cloakmakers to form a national union
in 1892 had failed pathetically. Factionalism had torn the union
to pieces in a few months. But by the turn of the century the air
had cleared. The new socialist movement of Debs and Hillquit,
with which the garment workers were in close sympathy, set its
face against dual unionism. The workers no longer had to choose
between the AFL and the Knights of Labor—because the Knights
were dead. And times were changing. The vast majority of the
Jewish workers had become acclimated to American life. Moreover, sizable groups of Italians, Czechs, Poles, Russians and native Americans were entering the industry, and they had not
been through the bitterness of twenty years of inner discord. Another new factor was the steady influx of women and girls, who
by 1900 formed almost one third of the rank and file. They were
employed in the dress, shirtwaist, house dress and white goods
branches of the industry. And in spite of the indifference of the
men leaders, it became clear that they had to be organized if
unionism was to survive.

But probably the most significant fact making for a national
union was the growth of the industry itself. By 1900 it was one
of the major consumer goods industries in the country. In the
ten previous years the number of establishments had increased
from 1224 to 2701. The capital investment had grown from
$21,260,000 to $48,432,000, the value of the product from
$68,164,000 to $159,340,000, the number of workers from
39,149 to 83,739. The contract system was losing some of its

47

grip in the cloak and suit trade, and many small manufacturers were entering the expanding field.

It was thus in a far more auspicious atmosphere that the New York cloakmakers issued an appeal on March 11, 1900, for the formation of a national union of all the crafts of the industry. "In order to create a national organization," the appeal read, "it is necessary to hold a convention of all the workers in the trade, namely of those working at cloaks and suits, or at custom ladies' tailoring, or in skirt shops. With this end in view, we hereby call a convention to be held in New York City on June 3, 1900. We invite all workers in the trade in the United States and Canada, those who have unions and those who have none, to join us in our effort."

On the appointed day eleven delegates representing seven local unions with 2000 members convened at the Labor Lyceum, 64 East Fourth Street, in New York City. There were two delegates each from the United Brotherhood of Cloak Makers and from the Skirt Makers Union of Greater New York; two each from the Cloak Makers Protective and the Cloak Pressers Union of Philadelphia; and one each from the cloakmakers of Baltimore, Newark, and Brownsville, New York. The convention was opened by Joseph Barondess and by Hermann Robinson, representing Samuel Gompers.

The delegates decided to form an industrial union of all crafts in the women's garment trades, and to call it the International Ladies' Garment Workers' Union. Herman Grossman and Bernard Braff, both of them New York cloakmakers, were elected president and general secretary-treasurer, and a General Executive Board of five was chosen. The convention voted a per capita tax of one cent a week and each local union was assessed ten dollars for an operating fund.

On June 23 the AFL issued a charter to the new International. Of the seven founding unions four locals emerged: the New York Cloak Makers Union Local 1; the Philadelphia Cloak Makers Protective Union Local 2; the United Cloak Pressers of Philadelphia Local 3; and the Cloak Makers Union of Baltimore Local 4.

The International started its career with a capital of thirty dollars, and the New York cloakmakers generously provided it with desk space in their own modest office at 8 First Avenue. Neither the president nor the secretary received a salary, and they attended to their duties after work hours. The next year, however, the general secretary was voted five dollars a week, and a year later he got fifteen dollars, which enabled him to devote his full time to his official duties. In that year too the International rented an office of its own at 25 Third Avenue.

In the first three years of its life the organization grew lustily. Business conditions in the country were buoyant. Gigantic mergers such as the United States Steel Corporation were being formed. Our victory in the Spanish-American War had made us a world empire. Organized labor too forged ahead rapidly. In 1903 almost 450,000 new members flocked into the AFL. Labor intensified its organizational drives and its activities in general. Local bodies were merged into national and international unions, gaining everywhere in prestige, increased wages, reduced hours and improved conditions. The garment workers shared in this general upsurge and expansion. During its first year the International grew from four to nine locals; it doubled its membership to 4000. By 1903 it had fifty-one local unions with almost 10,000 members, of whom 3500 were women.

Strikes were now carefully prepared and called only as a last resort. Revolutionary unionism was beginnning to give way to business unionism. The International became interested in building up its financial strength, in death and sickness benefits for its members, in improving its day-to-day relations with the employers. It tried to model itself after the strong and successful unions in the AFL, such as the building trades and printing crafts. Yet the International differed profoundly from the conventional AFL crafts. The whole history of the women's clothing workers impelled them toward a more progressive attitude. The union prided itself on its liberal outlook and on its social consciousness. It advocated labor's independent political action and endorsed the new Socialist party. It joined the progressive and left-wing unions in the conventions of the AFL in opposition to the stand-pat attitude of the Federation oligarchy. From the very beginning the International was unmistakably one of the most advanced unions in American labor.

Much of the early growth of the International was outside of New York City. As the industry grew and diversified, locals multiplied throughout the country, giving the union a truly national character. A strong organization of cloakmakers rose even in San Francisco, powerful enough to force the International to ban Asiatic members, in spite of the horrified opposition of the Eastern radicals. By 1903 more than half of the union members were outside of New York, and at the convention of that year in Cleveland considerable opposition developed against New York "domination." Benjamin Schlesinger, who had made an enviable record as manager of the Chicago Joint Board of Cloakmakers,* was elected president.

Late in 1903 a severe depression hit the country. The employers launched a general offensive against organized labor. Anti-union industrialists banded together and founded the National Association of Manufacturers. Lockouts and injunction proceedings against labor became the order of the day. Within the next two years the AFL lost nearly a quarter of a million members. The International suffered heavily from the slump. At the Boston convention in 1904 Schlesinger was defeated for re-election to the presidency. He was accused of factionalism, and his close connection with the Socialist party and the *Jewish Daily Forward* was held partly to blame for the growth of unemployment and loss in union membership. James McCauley, a New York cutter, succeeded him, and Abe Brounstein, of Boston, was elected general secretary-treasurer to succeed Bernard Braff. The Schlesinger contingent could not very well object to McCauley, who was a leader of the strategically placed cutters, but they wouldn't accept Brounstein, who had been active in the

---

* A joint board consists of delegates from each craft in a major trade in one city, such as the cloak and suit trade or the dress trade. The New York Joint Board of Cloakmakers, for instance, consists of one or more representatives of the local unions of operators (who do the sewing), pressers, cutters and every other craft involved in the cloak and suit trade.

co-operative movement and whom they considered an outsider of dubious reputation. To avoid a knockdown drag-out fight with the socialists the McCauley forces agreed to call a special conference for the purpose of electing a new secretary-treasurer. And with the aid of Gompers, who was invited in as pacifier, John Dyche, a New York skirt maker, was chosen for the office, which he filled for a decade. During that period he was the outstanding leader of the International.

JOHN DYCHE

John Dyche was born in Russia and as a young man he went to England where, like Barondess, he was active in the trade unions. Though nominally a socialist, at least in his younger days, he always fought against partisan interference in organized labor, and in England he had acquired some reputation in a controversy with Sidney and Beatrice Webb, whom he criticized as pink politicos meddling in the trade union movement. After he came to this country in 1901 he got a job as a skirtmaker and soon became prominent among the garment workers as a "pure and simple" unionist. He was called the "Jewish Gompers," and in the course of his long career he moved steadily toward the right, toward an almost fanatical belief in strict business unionism. He decried all militancy as doctrinaire and unrealistic, opposed all partisan and revolutionary involvements, and advocated a steady, slow, conservative and "responsible" trade union policy. He came to despise the class struggle as a form of "ignorant bellicosity" and was against all "radical ravings" which precipitated "useless and avoidable" strikes.

Dyche was a man of great moral and intellectual integrity. Even when he was discovered in secret dealings with the manufacturers, no one doubted his motives; it was taken for granted that he acted for the good of the union as he saw it from his "reactionary" point of view. He was the first self-educated trade union leader in the modern sense, at least among the garment workers; his education was in industrial and labor economics. The self-educated labor leader a generation ago was apt to go in more for culture than for expert knowledge. He would often know a good deal about music and literature, but would look down his nose at the economics of his own industry or government reports. His desire for self-improvement was more romantic than professional.

Some time ago a distinguished professor of law told me how impressed he was with the personal culture of a certain labor leader whom I know well. What he meant was that this particular leader is a highly intelligent specialist. He is expert in the sense in which a competent economist is expert. But he is not a cultured man in the usual sense. He isn't particularly interested in symphony concerts or modern painters or creative literature. What he does read endlessly are government reports, economic and political studies of all kinds, magazines, newspapers. His information on what is happening in the country is enormous. It is this kind of training which the present-day self-educated labor leader acquires.

John Dyche was the first leader of this modern type in the needle trades. He kept track of everything. And indeed his very conservatism was based largely on his knowledge of the difficulties and complexities of economic society.

Dyche undoubtedly left his mark on the "safe and sane" forces in the International. But in retrospect it is clear that his conservatism, his constant effort to see the employer's side, was premature at that stage of the union's history. Today David Dubinsky can very well afford to see the employer's side, to look at the industry as a whole. The union is strong enough to be moderate; the industry is well enough organized for labor and capital to collaborate when necessary. But the union became strong by incessant struggles and not by incessant compromise. Dyche always wanted the International to maintain a round-table attitude at a time when the employers were still holding all the aces. And though respected by everyone for his character, he was also thoroughly disliked for his conservatism, especially since his "common sense" was usually expressed contemptuously and intemperately. He was stubborn and opinionated and had a genius for rubbing his own people the wrong way. He was the kind of man who felt that perfect frankness—and he was seldom less than frank—called for complete disregard of the other fellow's feelings.

HARD TIMES

By the summer of 1904 the International began to feel the full effect of the depression. The Chicago cloakmakers went out on strike for six weeks, lost, and did not recover from the blow for half a dozen years. The Cleveland cloakmakers also struck, against the express orders of the International, and got nothing for their pains; the cutters refused to go out with them, and both local unions were seriously weakened.

In Cincinnati and St. Louis a number of locals disbanded and the rest merely dragged on. The Cloakmakers' Union in New York dwindled to about 300 members, and the skirtmakers and pressers shrank to less than 100 each. The effect on the International seemed disastrous. The local unions paid less and less attention to national headquarters and declared strikes all over the country without even notifying the International.

At the New York convention of the International in 1905 James McCauley declined renomination for the presidency and the state of the union was no doubt accurately reflected in the personality of his successor, Herman Grossman, who had been the first president of the International and was still its leading nonentity. In complete discouragement the convention passed a resolution to merge the International with the United Garment Workers, the men's clothing union in the A.F.L. Fortunately a referendum of the rank and file rejected this counsel of despair. Nonetheless the union appeared to be on its last legs. The per capita tax collected from all affiliates decreased from $4166 in 1903–04 to $1749 in 1905–06 and the number of locals shrank from sixty-six in 1904 to thirty-four in 1906.

John Dyche blamed the local unions for their many "useless and avoidable strikes," for their lack of "diplomatic skill," for their "irresponsibility" in general. His solution was to curb their autonomy. And the convention of 1906 went a long way toward augmenting the power of the International over its affiliates. It gave the parent body the right to audit the books of a local union and to expel it for non-payment of dues. It also prohibited unauthorized strikes.

THE IWW

To add to its troubles the International became involved in a bitter struggle with the IWW. The IWW were organized in 1905 as a coalition of the Western Federation of Miners, of which Bill Haywood was the outstanding leader, Daniel De Leon's zombie Socialist Labor party and other ultrarevolutionary groups. They promptly set to work to wreck the AFL. The International, with its long radical background, seemed to them an easy mark. For four years, they harassed and raided the women's garment workers. They created rival cloakmakers' unions in Montreal, Cleveland, Chicago and St. Louis. And they were especially active in New York, where De Leon and his gang thought they had a chance to become once more a power in the labor movement. Joseph Schlossberg, who was now editing the Jewish weekly, *Arbeiter,* kept up a steady bombardment against the International, concentrating his fire on Benjamin Schlesinger, who was then the manager of the New York Joint Board of Cloakmakers. The IWW formed four unions among the New York garment workers—two unions of cloakmakers, one of dressmakers and one of pressers. In 1906 they fused into a single industrial union—Local 59, IWW. Dualism and factionalism once more ran riot. But for all the sharpness of the conflict, the International was at no time in danger of being wrecked by the Wobblies. The workers had had their fill of rival unionism in the nineties.

The IWW brought forth one of the great leaders of the International, Morris Sigman, then a presser in a cloak shop. Sigman objected to the "corruption of the bureaucracy" in the International and to its "high" initiation fee of five dollars. In 1904 he organized a local of his own, the Independent Cloak Pressers Union, charging only a dime admission, and got several

hundred members. A year later he took this local into the IWW
and became its general organizer in the New York garment field.
He remained in the IWW until 1907, when he and his followers
rejoined the International. Twenty years later, as president of
the International, Sigman was the leader of the "civil war"
against the communists, the union wreckers of a later day.

UPHILL ROAD

Of the many strikes during this period two had a considerable
influence on the future development of the union. One was a
strike of cloakmakers in Boston in 1907, called against the order
of John Dyche, which was finally defeated after a bitter struggle
of four months. It was broken by a series of injunctions obtained
against the union by Louis D. Brandeis, counsel for the employers. The basic issue of the strike was the closed shop. Brandeis
suggested a novel compromise, which later became famous as
the "preferential union shop." Under this scheme union men
would receive first chance at employment, other things being
equal. The Boston cloakmakers rejected the idea. But three
years later the great New York cloakmakers' strike was settled
on the basis of the Brandeis formula. The Boston strike marked
the debut of Mr. Brandeis as a Great Liberal and professional
sage.

The other conflict in 1907, which seemed more important at
the time, was a strike of the New York reefer makers. The conditions of these workers in children's wear were the most miserable in the entire industry. Children's clothing was still being
manufactured under the worst sweatshop conditions of a decade
before. Most of these workers were recent immigrants, unskilled
and ignorant and easily exploited. After a conflict which lasted
over three months the strikers won all their demands. The employers agreed to a union shop, to a 55-hour week, and promised
to "furnish free of all charges materials, tools, and appliances."
The settlement also provided for a board of arbitration.

The success of the reefer makers' strike encouraged the harassed International tremendously. Even Dyche, the perennial

hypochondriac, exulted at the Baltimore convention in 1907 that "the tide of unionism among our work people in our trades at last turned in our favor, and we have every reason to believe that our International Union is now facing a period of prosperity."

But unfortunately for President Grossman and Secretary Dyche the socialist crowd in the union, led by Benjamin Schlesinger, had played a far more vital role in achieving the victory of the reefer makers than John Dyche with his Fabian counsels. It was not easy to unhorse Dyche, but Grossman could be—and was—repudiated by the convention. Mortimer Julian, a well-known figure among the New York cutters, became the new president.

Julian's election brought into the open the latent hostility between the cutters and the cloakmakers. Many of the cutters were native Americans or Americanized Irishmen, Germans and Jews who were proud of being highly skilled craftsmen and contemptuous of all the other trades in the industry. Their Local 10 was the best-disciplined and strongest union in the International. The cutters paid their dues and assessments regularly, they conducted their business in English, they had long experience as trade unionists and they were in close touch with the rest of American labor. It was difficult to get them to co-operate with the other crafts during strikes and there was constant mutual recrimination about scabbing and "irresponsibility." Julian was a typical cutter, a right-wing craft aristocrat, and he represented the point of view of the cutters with vigorous prejudice. His position as president of the International soon became untenable and he resigned before his term was up. Later, at the convention of the AFL in 1908, he introduced a resolution demanding a reorganization of the International. The International, which in those years was still dominated by the cloakmakers, revenged itself on the cutters by revoking the charter of Local 10, accusing its leaders of "obstructionism."

In the Philadelphia convention of 1908 Abraham Rosenberg, a very active member among the New York cloakmakers, was elected president. He came to office at the height of the depression which had set in the year before. Shop after shop closed down, many of them went into bankruptcy and thousands of workers walked the streets. Local unions throughout the country passed out. During some months of that year the per capita tax collected by the International amounted to no more than sixty or seventy dollars. The union was in desperate straits. Dyche would sneak into his office early in the morning, grab the mail and rush out again for fear of the landlord and bill collectors. But by the middle of 1909 the depression was gradually lifting. The local unions in the various centers began to revive. The dispute with Local 10 was adjusted and the cutters were re-admitted into the International. As always, the revival of the union was partly conditioned by the revival of the industry. But by no means a negligible factor in this upswing was the personality of Abraham Rosenberg.

ABRAHAM ROSENBERG

Rosenberg, who held office until 1914, was the archetypal cloakmaker, close to the rank and file because he was one of them. He completely lacked the usual prima donna touch of the leader and his common sense was never suppressed or sublimated by ambition. He was a wonderful storyteller, the beloved kibitzer of the masses. Today many people in the union speak of him as having been Dyche's happy stooge, who kept the workers amused while Dyche ran the show. But old-timers, who knew Rosenberg well, have an entirely different picture of him. Rosenberg, they insist, was the perfect complement to John Dyche. Both men had the same outlook and believed in the same policies. Unlike Dyche, Rosenberg was a man of little education but mellow, witty, patient and shrewd in his knowledge of people. Dyche was the "business unionist" and represented the International before the public, while Rosenberg did the quiet manipulating, persuading and fixing within the union. Together they made an excellent team—Dyche out in front and Rosenberg in the background; Dyche belligerently impatient with the members and Rosenberg smoothing down their feathers. The two men worked as one to keep the union clear of political entanglements, to build slowly, to avoid strikes and never to rock the boat. Like everybody else, the trade union leader does not stand still. The conservative leader is apt to move more and more to the right. In time the Rosenberg-Dyche team became too "sensible," too safe and slow for that particular period in the life of the International. But both men deserve the grateful memory of the American women's tailors, for one may well argue that if they had been as "advanced" as their critics there might be no well-knit International today.

IV

Two Great Strikes

Ｉ N 1909 and 1910 two strikes in New York City turned the
eyes of the nation upon the women's garment workers. These
two strikes revealed that the International, in spite of its ups
and downs and internal fights, had been storing up tremendous
latent powers of solidarity and organization.

The first of these strikes was called by the shirtwaist makers,
of whom 80 per cent were women. The vast majority of them
were girls between sixteen and twenty-five. Their strike lasted
from November 22, 1909, until February 15, 1910.

The second strike was called by the cloakmakers on July 7,
1910, and was settled on September 1.

THE UPRISING OF THE TWENTY THOUSAND

The shirtwaist industry had its modest beginnings in the
1890s. But in the first decade of this century ready-made blouses
and skirts became the rage and the industry expanded rapidly.
A great many of the workers were recent immigrants from Russia
and Poland, deeply radicalized by the revolution of 1905. And
they communicated a smoldering unrest to the rank and file, who
by this time were no longer overwhelmingly Jewish. About 35
per cent were Italian and almost 10 per cent were native-born
of various stocks. These girls were exploited unmercifully. Hours
were fifty-five a week or more. Wages averaged from seven to
twelve dollars a week for regular operators, but nearly a quarter
of these girls were classed as "learners" and earned between three

and four dollars a week. They were the victims of a vicious system of "inside subcontracting," under which a man worker would hire a number of girl helpers on his own hook. What such a padrone really did was to run a contract shop on the premises of an inside manufacturer. At this period there was comparatively little outside contracting in this branch of the industry. Most of the firms employed from 50 to 100 workers and some of them as many as 500. But the conditions in the shops were not much better than in the old sweatshops of the last century. The workers were charged for needles, for the use of electric power, and in some shops even for their chairs and lockers. A racket of arbitrary fines sometimes cut their wages in half.

Back in 1901 the shirtwaist makers had organized the Ladies Waist Makers Union Local 12. But in 1905 it disbanded from sheer inanition. In the same year a new union, Local 25, was formed but it too failed to thrive. In 1909, on the eve of the strike, Local 25 had only about 100 members and four dollars in the treasury. But business conditions were on the upgrade and the union began to stir. Shop disputes and walkouts, characteristic of a business upswing after a deep depression, were frequent. The trade was surcharged with restlessness. The workers were tense, angry and impatient for action. In the fall of 1909 Sam Shindler and Abraham Baroff, the secretary and the organizer of Local 25, raised the daring slogan of a general strike* and in October the executive board of the local officially approved the idea. But Secretary Dyche and the other leaders of the International frowned on such "recklessness" and suggested instead the perennial alibi for inaction—a committee to investigate the conditions in the trade.

At this point moral support came from an entirely new quarter. The Women's Trade Union League, founded not long before for the purpose of aiding the unionization of women, offered to help. Encouraged by this sympathy, a number of spontaneous strikes broke out. The entrance of the League upon the scene drew public attention to the condition of the shirtwaist makers,

* In the International a "general strike" means a walkout of all the crafts—operators, pressers, cutters, finishers—in one branch of the industry.

and when Mary Dreier, president of the New York chapter of the League, was arrested on the picket line in front of the Triangle Waist Company, the metropolitan press sat up and took notice.

The Women's Trade Union League was never part of the official labor movement. It was organized and supported by socially-minded upper-class and professional women such as Miss Dreier, Ida M. Tarbell, one of the leading muckrakers of the day, industrial students such as Martha Bensley and Helen Marot, Mrs. Mary Kingsbury Simkhovitch and Lillian D. Wald, the well-known settlement workers, and Rose Schneiderman, the only one of the lot who was a wage earner. The League was really part of the feminist movement, concentrating on labor legislation and trade union organization among women. The AFL oligarchy paid it little mind, and most of its connections were in the worlds of liberal opinion, social reform and society with a capital S. When these ladies took their stand at the side of the shirtwaist makers the girls felt that they had strong and glamorous allies. They even felt brave enough to defy Secretary Dyche, who was very snooty about this alliance between high-brow "butters-in" and "irresponsible little girls." A rash of strikes broke out all over town.

On November 22 the shirtwaist makers held a mass meeting at Cooper Union. The story of that meeting has been told and retold until it has become one of the legends in American labor. An imposing array of speakers was invited, including Samuel Gompers, Mary Dreier, and the socialist leaders Meyer London and Jacob Panken. The meeting had gone on most decorously for about two hours. The situation was discussed soberly and cautiously. Rosenberg and Dyche were all for "realistic restraint." Then suddenly Clara Lemlich, a young striker with a fine record of fighting cops on the picket line, asked leave to speak. She was "a wisp of a girl still in her teens." Every instinct warned the trade union bureaucrats that here was a half pint of trouble. So when Clara asked for the floor there was considerable commotion on the platform. But Chairman Benjamin

Feigenbaum, a well-known socialist and a staunch democrat, felt that she had a right to be heard. He recognized her, and Clara Lemlich burst into an impassioned "philippic in Yiddish."

"I am a working girl, one of those who are on strike against intolerable conditions. I am tired of listening to speakers who talk in general terms. What we are here for is to decide whether we shall or shall not strike. I offer a resolution that a general strike be declared—*now*."

The effect of this challenge is described in the *Souvenir History of the Shirt-Waist Makers' Strike:*

Instantly the big gathering was on its feet, everyone shouting an emphatic affirmative, waving hats, canes, handkerchiefs, anything that came handy. For five minutes, perhaps, the tumult continued; then the chairman, B. Feigenbaum, made himself heard and asked for a seconder of the resolution. Again the big audience leaped to its feet, everyone seconding. Carried off his feet by the emotional outburst, the chairman cried: "Do you mean faith?" . . . And up came two thousand hands, with the prayer: "If I turn traitor to the cause I now pledge, may this hand wither from the arm I now raise."

Thus began the historic Uprising of the Twenty Thousand. Over 15,000 waist- and dressmakers came out in this mass rebellion. Five hundred shops were emptied. For a few days there was immense confusion, simply because there was no organized machinery to handle this vast eruption. But support poured in from all sides. The United Hebrew Trades, the Socialist party and the Women's Trade Union League assigned prominent members to assist the strikers. The general public too came to their defense, shocked by the revelation of the sweatshop conditions under which these girls were compelled to work. The public and a large section of the press were especially outraged by the conduct of the magistrates and the police. A magistrate named Olmsted, in sentencing a picket, shouted, "You are on strike against God." In a letter to the newspapers Professor E. R. A. Seligman of Columbia, Lillian Wald, Mary Kingsbury Simkhovitch and Ida Tarbell claimed that there was "ample evidence to warrant a statement that the employers have received co-operation and aid from the police."

Now that it was clear that the strike enjoyed public approval and was likely to succeed, the leaders of the International and of the cloakmakers threw themselves into the fight. Whenever a strike gave promise of strengthening the union Rosenberg and Dyche were tireless in its support. Sigman of the pressers gave his full time for the duration. But what gave the Uprising verve and drama was the magnificent devotion of hundreds of girls, who sprang up overnight as leaders, organizers, speakers, administrators. They kept up the spirit of the strikers, rushing from hall to hall to address them, they fought the cops and the "gorillas" hired by the employers, they raised money for relief. They seemed to get along without sleep or food. Bessie Switski, a member of the Executive Board of Local 25, and her sister would attend meetings until four and five in the morning and then bright and early show up on the picket line. Daily, as a matter of routine, they would be arrested, bailed out, and then rush back to the fray, selling newspapers that supported the strike or addressing meetings of clubwomen or feeding the families of the strikers.

On December 5 a mass meeting was held at the Hippodrome. It was arranged by Mrs. O. H. P. Belmont, the society leader of the day. The chairman was John Howard Melish, rector of Holy Trinity Church in Brooklyn. Among the speakers were Monsignor Lavelle, representing Archbishop Farley, City Controller Metz, Superintendent of Schools Dr. Maxwell, the Rev. Dr. Anna Shaw and other prominent citizens.

Ten days later a committee of women, among whom were Mrs. Belmont, Miss Anne Morgan, the sister of J. P. Morgan, and Miss Elisabeth Marbury, organized a meeting at the Colony Club to present the case of the strikers to high society. Wellesley College girls donated $1000 to the strike fund. All the newspapers were friendly, and some of them, such as Hearst's New York *Evening Journal* and the two socialist dailies, the New York *Call* and the *Jewish Daily Forward,* became virtually official strike publications.

Conferences began and broke down. The employers would not consider union recognition or a pledge to rehire all workers without discrimination, two cardinal points on which the union insisted. The union offered to submit to arbitration, but the employers refused. With the new year the struggle settled down to a quieter course. The strike committee concentrated on individual settlements but continued negotiations with the Waist and Dress Manufacturers Association. Meanwhile the strike had spread, on a much smaller and less dramatic scale, to Philadelphia.

Finally, on February 15, 1910, the New York strike came to an end. (In Philadelphia it ended on February 3.) The settlement was by no means a complete victory for the union but it established it on a permanent basis. The Manufacturers Association refused recognition, but 339 individual firms out of the 352 members of the Association—and among them all the big firms—agreed to deal with the International. The employers undertook to furnish needles, thread and all necessary appliances free of charge. During the dull seasons work was to be divided as far as practicable. The union won a 52-hour week and wages were to be arranged in each shop between the employer and a committee of workers. Finally, all strikers were to be taken back without question.

But the strike had an importance far beyond these tangible gains. It was the first successful mass strike in the needle trades and it revealed the immense potentiality of the International. To the leaders of the union it showed that women workers had to be organized as well as men. Moreover, the strike brought forth a vague but significant alliance between socially-minded women of the middle and upper classes and the American workingwoman; in fact, between the liberal community as a whole and organized labor. This loose and almost intangible alliance was to grow through the years into an influential force in public life. It was this liberal force which was most articulate in supporting the progressive tendencies of Theodore Roosevelt's Bull Moose movement, of Wilson's New Freedom and finally of the New Deal.

THE GREAT REVOLT OF 1910

Five months after the rebellion of the shirtwaist makers ended, the New York cloakmakers also decided on a general strike. In this trade too tension had reached the breaking point. The rapid growth of the cloak industry since the opening of the century was characterized by the spread of innumerable small shops, which were not contracting shops but independent establishments, whose standards were if anything worse. They were known as the East Broadway "moths" because they all concentrated, like the old sweatshops, on the East Side where the workers lived. The conditions in the trade constantly deteriorated. And even before the Uprising of the Twenty Thousand, the feeling among the cloakmakers had been that a general strike was the only way out.

With the revival of business in 1909 the agitation for a complete stoppage in the cloak industry spread and intensified. But unlike the waistmakers, the veteran cloakmakers prepared carefully and systematically. Their Joint Board levied a two dollar strike tax and early in 1910 began the publication of the *New Post* in English, Italian and Yiddish, an official bulletin whose sole purpose was to lay the groundwork for the impending conflict. Workers in the trade rallied to the union and by June 1910 the Joint Board could boast 10,000 members. In the same month the Boston convention of the International voted to approve a general strike in the New York cloak market. The AFL sent its pledge of support.

As soon as all these detailed preparations had been made and the strike machinery set up, a great mass meeting was called at the old Madison Square Garden, the first labor meeting to be held in that historic place. The Garden couldn't hold the crowds, and thousands of workers overflowed into the square and the adjoining streets, where speakers addressed them from trucks hastily pressed into service. According to Frank Morrison, the secretary of the AFL, it "was the greatest outpouring of the workers of any trade that has been seen." Gompers and other nationally known labor leaders spoke and "the enthusiasm was indescribable."

The strike was called for the afternoon of July 7. Between 50,000 and 60,000 cloakmakers left their jobs, which was beyond the most sanguine expectations of the leaders. The union demanded the abolition of the subcontracting system, equal division of work during slack seasons, abolition of payment for electric power, the 49-hour week and union recognition. The employers refused. When the New York State Board of Mediation proposed a conference, they agreed to meet the strike leaders only if the union waived in advance its demand for a closed shop. But the strike committee began to sign up the smaller shops and by July 22 about 22,000 workers had gone back.

To break the deadlock, Dr. Henry Moscowitz, a well-known New York reformer who later became adviser to Governor Smith, went to Boston to secure the good offices of A. Lincoln Filene, a department-store merchant and professional public figure who was a big buyer of women's wear. Filene in turn induced Louis D. Brandeis, attorney for the Boston women's garment manufacturers, to approach the New York employers. Toward the end of July the conference between the manufacturers and the cloakmakers' Joint Board was resumed under the chairmanship of Brandeis. But nothing could overcome the resistance of the employers to the closed shop. Finally Brandeis trotted out his old formula of the "preferential union shop" which the Boston cloakmakers had refused in 1907. The manufacturers rejected the plan and once more negotiations collapsed.

Meanwhile trouble had developed in union ranks. John Dyche, the arch-Fabian, had privately informed the employers that the demand for the reinstatement of the strikers might be subject to negotiation. The strike committee indignantly repudiated Dyche. An ugly row threatened between the International and the Joint Board. Benjamin Schlesinger, who was at the time manager of the *Jewish Daily Forward*, was added to the strike committee by the lefts in order to strengthen the anti-Dyche element, while the International called in Sam Gompers to bolster their side. Just at this moment Justice Goff, a violent reactionary, handed down a sweeping injunction which declared all picketing to be a conspiracy and which virtually outlawed the strike. The cloakmakers defied the injunction and scores of them were arrested and fined. Violence flared up, and in August the employers announced that they intended to open their shops with strikebreakers. The situation was full of dynamite.

At the end of August Louis Marshall, a well-known constitutional lawyer, entered the picture. Louis Marshall was a man of tremendous power and moral authority in American Jewry. He was thoroughly disgusted with the stupid intransigeance of the employers, most of whom were Jews and, in Marshall's opinion, injuring the good name of the Jewish community. In his usual domineering way he virtually browbeat the manufacturers into resuming negotiations with the union. And on September 1 a settlement was finally reached. It was the famous Protocol of Peace.

The agreement provided for the installation of electric power in all plants and for its free use by the workers; the abolition of all homework and inside subcontracting; a six-day week of fifty-four hours with ten paid holidays through the year; weekly pay in cash; piece rates to be fixed by a joint committee of employers and the union; a maximum of two and a half hours overtime and that only during the busy season; the establishment of a Joint Board of Sanitary Control which was to supervise conditions in the plants; the preferential union shop, carefully defined; and finally, the establishment of a machinery for the conciliation and arbitration of disputes and grievances.

It was a great victory for the cloakmakers and for the International.

V

The Protocol of Peace

THE PROTOCOL OF PEACE marked a decisive turning point in the history of the International. Its basic idea was later copied by the other needle trades, notably the Amalgamated Clothing Workers. And in time its influence spread throughout American industry.

The Protocol generated a new conception of industrial relations. It was hailed as something more than ordinary collective bargaining, indeed as a new era in industrial statesmanship. It introduced the notion that labor had a stake in industry beyond wages and hours, a stake in its efficient management, continuous prosperity and social responsibility. The Protocol assumed a benevolent partnership between capital and labor, a sort of joint industrial syndicate of boss and worker.

The preferential union shop, which in effect was the closed shop, implied that the worker had the right to his job and that therefore his union had no right to weaken or jeopardize the industry which provided that job. The Joint Board of Sanitary Control was also a brand-new idea. It was a system of voluntary factory inspection and self-imposed regulation for the good of the industry, the workers and the public at a time when there was virtually no factory inspection. Finally, the Protocol provided a permanent machinery for conciliation and arbitration, again a voluntary and self-imposed government accepted by both sides. In short, the Protocol of Peace was almost a perfect anarcho-syndicalist charter: it established, in theory, a self-governing economic unit with which the state would have no cause

68

or pretext to interfere. And it had the characteristic anarchist utopian touch of permanent peace and good will among men; it banned all strikes and lockouts and it had no time limit. It was to last forever and a day.

(It is interesting to note that Mr. Brandeis, the "father" of this anarcho-syndicalist charter in industry, almost a quarter of a century later became one of the leading architects of the New Deal, which went a long way toward institutionalizing government control of the national economy. The anarchist, conscious or unconscious, once he acquires power, invariably tends toward the omnipotent state, for in the long run only the bureaucrat can give him the illusion that his dreams are coming true. That is the permanent irony of anarchism.)

The Protocol was a genuine social invention—in its minor way just as much a social invention as Rousseau's "natural man" or Marx's "dictatorship of the proletariat." Now, whose social invention was it? The fact is that the Protocol was created neither by capital nor by labor. It was a device which expressed the prevalent attitude of the liberal and progressive mind, of the social pacifist who thought of industrial conflict as the result of ignorance and misunderstanding rather than as a conflict of group interests.

As a matter of fact, the Protocol, both in its constitution and in its administrative complexity, was never psychologically accepted by the workers. The cloakmakers accepted it not as a charter of industrial statesmanship but simply as a favorable settlement of their great strike of 1910. But they sensed from the very beginning that the machinery of the Protocol would necessarily register the actual correlation of forces between capital and labor, and that the union was bound to suffer since it was far weaker than the employers in this balance of power. The manufacturers too accepted the Protocol for opportunistic reasons. It offered them protection against strikes, it equalized production costs and working conditions in the shops, and it gave them a more respectable standing in the community. It transmogrified Messrs. Potash and Perlmutter, whose opinion of themselves had never been any too high, into enlightened leaders of

American industry. As the counsel for the manufacturers, Julius Henry Cohen, said, they wanted to "put the industry upon a higher plane and to make of the business something that would not make them shamefaced when admitting to their neighbors or children that they were cloak manufacturers."

These motives were not strong enough to develop the Protocol of Peace into a creative institution. It was finally wrecked by the explosive forces of industrial democracy. Democracy in industry can come only from the gradual process of adjustment between its actual participants, between capital and labor. Imported good will, which the Protocol represented at that stage of our economic evolution, can only be imposed, and imposition destroys the democratic process. Moreover, as we shall see, the Protocol machinery was completely ineffective even in imposing its will. Thus the Protocol of Peace inevitably led to continuous war. Both parties, but especially the union, found it less an instrument of mutual appeasement than a mechanism of joint frustration. And in social politics frustration is bound to create tensions and explosions.

THE PROTOCOL SETUP

The Protocol machinery consisted of two parts: a Board of Arbitration, which was the highest authority, and a Board of Grievances. The real administrative agency was the Board of Grievances. It was composed of five members from each side. Among the labor members were Abraham Rosenberg, John Dyche and Benjamin Schlesinger. The executive officers were a chief clerk for the union and another for the cloak manufacturers. Sol Polakoff was appointed chief clerk for the cloakmakers.

The Board of Arbitration consisted of three members, who served without pay. They were Louis D. Brandeis, who represented the employers, Morris Hillquit, who represented the workers, and Hamilton Holt, editor of the *Independent,* who represented nobody—that is, the public. Brandeis and Hillquit were undoubtedly very able men. But in collaborating on an unreal program they made little headway. Reflecting the wary attitude of their principals, they established a modus operandi of evasion and escape. And Mr. Holt, the typical confused liberal, was more of a supernumerary than an umpire.

The Board was meant to deal only with high policy and the most important issues. The arbiters were quite olympian in their attitude and were in fact too busy with their own affairs to pay much attention to the day-to-day problems of industrial relations. Accordingly everything was left to the Board of Grievances. Difficulties arising in the shop were dealt with first by the shop steward and a representative of the firm. If they could not agree, a complaint was filed either with the chief clerk of the union or the chief clerk of the manufacturers, depending on who did the complaining. They or their deputies would jointly look into the matter and try to adjust it. If they failed the issue would come up before the Board of Grievances.

Under this arrangement everything depended on the process of *conciliation* and only a deadlock on the most important questions of policy was referred to the higher body for *arbitration*. In short, the specific weight of the whole machinery rested on the mechanism of conciliation, which in its nature can settle only minor disputes. Brandeis was a strong believer in conciliation as against arbitration, in the round-table method of "reasonable discussion." To him discussion meant "industrial democracy and self-government."

THE ARBITERS

Louis Brandeis, the "Father of the Protocol," was an extremely successful Boston attorney for Big Business in private, and one of its severest critics in public, a jurist who smoothly combined the best features of the smart lawyer and the fashionable reformer. Noiselessly he amassed millions, which enabled him to function for the rest of his life as a censor of social and business morals.

Even in those days Brandeis was the leader of a small coterie of self-appointed Brain Trusters, a pioneer in this youngest profession. He was a master of the kind of reform which obliquely seeks power—and he became the idol of the social workers and professional liberals of his day. Learned and extremely intelligent, he was a brilliant and cautious opportunist, with a gift for conveying the impression of mellow sagacity and humble goodness. The Protocol of Peace, in whose failure he played the leading role, clinched his reputation as a constructive statesman, and in 1916 he was elevated to the Supreme Court of the United States, later becoming the leading elder statesman of the left-wing New Dealers. He had a veritable genius for bureaucratizing good will among men.

Morris Hillquit, the labor representative on the Board of Arbitration, was of a very different breed. By 1910 Hillquit was, next to Debs, the leading figure in American socialism and one of the most distinguished members of the American bar. He was a man of great intellectual integrity, matched only by his intellectual pride. Cynical without the least touch of moral corruption, idealistic without romanticism, shrewd without ulterior motives, he spent his days in the midst of men and movements and yet remained all his life remote and spiritually inaccessible. He lacked the driving ambition so necessary to leadership, because his intelligence was far too objective and because his energies were drained by a lifelong struggle against tuberculosis.

From 1914 until his death in 1933 Hillquit was counsel for the International. But that does not suggest his function or significance in the history of the union. Way back in the eighties he had been one of the founders of the trade union movement among the garment workers. And he maintained this intimate association all through life. From Barondess to Dubinsky the union leaders, big and little, came to him with their problems and often with their personal troubles. They relied on his shrewd, worldly and disinterested judgment. And the rank and file was proud of his position as the intellectual leader of American socialism and of his prestige in public life. Yet in spite of his socialism, which is a prophetic business, there was nothing of the prophet or popular leader in Morris Hillquit. For that he was too aristocratic in his human passions. He was the sage behind the scenes, the Gray Eminence of the conference room. No amount of research can trace the extent of his influence on the International. From his early manhood until the day he died he was as important as any figure in its destinies.

Hamilton Holt, at the time editor of the *Independent* and now president of Rollins College in Florida, was then at the height of a distinguished public career about nothing in particular. With his amiable bewilderment he aptly represented on the Board an amorphous "public." He was the odd man of a futile trinity.

During the life of the Protocol the personnel of the Board of Arbitration underwent several changes. In 1916, when Brandeis moved up to the Supreme Court, Federal Judge Julian W. Mack, a naïve liberal who worshiped Brandeis, took his place as chairman. In 1911 Hillquit resigned as the labor representative and was followed by Walter E. Weyl, who became one of the founders of the *New Republic* and a master of the turgid essay. He in turn was followed by William O. Thompson, a Chicago lawyer who had been the partner of Governor Altgeld and Clarence Darrow and was later the impartial chairman of the arbitral machinery at Hart, Schaffner and Marx. Thompson was a well-meaning, friendly man, none too bright, who had a romantic feeling for labor which he indulged by developing crushes on labor leaders. He was one of the discoverers of Sidney Hillman and helped launch him on his career as labor statesman. It was he who in 1914 persuaded the New York cloakmakers to import Hillman from Chicago to become chief clerk of their Joint Board.

THE PROTOCOL SPREADS

The Protocol of Peace acted as a tremendous stimulant to the New York cloakmakers, who still represented three fourths of the International. The provisions of the strike settlement of 1910, which were embodied in the Protocol of Peace, were carried out at first with considerable gusto on both sides. Inside subcontracting practically disappeared, sanitary conditions in the shops improved enormously, the wage and hour clauses of the contract were respected. Workers poured into the union and stayed there. By 1912 the membership had increased to 50,000, about fivefold in less than three years. Ninety per cent of the cloak trade in New York City became organized.

The manufacturers too extended their organizations. The bigger one—the Cloak, Suit and Skirt Manufacturers Protective Association—increased its membership to nearly 200 firms employing over 30,000 workers. The cloakmakers also had Protocol agreements with the United Association of Cloak and Suit Manufacturers, who employed 10,000 people, and with independent concerns, employing about 7000. Out of a total of 1829 shops the union had agreements with 1796. The income of the Joint Board ran into thousands of dollars a week, it had branch offices in various parts of the city and employed a large staff of business agents. The future looked bright.

The successful strike of the cloakmakers, and especially its culmination in the glamorous Protocol of Peace, set off a wave of union organization in other centers and in other trades of the industry.

The second largest cloak and suit market in the country was Cleveland. It was a market of large inside shops against which the union had never been able to make headway. Shop conditions were very much like those in New York before the 1910 strike. Wages were low, hours long, inside subcontracting was rampant, and three fourths of the workers were classified as "helpers." The Cleveland cloakmakers felt that only a general strike could help them, and for once John Dyche agreed. On June 3, 1911, the union presented its demands to the employers individually. It called for a 50-hour week, for the abolition of inside subcontracting, for free use of all machinery and appliances and the establishment of joint price committees to fix wage rates. The employers promptly and arrogantly refused these terms, and three days later 5000 workers, among them 1000 young women, went on strike.

At first the strike was orderly, confident, almost gay. The International and its local unions throughout the country poured thousands of dollars into Cleveland; by the time the strike was over they had contributed over $200,000. The public and the press were extremely friendly. But the employers were well organized and adamant. They charged that the International and the New York manufacturers were "in a criminal conspiracy" against the Cleveland market. They employed scabs, and one of their undercover agents, named Morris Lubin, managed to get control of the picket committee two weeks after the strike began. Violence broke out. Later Lubin confessed that he had acted as a provocative agent, and served a term in prison.

Brand Whitlock, mayor of Toledo, and one of the great liberals of his time, Mrs. Harriet Upton Taylor, president of the Ohio Suffrage League, and other civic leaders urged the strikers to hold out. But the outbreak of violence turned the public as a whole against them, and the manufacturers were able to get their orders filled in New York City. In October the International decided to call the strike off. The union mapped out a vigorous campaign to boycott the Cleveland market, but of course failed. For the next seven years the International got nowhere in that city.

Simultaneously with the Cleveland strike a much smaller conflict took place in Chicago, where the cloakmakers' Joint Board had influence only in the small outside contracting shops. The officers of the International advised against precipitate action, but the Chicago union insisted on going ahead. It called a strike against Palmer and Company, one of the largest firms, in the hope of breaking into the big inside shops. Again the strikers at first enjoyed considerable public support and a favorable press. The Chicago Federation of Labor, the Women's Trade Union League and the progressive forces in the city helped all they could. But Palmer and Company were able to hire strikebreakers from the United Garment Workers and even from a local of the International, the Ladies Tailors, who were not members of the Joint Board. The strike was lost.

During 1912 there was quiet on the organizing front. The failures in Cleveland and Chicago, coupled with difficulties over the Protocol in New York, for a time discouraged further union expansion. But early in 1913 the strike movement revived. In February the cloakmakers and the dressmakers of Boston struck. Both walkouts were successful and a few weeks later Protocol agreements were signed.

Much more significant was the series of strikes in the New York "women's trades"—those branches of the industry in which women and girls predominated. These women workers had been in a restless and rebellious mood ever since the tragic Triangle fire on March 25, 1911. The Triangle Waist Company operated a large factory on an upper floor of a condemned loft building in New York City. When the fire broke out the girls were trapped high above the street with the exit doors jammed. Most of them were burned to death, others jumped out of the windows; altogether 146 of them perished. The catastrophe was a profound shock not only to labor but to the entire country. The New York Legislature set up a Factory Investigating Commission whose first executive officer was Frances Perkins. In time Miss Perkins and her colleagues roused the whole nation to the need of effective factory inspection and safety legislation. The reaction of the International to the Triangle fire was to redouble its efforts to organize the women in the industry.

At the eleventh convention in Toronto in June 1912 the International decided to make an intensive drive to extend the Protocol system to the women's trades. Rosenberg and Dyche began a series of discussions with the larger manufacturers, and these conferences were also attended by high AFL officials. After several weeks of negotiation a tentative agreement was reached with the Dress and Waist Manufacturers Association. The understanding provided that the union was to demonstrate its control over the workers by calling a general strike in the waist and dress industry, and that the strike was to be settled immediately with the Association, and then with the rest of the employers on condition that they would join the Association. If the union could show that a majority of the workers supported it, and the Association could garner in the majority of the manufacturers, a protocol similar to that in the cloak industry was to be adopted. This technique of prearranged strikes and settlements has since been used quite frequently in the women's clothing industry, as a rule with constructive results.

The plan went through without a hitch. On January 5, 1913, a general strike meeting was held at the Hippodrome in New York, and ten days later the strike was called. The next day the union and the Association met in conference, and on January 18 a Protocol of Peace for the dress and waist industry was signed. The whole maneuver had lasted less than two weeks and proved successful. This was a very different sort of agreement from the one that ended the Uprising of the Twenty Thousand in 1909. Now the biggest of the women's trades, the waist- and dressmakers also had a complex arbitral machinery to deal with their problems.

In the lesser women's trades—the wrapper, kimono, house dress and white goods branches—there was just as keen a desire for a protocol. These trades were small and poorly organized, and their workers had very little trade union experience. The employers were typical small-fry sweatshop bosses. In New York sporadic and feverish conflicts broke out in all these trades, especially among the underwear workers, led by Samuel Shore and Fannia M. Cohn, who are still prominent in the International. As usual, public sympathy was with the girls. Again the Women's Trade Union League was there to help; Rose Schneiderman, secretary of the League, had herself been a worker in the needle trades. Freda Kirchwey, now publisher of the *Nation* and then an undergraduate at Barnard, and Fola La Follette, the Senator's daughter, were active on the picket line. Mayor Gaynor and Theodore Roosevelt expressed their good will. By the middle of February 1913 the employers gave in and signed protocol agreements with the various local unions in all the minor women's trades in New York.

Between 1910 and 1913 the International had been able to advance on the crest of a rising business cycle. Good business and protocolism combined to make this three-year period a success. In June 1910 the International had less than 30,000 members in all its various crafts throughout the country. In June 1913 it had 90,000, and 80 per cent of them were covered by protocol agreements. At this high point the International was able to employ forty organizers, its finances were sound, and it was growing in public esteem. Magazines and newspapers sang its praises as the advance guard of American labor.

But in the second half of 1913 a business recession set in and almost overnight the picture changed, as was so often the case in the earlier history of the union. The cloakmakers of Philadelphia, Baltimore, St. Louis and San Francisco went out on strike, demanding conditions similar to those prevailing in the New York market. They wanted an increase in wages, the 50-hour week, the abolition of homework and especially of inside subcontracting. But all these strikes were lost. The Philadelphia strike alone cost over $250,000. These losses in money and morale affected all the women's garment trades. By 1914 the membership of the International had dropped to 70,000.

And by 1914 the Protocol of Peace was already on its way out.

SEEDS OF WAR

The Protocol of Peace in the New York cloak trade lasted six years. Concrete difficulties developed from the start. The Board of Grievances was perpetually bombarded with complaints. Evenly divided between workers and employers, its vote was almost invariably tied even on the pettiest issues. Moreover, it had no final arbitral authority. Only the Board of Arbitration had this power, and it refused to be bothered about small matters. The result was that the docket of the Board of Grievances was chronically jammed with unfinished business.

Let us suppose that Joe Kaplan, a cloakmaker, was fired and his complaint finally reached the Board of Grievances. The

Board was likely to be tied in its decision. In theory the next tribunal was the Board of Arbitration. But the arbitrators, dominated by Brandeis' conception of their function, refused to go into Joe's problem unless it involved some general principle affecting all the Joe Kaplans in similar circumstances. Unfortunately, by the time Joe's case assumed the dignity of a principle, Joe himself had been out of work for three months. This sort of delay and stalemate characterized the whole grievance process, whether it was the union or the employers that initiated the complaint.

In time these daily worries and annoyances created an undercurrent of skepticism and suspicion toward the Protocol on both sides. The workers came to resent the loss of the right to strike, and the employers came to feel that they had been finagled into giving up their basic privilege of managing their own business. However, both sides were so anxious to make a go of the experiment that during its first two years it seemed to run well enough. There had been so much public ballyhoo about the Protocol as a Magna Charta of industrial democracy that neither side was willing to come out against it.

Sol Polakoff, the first chief clerk of the cloakmakers' Joint Board, soon proved that he was not cut out for the job. He was a man of little education and lacked the necessary technical equipment. He had been a loyal Jimmie Higgins on the picket line; the complicated machinery of the Protocol was too much for him. In 1911 Abraham Bisno, then manager of the Chicago cloakmakers, succeeded him.

ABRAHAM BISNO

Bisno was already a well-known figure among the garment workers. An active trade unionist, he had been appointed factory inspector in Chicago by Mrs. Florence Kelley, chief factory inspector and one of the great industrial reformers of the day. He was a self-educated workingman who had a good command of English, knew the ins and outs of the labor movement, and had acquired sufficient general culture to set up as a philosopher of life and labor. He had the cloakmaker's propensity for ideological hairsplitting and interminable gab. Extremely likeable and ludicrously absent-minded, he could be brilliant on occasion. He loved power without knowing what to do with it, and would have made a perfect New Dealer of the benign variety. He saw what was wrong with the system but could not implement his insight.

Immediately upon his arrival in New York he set up a board of directors for the New York Joint Board of the cloakmakers, with himself as chairman, thus becoming the leader not only of the Joint Board but almost of the International. And he at once proposed an extensive program of reform which met with considerable response from both the workers and the employers.

His main idea was to clean up the demoralizing conditions in the industry brought about by the contracting system. He wanted all contractors to be registered with the union so that they could be controlled and supervised in their relation with the big inside shops. The fly-by-night contractor as well as the stooge submanufacturer, attached to a single large concern, were to be eliminated altogether as industrial termites. "Out-of-town shops" in the vicinity of New York City were to be corraled under the jurisdiction of the Protocol. His slogan was, "Don't let the bundles roll out of New York City." A joint price-fixing committee to stabilize wages was to be established by the union and the employers. Finally, Bisno wanted to introduce an effective discipline against all violators of the Protocol system.

No one could possibly object to these reforms. But the trouble with Bisno's program was that it was too fundamental to be realized by a process of conciliation. It meant the virtual reorganization of the cloak and suit trade, which indeed needed reorganization. But the machinery of the Protocol, a round table for discussing surface disagreements, was no agency for basic reform.

Whatever Bisno's faults, he was no fool. He quickly realized that conciliation didn't work, that what was needed was a competent full-time impartial chairman presiding over an authoritative board of arbitration. Naturally this idea annoyed Mr. Brandeis, who clung to his faith in benevolent conciliation, and it infuriated John Dyche, who was congenitally against anything that might come up, especially if it involved drastic changes. Dyche hated to rock even a stranded boat.

Bisno stiffened in his campaign against the impotence of the Protocol and became the champion of the restless cloakmakers against the manufacturers and against the Dyche machine in the International. In the 1912 elections of the cloakmakers he was chosen both as general manager and chief clerk of the Joint Board, and he immediately unseated Dyche, Rosenberg and Polakoff from its board of directors. He thus got rid of the influence of the International in the governing body of the cloakmakers.

The new Joint Board vigorously attacked the leaders of the International as fellow travelers of the bosses. The *New Post*, official weekly of the cloakmakers, went to town on the issue. "A union which obtains the support of the manufacturers' association has no moral right to exist," it declared—obviously a specious bit of nonsense coming from a signatory to the Protocol of Peace. Dyche, never one to mince words, came back in the official organ of the International, the *Ladies Garment Worker*, accusing Bisno and his crowd of "ignorance and dogmatism plus demagogy."

In the long run Bisno could not buck both the International and the manufacturers. The manufacturers simply announced that they would not deal with him as chief clerk. The cloakmakers had to give way, and in the fall of 1912 John Dyche became temporary chief clerk, though Bisno continued as general manager of the Joint Board. Finally, on January 11, 1913, Meyer Perlstein, then secretary of the Joint Board and now an important leader in the International, proudly announced that the union had been "fortunate enough to secure one of the best men in the country," Dr. Isaac A. Hourwich, to take Bisno's place.

THE AMAZING DR. HOURWICH

The moment Dr. Hourwich became chief clerk, *l'affaire Hourwich* began. Indeed, *l'affaire Hourwich* began at the hour of his birth. For Dr. Hourwich was 100 per cent Personality, inspiring total loyalty or total exasperation.

Isaac Hourwich was born in Vilna in 1860, where his father was one of the first of the modern Jewish intellectuals in czarist Russia. Young Isaac graduated with the highest honors from the Law School of the University of St. Petersburg, and along with his diploma he received a sentence of four years' exile to Siberia. For in the university he had divided his vivid energies between scholarship and insurrection. On his return from Siberia he settled in Minsk, where he combined the rather contradictory professions of leading lawyer and leading revolutionary. The police were again on his trail and he fled the country, going first to Sweden and then to the United States.

In America he immediately started the first Russian paper in the country, called *Progress,* and at the same time took graduate work at Columbia University in history, law and statistics, receiving his Ph.D. in economics. In 1893 he taught at the University of Chicago; other academic invitations followed. But he decided to give his time to the socialist movement as a writer and lecturer in English, Russian, German and Yiddish. Books, pamphlets and articles poured from his pen. He became one of the leading statisticians in the country, and eventually the outstanding authority on immigration. He served for a number of years in the federal government as an economist and mining analyst, managing to be a stormy petrel even as a government expert. In 1922 he visited Russia, full of enthusiasm for the Bolshevik revolution. But his enthusiasm quickly turned into a bitter anti-Bolshevism, and he came to consider Lenin and Trotsky as the fathers of modern totalitarianism.

Dr. Hourwich was brilliant, profound, catholic in his learning and interests—and impossible to get along with. If you didn't cross him, he was charming: cultivated, a connoisseur of good thinking and good living. He was elegantly turned out, his black mustache and gray beard were trimmed to the last brisk hair, and when he walked into a room he radiated such dignity and energy that he seemed to magnetize the very atmosphere.

Once I spent an evening with him that I wouldn't have traded for one of Boswell's sessions with Dr. Johnson. Like Dr. Johnson, he was full of wit, sagacity and the astute prejudices of a rich and well-assimilated experience of life.

No matter what his temporary interests, Dr. Hourwich considered himself first and foremost a lawyer. He walked through life as the counsel for his own ideas, acting as if his convictions were forever on trial—one reason why he could never make a living practicing law. For the cloakmakers, who love argumentativeness, contrariness and intellectual pyrotechnics, Dr. Hourwich was made to order. He became their knight in shining armor, without fear and without reproach.

Though chief clerk of the Joint Board, Dr. Hourwich made it very plain that he did not consider himself part of the trade union movement. His job, he insisted, was that of "counsel" for the cloakmakers, and it was his duty to protect them in their contractual dealings. They were his "clients." And the employers, in this picture, became the defendants in the case. In his political views he was quite moderate. In 1912 he bolted the Socialist party and supported Theodore Roosevelt for President and himself ran for Congress on the Bull Moose ticket. But as "counsel for the cloakmakers" he was an intransigeant Defender of the Faith, which to them meant a revolutionary leader.

As soon as he became chief clerk he attempted to overhaul and systematize the Protocol machinery. Unfortunately he inherited the hostilities between the Joint Board and the International, the tensions between the cloakmakers and the manufacturers, the growing discontent of his "clients" with Brandeis and Company, and the permanent deadlock of the Board of Grievances. And since he viewed the whole mess in legalistic terms he was far more effective in systematizing these hostilities and tensions than in reforming the system itself.

Under Dr. Hourwich's influence the earlier constructive criticism of the Protocol became an outright movement against it.

Like Bisno, he denounced conciliation as "impotent" and demanded an arbitral machinery with teeth in it. But he added that a real arbitral system could not be had by merely tinkering with the Protocol. This militant attitude, of course, annoyed Mr. Brandeis, and anything that annoyed Mr. Brandeis delighted Dr. Hourwich. Brandeis' oblique methods grated on him and he did not fail to say so. He denounced Brandeis as essentially hostile to the union, as paternalistic and deviously dictatorial. The cloakmakers gladly believed these accusations.

By the middle of 1913 the fight over the Protocol had developed into a major battle. Today it is difficult to imagine the fanatical partisanship and almost hysterical excitement which gripped the cloakmakers and spread through the International over this issue. The Cloak and Suit Operators Union Local 1 and the Cloak Finishers and Tailors Union Local 9, the two most important and radical groups in the International, were imbued with the spirit of crusaders against the Saracens of the cloak and suit industry, with Dr. Hourwich as their Richard the Lionhearted.

But among the officials of the cloakmakers' Joint Board rifts began to appear. Bureaucrats are congenitally never as unswerving in their loyalty to a leader as the rank and file. Some of the executive members of the Joint Board began to waver and formed a moderate faction between Dr. Hourwich and his enemies. They were afraid that his extremism was endangering the entire structure of the union and its industrial relations. John Dyche, who had been melancholy about Dr. Hourwich from the first—and indeed considered him a learned lunatic—now tried to get rid of him by having him kicked upstairs into the Industrial Relations Commission. But Dr. Hourwich was not tempted.

In November *l'affaire Hourwich* was approaching its climax. Meyer London, who was the official counsel for the Joint Board, resigned in exasperation. For one thing, Dr. Hourwich's conception of himself as the Cloakmakers' Advocate had in effect absorbed London's function. Moreover, London's faithful efforts

to reconcile the warring parties were constantly upset by Hourwich's genius for stirring things up.

MEYER LONDON

Meyer London enjoyed great moral prestige among the
workers, both in and out of the Socialist party. He was cut after
the Debs pattern, an unreconstructed idealist, one of those rare
spirits whose goodness was felt by all who came in contact with
him, the type of man who has to be browbeaten into accepting
a fee for his services. London was incapable of engaging in
jealous bickerings or of maneuvering for personal advantage.
Compared to Rosenberg and Dyche he had no ambitions; compared to Brandeis and Hillquit he had no mind; compared to
Hourwich and Cahan he had no fight. He was a saint, but not
of the Gandhi type who makes a career of it. Rather transparent
and naïve, when the socialist movement emerged from its early
idealism into real social politics, London was out of his depth.
In both the Socialist party and the trade union world he gradually became less and less the lawyer and more and more the
beloved friend.

Dr. Hourwich was the stormy petrel of the cloakmakers for
one tumultous year. Meyer London was their good shepherd
for three decades. He grew up among them on the East Side,
and three times they elected him to Congress, turning their backs
on Tammany, the golden calf to which these traditional socialists
often paid the tribute of their vote. The garment workers literally worshiped Meyer London. It was he who induced them to
try the Protocol of Peace, and he did everything in his power
to make it work.

But even he resented being placed in a false position as peace-
maker between Dr. Hourwich and Mr. Brandeis: as hero of the
radical cloakmakers he should have sided with Dr. Hourwich,
yet his abhorrence of destructive passions turned him toward
the liberal Brandeis. To the left-wing cloakmakers in their in-
flamed state of mind he seemed like a deserter from "revolutionary" socialism. This wounded his moral self-esteem, and he

showed his disgust with the whole mess. His resignation as counsel to the Joint Board made quite a stir; if even London was against Dr. Hourwich, many people felt, the fault must lie with the doctor.

EXIT DR. HOURWICH

The London resignation swung the majority on the Joint Board, who were mostly socialists, against Dr. Hourwich, and they refused to reappoint him as chief clerk. But the rank and file overruled the Joint Board in a referendum, sustaining Dr. Hourwich by a vote of 6553 to 1948. Whereupon the employers went over the heads of the cloakmakers and officially called on the International to remove Dr. Hourwich, stating that under no circumstances would they participate in any proceedings under the Protocol at which he was present.

When bricklayers or carpenters have an intraunion fight the different factions do not engage in journalistic polemics. The official union organ simply suppresses all opposition and criticism, and that's that. But the garment workers, and especially the cloakmakers, have always had a string of factional journals at their disposal. Hence the fight over the Protocol and the Hourwich affair could be waged with vim, vigor and vituperation in the radical press, particularly in the Yiddish press. Dr. Hourwich poured forth his philippics in the *Wahrheit*, an independent left-wing daily, and in the *Freie Arbeiter Stimme,* the anarchist weekly. Abraham Cahan could let himself go in all directions in the *Jewish Daily Forward.* He was against Dr. Hourwich as an "impossible fanatic" and against Dyche and Rosenberg as non-socialist "pure and simpletons." The lusty fight in the radical press was taken up by the metropolitan newspapers and magazines, which were overwhelmingly anti-Hourwich. Dr. Hourwich had no one on his side except the vast majority of the cloakmakers. And they expressed their loyalty by mass meetings, street demonstrations, and by invading union headquarters and wrecking the furniture.

Finally John Dyche declared that the International would not continue as the "guarantor" of the Protocol as long as Dr. Hour-wich remained chief clerk. The Joint Board, though ready to oust the doctor, promptly moved for a special convention to impeach Dyche and Rosenberg for invading its autonomy. Samuel Gompers and John Mitchell, president of the United Mine Workers, were called in to pour oil on the troubled waters, but they could do nothing. The entire cloak market was in an uproar. The employers threatened a general lockout and the workers talked of a general strike.

At this point, early in 1914, Bisno, still the general manager of the Joint Board, offered a compromise. He suggested that Dr. Hourwich resign on condition that the Protocol machinery be converted into a strictly arbitral mechanism by the appointment of a full-time professional impartial chairman. Brandeis gave in, and all parties agreed. Dr. Hourwich tendered his resignation and it was accepted on January 21, 1914, after a stormy session which lasted until 5 A.M.

Three days later the Board of Arbitration set up the new machinery. A committee was created consisting of two repre-sentatives of the employers, two of the union, and an outside full-time impartial chairman. This post was filled by John Williams, who had served in a similar capacity at the Hart, Schaffner and Marx plant in Chicago. Morris Hillquit became the attorney for the union and Benjamin Schlesinger replaced Bisno as manager of the Joint Board. The new chief clerk was Sidney Hillman, who had been the labor representative at Hart, Schaffner and Marx. In Chicago Hillman had been the pro-tégé of the social reformers, especially of Jane Addams, Florence Kelley and William O. Thompson. They recommended him to Abraham Cahan, who put him over with the Joint Board.

SIDNEY HILLMAN

The story of Sidney Hillman among the cloakmakers is brief and colorless. On arriving in New York he went to live in the Henry Street Settlement and soon became the white-haired boy of the city's leading social workers, such as Miss Lillian D. Wald and Paul Kellogg, the editor of the *Survey,* the official organ of organized benevolence and undoubtedly the dullest journal in Christendom. The cloakmakers were left cold by Mr. Hillman's personality, his associations and his interests. They didn't know what he was all about and didn't care. And he in turn did not understand them. He was no Bisno or Hourwich. He has always been incapable of dealing democratically with ordinary workers. The cloakmakers, who came to his office with their innumerable complaints, were in the habit of arguing things out, usually at the top of their lungs, and with no brakes on their language. To Hillman they seemed uncouth, and to them he seemed a complete outsider. To this day the older cloakmakers think of him not as a leader of labor but as a man who has risen to the presidency of the Amalgamated Clothing Workers as one might rise to the presidency of the National City Bank.

Not long ago I had a talk with an old-time cloakmaker. We discussed Hillman and compared him with other labor leaders, particularly David Dubinsky. "I don't remember much about Hillman," he said. "As chief clerk he acted like he was some sort of Home Relief investigator. We didn't bother about him much. Besides, there's no comparison between him and Dubinsky. Dubinsky grew out of the movement and Hillman was never in it. He worked at pants for a couple of months and then he became right away a statesman. And what's become of him since then you know yourself. If that's a labor leader, then I'm President Roosevelt."

THE PROTOCOL ON THE WAY OUT

The revamping of the Protocol machinery made it possible for the real problems of the cloak and suit industry to rise to the surface. The main problem was how to reconcile "the right to the job" with efficient management and a fair distribution of work. Another aspect of this same problem was the right of the employer to "reorganize" his shop—today we would call it rationalize his shop—a right which almost invariably involved the discharge of some workers. The union did not object to reorganization in principle, but it claimed that in most cases it was merely an alibi for getting rid of active unionists.

Morris Hillquit brilliantly presented the union's case before the Board of Arbitration. The union, he said, was willing to concede to the employers the right to reorganize provided it was done in good faith. The employers rejected the Hillquit position, insisting that he was merely quibbling and that they should have the right to run their business as they pleased. Finally, in January 1915 the Board of Arbitration rendered a decision which seemed to sustain the union but was so vague as to be meaningless. And on May 20 the Protective Association, the leading body of the manufacturers, broke off relations with the Joint Board of the cloakmakers.

Benjamin Schlesinger, who had been elected president of the International the previous June, did his best to avoid a strike. He appealed to Mayor John Purroy Mitchel, one of the gilded liberals of the period, to appoint a citizens' committee to settle the issue. Mitchel appointed a Council of Conciliation of six members. They were Dr. Felix Adler, the leading promoter of ethical culture, Louis D. Brandeis, Henry Bruère, now president of the Bowery Savings Bank, Dean George W. Kirchwey of the Columbia Law School, Charles L. Bernheimer, a prominent member of the New York State Chamber of Commerce, and Walter Noyes, a federal circuit judge. This distinguished body took up everything, but they left the main issue of job security versus plant efficiency exactly where they found it. They recognized the employer's right to reorganize his shop and to hire and fire as he pleased, but they urged him to be fair and decent about it. Such appeals are, of course, pointless. Yet the mayor's committee could not be blamed, for as long as the utopian Protocol of eternal peace remained, as long as the workers could not strike and the bosses could not fire, agreements on the basis of actual power relations were impossible—at least at that stage of economic evolution in the country.

Neither side to the dispute dared to challenge the august Council of Conciliation. But nothing was settled just the same.

For the rest of the year an armed truce prevailed in the cloak and suit trade. Then, in the spring of 1916, the Protective Association suddenly locked out 25,000 workers. The union immediately answered with a general strike. Over 60,000 cloakmakers walked out. The lockout-strike was fought with extraordinary bitterness for fourteen weeks. On August 4, 1916, it came to an end—and with it the Protocol of Peace. The new agreement provided for a 49-hour week, for a somewhat higher range of wages and for minor improvements in conditions. But all this was comparatively unimportant. The important thing was the abolition of the entire Protocol system in the cloak and suit market in New York City. The impartial chairman, the chief clerks and their deputies, the Board of Grievances, the Board of Arbitration, the Committee on Immediate Action, all were swept away. The workers regained their right to strike and the bosses their right to hire and to fire.

Soon the cloakmakers of Philadelphia, Boston, Chicago and others centers followed suit. The protocols were abrogated and replaced by the usual type of collective bargaining agreements.

In the waist and dress industry almost the identical process of Protocol liquidation took place, and almost at the same time. In this trade the main issue was the haphazard system of fixing piece rates, which led to constant friction. The union and most of the employers wanted to revamp this system, but unfortunately the Dress and Waist Manufacturers Association controlled only a fraction of the trade, the rest of the manufacturers being independent. And the union was none too sure of its control of the workers in the independent shops. Accordingly the union ordered, in February 1916, a "demonstration strike"— called by prearrangement with the employers for the purpose of consolidating the position of both sides so that they could deal with each other responsibly.

The strike lasted a few days, both sides strengthened their positions and then proceeded to patch up the Protocol. A Board of Protocol Standards was set up and made a thorough study of the economic conditions in the trade. In September this Board issued its report, which showed very clearly that conditions in the Association shops under the Protocol were distinctly worse than in the independent shops outside the Protocol. This killed the Protocol system in the dress industry—and in the other women's trades—though it was not officially buried for another year or two.

BALANCE SHEET OF PROTOCOLISM

In spite of its failure at the time, the Protocol of Peace was one of the most important charters in American industrial relations. It laid the groundwork for the present vast and effective system of arbitration in all the needle trades, covering over 700,000 workers. Its ideological influence on American industry as a whole proved to be immense. In many ways it foreshadowed such contemporary institutions as the National Labor Relations Board, the Railway Mediation Board and even the War Labor Boards of both World Wars.

What ailed the Protocol of Peace was the optimistic naïveté of all seminal movements. It tried to civilize the struggle for power between capital and labor without daring to assume the power of an umpire. It failed functionally because it relied on conciliation instead of arbitration. And it failed morally because it attempted too much too soon; it asked both the employers and the workers to have their being in a blueprint universe, not in the world of economic realities. Since then much of the blueprint *has* become reality, and one of the reasons is that these immigrant workers had the courage to try out the Protocol experiment and the courage to discard it when it was found wanting. But the experience itself was invaluable to them when later they set up a practical and effective system of industrial arbitration.

Progress and Publicity: Benjamin Schlesinger

Benjamin schlesinger was elected president of the International for the second time at the Cleveland convention in 1914. This time he was to remain in office for nine years. The convention was dominated by the socialists, marshaled by the redoubtable Abraham Cahan. Flushed with their recent victory over Dr. Hourwich, they meant to "clean house" or, in plain words, to seize power.

Schlesinger was their man, for he was prominent both in the union and in the Socialist party. His career was a dual one: he alternated between high office in the International and a big job on the *Forward*, which was an official socialist organ. He was in effect a fusion figure, representing socialism in the union, and the union in the socialist movement. In the AFL he was regarded as the leading spokesman—though never very outspoken—of socialist ideas.

Mr. Cahan's housecleaning job was comparatively simple. Now that Dr. Hourwich was out, the problem was to eliminate Messrs. Rosenberg and Dyche. This could be done by a weak endorsement of the policy they had pursued against Dr. Hourwich, coupled with a strong condemnation of the allegedly incompetent, tactless, divisive and reactionary methods they had used to fight him. This maneuver was brilliantly successful. The Hourwich devotees among the delegates had come to hate John Dyche, and welcomed his sacrifice as an expiation of his "persecution" of their hero, while many others were sick and tired of Dyche's ultraconservatism and testiness. The union needed a change, and the mood was toward the left. And so they elected the socialist Ben Schlesinger president and the ex-IWW Morris Sigman secretary-treasurer. For many years to come these two men were the most powerful leaders of the women's garment workers. It was their fate to be linked for the rest of their lives in disagreement and mutual dislike.

The forceful Dyche had made the office of secretary-treasurer the most important in the International during his decade of tenure. It was Schlesinger, a man of equal force and much more ambition, who made the presidency of the union what it is today.

Schlesinger took office in the middle of a business depression which was to last for another year and a half. Moreover, the collapse of the strikes in the fall of 1913 and the struggle over the Protocol of Peace had weakened the union considerably. The industry was in a bad way, standards were falling and unemployment was spreading.

It was at this critical period that the International had to weather a sinister experience far worse than the Jamaica and Papkin troubles in the days of Barondess. A certain Max Sulkes, a private detective, had organized the International Ladies Garment Workers of the World, an outright racket designed to provoke violence and disruption. In April 1914, at the instigation of Sulkes, the Grand Jury indicted without warning eight members of the International, charging them with the murder of Herman Leibowitz, a strikebreaker who had been killed during the cloakmakers' strike of 1910. The accused were Morris Sigman, Saul Metz, then one of the leaders of the cloakmakers and later manager of the teamsters' Local 102; Isidore Ashbes, Julius Wolf, A. Wedinger and Max Singer, all cloakmakers; Morris Stupniker and Louis Holzer, waistmakers.

Sigman and his codefendants were represented by Morris Hillquit, who associated with himself W. M. K. Olcott, one of the most prominent lawyers in the city, and two outstanding members of the criminal bar, Abraham Levy and Henry W. Unger. The case did not come up until late in 1915. All the men were acquitted, and Hillquit's defense has gone down as a classic in the legal annals of the state. But for over a year the "Sulkes affair" plagued the International. It had to spend most of its energies and much of its cash in defending itself against an obvious frame-up at a time when economic conditions demanded all its attention.

Exploiting the union's predicament, District Attorney Perkins, of New York County launched a general investigation of the International, and brought an indictment against five of its officers "for hiring thugs to terrorize employers and workers." They were Vice-Presidents Abraham Baroff, Henry Kleinman, Jacob Halperin and Samuel Lefkowitz, and a business agent named Silver.

The garment workers, and for that matter the whole of New York labor, were aroused to fever pitch by these attacks. They organized protest meetings, raised defense funds, spoke on street corners and held a gigantic mass demonstration in Madison Square Garden on June 12, 1915, at which Samuel Gompers, President Schlesinger and other notables spoke. Baroff and his codefendants were later acquitted. But the whole American labor movement was disturbed by the Sigman and Baroff cases almost as much as it had been by the famous McNamara case a few years before.

In 1916 business conditions improved, and in 1917 we were in the midst of war prosperity. The sudden stoppage of immigration led to an increasing labor shortage and to a growing spirit of security, power and aggressiveness on the part of labor. Local unions in the women's garment industry everywhere agitated with considerable success for the 8-hour day and for better wages and conditions. At the same time the International launched an organizing drive among the workers in the women's trades and among the cloakmakers outside of New York City. These drives were quite effective, especially the strike of the cloakmakers in Cincinnati. (Until the NRA in 1933, organizational drives had to be undertaken again and again to maintain unionism in the garment trades.)

Morris Sigman was not happy as secretary-treasurer of the International and late in 1915 he resigned. He was a man of action, not of figures. In 1917 he became manager of the cloak-makers' Joint Board in New York, where his tenacious driving force could count. He was interested in a broad program of reform, which in the International always meant cleaning out the irresponsible contractors, the inside submanufacturers and other such industrial parasites. But his immediate objective was to replace piecework with week work. For some time this had been a burning issue among the workers. The piecework system had proved thoroughly unsatisfactory, because no scientific method of determining piece rates had been worked out. The constant haggling over wage rates had become a chronic source of irritation, and many regarded it as the main cause of all the troubles in the industry.

Under Sigman's leadership the Joint Board came out for a 48-hour week and a straight minimum weekly wage. Some of the leading figures on the Joint Board, such as Israel Feinberg, Harry Wander and Jacob Halperin, were convinced that week work would mitigate considerably the evils of contracting, sub-manufacturing and other forms of cutthroat competition, that it would ease the tension of the speed-up system and distribute work more evenly throughout the year and among the membership.

The only leader of importance who opposed the abolition of piecework was Jacob Heller, the manager of Local 17, the reefer makers. President Schlesinger was at first dubious about week work as a cure-all, but as the discussion went on he gradually gave way. The debate lasted until the Boston convention in May 1918, when the week-work advocates won hands down. The delegates also voted for a 44-hour week and for minimum wage scales.

In the meantime serious internal difficulties had developed. A confused but powerful left-wing opposition was growing among the New York Waist and Dress Makers, the biggest single union in the International. Even worse, a bitter jurisdictional dispute broke out between the cloakmakers of Local 1 and the children's cloakmakers of Local 17. It was almost impossible to delimit the twilight zone between the two branches of the trade; the same shop would often manufacture garments for misses as well as children. Was a husky tomboy of sixteen a child or a woman? Local 1 considered her fully grown up, while Mr. Heller, of Local 17, to this day a jurisdictionally very disputatious gentleman, thought of her as a mere child. His local would sign agreements with shops which manufactured garments all the way up to "50 stouts."

This struggle, which was to rage in the International for almost two decades, was worse confounded when the unreconstructed rebels of the old Hourwich bivouac seized control of Local 1 in July 1916. Under the crackpot "revolutionary" leadership of Moishele Rubin, Local 1 bolted the Joint Board. The International finally had to intervene and revoke the charter of Local 1 and then reorganize it in order to enforce peace. All these difficulties hampered the union in the work of rationalizing its own organization.

THE WAR YEARS

In April 1917 the United States entered the first World War. The International had always been a quasi-socialist union, verbally radical even in its business unionism, traditionally committed against "capitalist war." Still, the much-vaunted socialism of the International was by no means intransigeant and red. Its officers and members were certainly against imperial Germany, especially after the overthrow of czarism in the February revolution of that year. And when America entered the war the International eagerly pledged its loyalty to the war effort. But in the hysterical atmosphere of the time it did not escape the suspicion of harboring pacifist and even subversive elements.

The war helped the union enormously. The garment industry shared in the general war prosperity, and the International profited greatly from the friendly attitude toward labor shown by the National War Labor Board under the effective and enlightened cochairmanship of ex-President Taft and Frank P. Walsh. Both the Wilsonian New Freedom and the demands of the war stimulated trade union organization. With the rest of organized labor, the International was able to use the war situation to extend its membership without resorting to strikes. The organizations in Cleveland, Chicago, Boston and Philadelphia flourished like the green bay tree.

Immediately after the Armistice the International mapped out a comprehensive and vigorous campaign to implement the program it had adopted in the convention of the preceding May, and to retain and extend its wartime gains. The offensive was carefully planned and organized and it unrolled in three big waves.

First the union went after the women's trades in the New York market. On January 21, 1919, a strike was declared in the waist and dress industry; on February 8 the kimono workers were called out; and on February 24 the children's dressmakers. These strikes ended during March and April with wage increases and a 44-hour week.

The second drive was in the cloak and suit trades. The New York cloakmakers went out on a general strike on May 4, demanding wage increases, a 44-hour week and week work. The struggle spread to other centers—Baltimore, Chicago, Boston, San Francisco, Toronto, Montreal—to virtually every market in the industry. The strikes were all successful and were settled on the basis of the original demands.

The final campaign was conducted from July to November in the rest of the industry, in such miscellaneous trades as corsets, raincoats, undergarments and embroidery. In these trades too the International signed victorious settlements which included week work, the 44-hour week and wage increases.

This sweeping 1919 offensive, superbly executed under Schlesinger, extended unionism and strengthened collective bargaining in most branches of the industry. The union felt strong and confident. Dues were increased and regularly collected, strike funds were set up and earmarked. The International and various locals initiated or extended all sorts of benevolent, educational and recreational activities. Many local bodies bought or built their own headquarters. Vacation homes, notably Unity House, were founded.

The various local union and joint board publications were merged with the *Ladies Garment Worker,* and the new official organ of the International was renamed *Justice.* It appeared in three editions, English, Italian and Yiddish, under the general editorship of Saul Yanovsky, a veteran philosophical anarchist of great personal culture and high standing in the world of labor. It was in those days that the International began to contribute to various labor, progressive and philanthropic causes in such a princely fashion that it became known as the Rockefeller Board of the labor movement. Large sums were donated to various charities in this country and to the victims of the European war. The union voted $150,000 for East European relief and it gave $100,000 to the Great Steel Strike of 1919, more than any other labor organization.

The 1920 convention at Chicago celebrated the twentieth anniversary of the International. It was one long demonstration of rejoicing, solidarity and exuberant optimism. The union could boast over 105,000 members in good standing and it was now one of the most important unions in the country. Its prestige both in the labor movement and in public life was unique.

The hero of the hour was Benjamin Schlesinger.

BENJAMIN SCHLESINGER

Schlesinger was born in Krakai, Lithuania, on December 25, 1876. His father was a small-town rabbi, a man of great poverty, dignity and little learning. Such homely leaders in the ghettos of Eastern Europe were a good deal like the colored Baptist preachers in the backwaters of our own South a generation ago. As a youngster Ben Schlesinger went to the local *Kheder,* the typical parochial school of orthodox Jewry, where secular learning was taboo and the only subjects were a semiliterate Hebrew and the Old Testament, absorbed by rote and rod. At twelve he was an orphan.

He came to this country in 1891 as a boy of fifteen, and his first job was peddling matches in the Chicago slums. Within a few weeks he went to work for a cloak contractor as a "floor boy," the Oliver Twist of the sweatshop. He swept up, ran errands, carried bundles and learned the cloakmaking trade. At this period the sweatshop was at its lowest depths. Endless hours, starvation wages, unspeakable conditions turned the boy into a flaming rebel. He was also a born agitator, and at seventeen he led a strike in his shop and settled with the boss. By that time he was, of course, a Marxist, way on the left, and a devout disciple of Daniel De Leon. He remained a socialist all his life, though as the years went by his socialism became more and more nominal and conservative. He was always the socialist trade unionist par excellence. He became one of the important figures of the opposition to Gompers in the AFL—the typical social-democratic minority leader like MacDonald and Morrison and Bevin in the British Parliament. The truth is that right-wing socialism is indistinguishable from a general belief in industrial democracy. The socialist dignitary is if anything slightly on the right of the average progressive, and Schlesinger was very much the dignitary.

The really dominant emotional undertone in Schlesinger's long career was a deep, almost fierce devotion to this country and its democratic institutions. In this he was typical of the Jewish immigrants of his generation who, however wild their political utopias, knew one thing: America was liberty. Pogroms were impossible, education was free, and opposition was not only permissible but sound American doctrine. In czarist Russia you couldn't discuss the powers that be above a whisper; here you could call Cleveland a "lackey of Wall Street" and McKinley "Mark Hanna's office boy"—and still be urged to vote for them at the next election. And by a curious twist of the human mind the American Government, which in the Marxist jargon was merely "a committee of the ruling class," became the very symbol of a functioning democracy. This simple, sentimental patriotism was as much part of the average old-time socialist workingman as the air he breathed. His radicalism—loud, highfalutin and humane—was completely different from the hard-boiled and spiritually corrupt nihilism of the modern left-wing totalitarian. If you really know the old-time cloakmaker you know that his love of American life and institutions is as deep as his love of family, and his outlook—for all his socialism—is thoroughly middle-class.

Schlesinger was very characteristic of this type. Behind all his orthodox socialist platform phrases—"class struggle," "capitalist exploiters," "class-conscious proletariat"—he was essentially the old-fashioned progressive. He was all het up about Bryanism, La Follettism, the Bull Moose movement, Wilson's New Freedom, though he always voted the Socialist ticket with the abiding conviction that all these movements had simply stolen the planks of the Socialist platform. It would be impossible to visualize Ben Schlesinger mounting Marxian barricades to overthrow the capitalist system which gave him the very opportunities he enjoyed as leader of "the toiling masses." In 1920 he visited Soviet Russia, and the terrorism in the revolutionary air chilled him to the marrow.

The present-day generation of leaders in the International do not need the socialist vocabulary to convince themselves that they live in a free society. David Dubinsky does not think in terms of the proletariat and the class struggle. Schlesinger—and this is crucial in placing his personality—was the last of the great *immigrant* leaders of the women's garment workers.

His childhood and his early sweatshop days marked him for life. He was a somber figure, melancholy without hypochondria, and in his personal relations touchy and impatient. Saul Yanovsky, the first editor of *Justice,* a shrewd observer of men, wrote:

I cannot recall having ever heard him laugh. In fact, I rarely saw him smile—even at the best of times, when everything seemed to be going smoothly. A sick man, a hard-hearted man, some of those who met Ben Schlesinger believed him to be. . . . But he was not unkind by nature. He undoubtedly was a very embittered person. The bitterness was the rust upon the iron of his soul, which had corroded it during his early youth, his first immigrant days in America. . . . The bitter want he had experienced in these years had placed its hard stamp upon his makeup for the rest of his life, and would not let him taste in full even the joys of success and the exultations of personal triumph which later years had brought him.

But Schlesinger functioned effectively in spite of these deep scars and his lifelong illness—tuberculosis and later an incurable endocrine imbalance. He was able, ambitious, dramatic and in-exhaustible—inexhaustible with the radium-like energy of a sick man living on his nerves. He won his great victories and his petty triumphs (and he was never able to distinguish between them, for everything was equally important) by wearing people down. Contact with him was like riding an electric horse. Once he called a union official to his home in the dead of night. He wanted to make sure that the man would side with him on some minor issue, though the poor fellow was one of his oldest friends and stooges. "Let's take a walk," Schlesinger said, "and talk things out." And for two hours they walked and walked while Schlesinger developed his position to its remotest contingencies. Every now and then his friend tried to interrupt him, but he couldn't get a word in edgewise. Finally Schlesinger, utterly exhausted, paused to inquire if he had made himself clear. "Why yes," said his victim. "I've been trying to tell you all this time that I absolutely agree with you."

"I know, I know," Schlesinger said. "But suppose you hadn't?"

Though arrogant and haughty, Schlesinger was democratic in his own peculiar way. No one was too insignificant to escape his domineering energy, which was bent on converting people to his position. He wanted to exact agreement, not obedience, a far more nerve-racking process. His dictatorial temperament had something of the quality of old Mr. Day in *Life with Father*. He looked upon himself as a union patriarch.

His son Emil, now a prominent labor lawyer, often speaks of his father's spiritual integrity, his many gifts, his wisdom. "But your father was pretty hard to get along with, wasn't he?" I once asked him. "Yes, of course," said Emil with affectionate pride. "Don't forget that Father was a tyrant. He wasn't the ordinary kind of democrat. He always had to have his own way. His democracy consisted in explaining his stubbornness in minute detail." Emil loved his father as the Day boys did theirs. But the General Executive Board of the International had no such filial devotion. To them Life with Schlesinger was one long headache.

I remember Schlesinger as one of the most fascinating-looking men I have ever seen. He was a handsomer version of Abe Lincoln. He was tall and gaunt and melancholy. His eyes were deep-set in a long, sad face, and he had that *Weltschmerz* look, as though he had taken on the heartbreak of humanity. This air of misericordia gave him a thoroughly unfair advantage in his dealings as a politician and negotiator, an advantage he exploited with consummate skill. And he used his illness as part of his technique. When negotiations with employers reached a stalemate, he would sometimes collapse. His fatigue was genuine enough, but his dramatic use of it was worthy of an Edwin Booth. He would lie down on a couch in utter exhaustion, making Messrs. Potash and Perlmutter feel like sadists and heels. Once a manufacturer who thought that Schlesinger had passed out cried, "For God's sake, let him have that goddamn nickel, or he'll die on our hands."

Even with his union colleagues who knew their Schlesinger this technique was usually effective, for they could never tell where illness ended and histrionics began. Neither could Schlesinger. When crossed, he always felt that he was being tortured beyond endurance.

Schlesinger was precocious in his leadership. In his early twenties he was already the outstanding personality among the Chicago cloakmakers, who were all personalities. At thirty he served for one year as president of the International. From 1904—07 he was manager of the cloakmakers' Joint Board in New York, then the second biggest job in the union. During the next five years he was business manager of the *Jewish Daily*

Forward. He never really left either the *Forward* or the union; he was always on a sort of unofficial leave of absence from one to the other. By temperament he was a superb journalist. For years he wrote a column in the *Forward,* talking to the Jewish workers, and especially to his cloakmakers, in their own special language. And whether they agreed with him or not they never missed his stuff. He knew the cloakmaker as Westbrook Pegler knows George Spelvin, American. And he fought his battles with his pen as intensely as he did everything else.

His stubbornness was exacerbating and incessant, with nothing of the unflinching quality which Sigman, his inveterate enemy, possessed. Schlesinger was not a fighter; he was a gifted prima donna. His vanity was incredible. Love of the limelight is the besetting sin of most leaders, and especially of labor leaders, who have risen through unusual aggressiveness from dismal poverty and narrowness of circumstances. Many of them have become fixed in a state of permanent astonishment and conceit at their own success. But in Schlesinger this egotism reached a point of exaltation. He was childishly jealous of power and hungry for publicity, which made association with him not only difficult but often embarrassing. He would fly into a tantrum if some other leader in the union got a big and perfectly justified play in the newspapers.

And yet, in spite of these traits, Schlesinger had genuine personal dignity. He was an emotional aristocrat, incapable of vulgarity in his official or private life—except for his avidity for the limelight. No one could get chummy with Schlesinger; he was too aloof, too preoccupied with great affairs, no matter how petty these affairs might actually be. No one called him Ben; it was always "Schlesinger." He was never one of the boys. He had no small talk in him. Personal gossip did not interest him, off-color stories pained him, and indeed, no one felt inclined to tell him any. His martyred air, his really noble face, his beautiful hands, which he used with eloquence—the whole business gave him a romantic quality, as if he were a Lord Byron among the labor leaders. And this got on their nerves, for they knew that Ben Schlesinger was no more Byronic than they were.

Schlesinger was a skillful negotiator, though he knew a great deal less of the industry than such men as Sigman or Dubinsky. His skill as a negotiator lay in his superb gall, in his dexterous opportunism and especially in his formidable talent for publicity. For above all Schlesinger excelled in his instinct for and understanding of public opinion. The dramatist in him infallibly created the sort of news that gave the union a good press. Newspapermen saw through him, but they couldn't help printing what he handed out. He knew how to enlist the great public figures of his day in strikes, negotiations and the struggles of the union.

Way back in the strikes of 1907 and 1910 he flabbergasted the cloakmakers by securing the sympathy and the active intervention of prominent outsiders in their behalf. Later he got governors and Presidents to appoint commissions to study the industry and senatorial committees to investigate conditions. He practically invented the Governor's Special Advisory Commission, first appointed by Governor Smith, which became a semipermanent institution in the New York cloak and suit market. The manufacturers came to dread his skill in securing the good will of the great and mighty whenever there was any trouble.

But his resourcefulness as a leader deserted him in any major crisis *within* the union, when compromise was out of the question. He had no stomach for desperate inside slugging. He was stubborn, but not hard-boiled. His strength derived less from inner character than from the strains of a neurotic personality. When he had his union solidly behind him against the outside world he had no end of self-assurance. But when the very life of the union was endangered by internal conflicts he couldn't take it. He folded up before such genuinely tough campaigners as Morris Sigman or Joseph Breslaw. In 1923, when the Communist campaign for control of the International was clearly leading to civil war, Schlesinger had to give way to Morris Sigman. Sigman, though infinitely less interested in personal power than Schlesinger, had that essential toughness of fiber which enabled him to weather the crisis. As president of the International, Sigman fought through this civil war. But when the struggle was over, Schlesinger was recalled to the presidency. He was the healing opportunist.

Though designed on a lesser scale, Benjamin Schlesinger reminds one a good deal of Woodrow Wilson. Like Wilson, he was an impressive phrasemonger, sensitive, proud, squeamish and omniscient in many things that weren't so. Above all, like Wilson, he was an egotist who was never able to identify himself with his cause but merely confused himself with it. It was this spiritual insufficiency that made both of them seem "sincerely insincere." They were both in love with power without the fundamental ruthlessness to wield it, domineering in personal relations and incapable of working well with others. They didn't know the difference between a stooge and a collaborator, and to them opponents always seemed "a little group of willful men."

And like Wilson, though again on a smaller scale, Schlesinger achieved much, died a broken man, and can be justly appreciated only in the perspective of history.

Soon after his death in 1932 I talked about Schlesinger with an old-time cloakmaker, a minor official in the International, who had known him well and long. "Ben Schlesinger," he said reverently, "was a son of a bitch. But he was *our* son of a bitch." From a cloakmaker that was a tribute.

RETREAT IN ORDER

Early in 1920 the International reached its highest point until the advent of the NRA. But by autumn things went into reverse. The postwar deflation was setting in, and organized labor was driven to the defensive. The AFL rapidly fell off in membership and influence. American industry swung into a nationwide campaign for the open shop—called the "American Plan." And the women's garment manufacturers went on a rampage.

In April 1921 the Protective Association in New York came

out for the restoration of piecework in the cloak market, for sharp wage reductions and regressive shop conditions. The union managed to fend off the full force of this reaction by making a "supplementary agreement" which called for a higher productivity of labor as a means of cutting labor costs. But the main offensive against the union came in the fall of 1921. A national conference of cloak manufacturers' associations, initiated by the New York crowd, met in Atlantic City and demanded a "readjustment" in the agreement. They were determined to reduce wages and go back to piecework and the 48-hour week. And the New York manufacturers announced that on November 14 they would begin to operate their shops on these new terms. The union answered with a general strike and 55,000 cloakmakers walked out.

Within the next few weeks the same pattern was repeated in the cloak industry in Philadelphia, Baltimore, Chicago, Los Angeles and Montreal. In Philadelphia the waist and dress trade also became involved, and a number of the minor women's trades in New York City went on strike. By December more than 75,000 garment workers were out.

The International met the employers' offensive with a new weapon. Morris Hillquit and Samuel Untermyer applied for a temporary injunction against the New York Protective Association for violating the collective agreement. The injunction was granted and made permanent by Judge Robert F. Wagner, who was to father the Wagner Act in the days of the New Deal. This unexpected move confused and disorganized the employers, and some of them broke ranks and individually came to terms with the union. By February 1922 the Protective yielded as a body and announced that its members would reopen their factories on the old basis. The other centers followed suit.

But the International lost ground in the women's trades and in the waist and dress industry. The Harding depression was now in full swing and by fall business conditions in general were extremely bad and unemployment mounted. The International, which had boasted a membership of 105,000 in 1920, had dropped off in two years to 93,000.

The retreat of the union was serious but it was not a rout. Far more serious was the menacing development of a new and growing left-wing opposition which was to lead to the so-called civil war in the International.

VII

Civil War: Morris Sigman

D URING THE DECADE after the Armistice the entire organized labor movement had to meet a sustained Communist offensive. This attack fell with special fury on the garment workers. Their unions had been arenas of factional conflicts for decades. And naturally, when the Bolshevik Revolution split the labor and socialist movements all over the world into warring camps, the International was hit harder than any other union in the country.

Among these workers the civil war between the right and left unfolded with classic precision and ferocity. It nearly wrecked the union and left it so exhausted that only the government pulmotor of the NRA could resuscitate it. But when the danger was over the International had developed an immunity to the totalitarian virus. Today this union is safe from Communist disruption. The issue was fought through to a finish, mostly because its outstanding leaders had had a long experience in appraising and dealing with factional feuds and were quick to recognize the menacing proportions of Bolshevism. To them Bolshevism was the old anarcho-Marxism, but in the terrifying form of a new and aggressive world power.

Morris Sigman, who was elected to the presidency for the purpose of fighting through this issue, was not the man to be appalled by the ominousness of the struggle. He saw the thing through without yielding an inch. Indeed he was almost too inflexible. Fortunately David Dubinsky, leader of the richest and most solid local in the union, the New York cutters, acted as Sigman's chief of staff. And Dubinsky had in abundance what Sigman lacked—tactical acumen. Under these two men both revolution and reaction were avoided; neither the Communists nor the die-hards came out on top. And though after the struggle the International was almost gone, what was left of it was healthy and progressive. Nowadays it can even afford, as can no other union, an occasional Communist local manager or business agent. They can no longer do harm as Bolshevik dervishes and union wreckers. In fact, they tend pretty strictly to union business.

CHICKENS IN A CHINA SHOP

The new left-wing movement began as far back as 1917, when a handful of waist- and dressmakers of Local 25 in New York City formed a Current Events Committee. Local 25 had come into its own with the Uprising of the Twenty Thousand in 1909 and it had a romantically militant tradition. These girls looked upon themselves as a sort of women's battalion whose mission it was to infuse a new spirit into the stolid regiments of cloakmakers and pressers.

Many of the waistmakers had come to this country from Russia soon after the revolution of 1905, and they had all the dedicated earnestness of the Russian revolutionary woman. Since America offered no Romanovs to vanquish, their fervor overflowed into all sorts of fads and movements. They were feminists, co-operative enthusiasts, suffragettes, dietary zealots, devotees of Margaret Sanger—non-conformists and insurgents of every hue and cry. They insisted that the union must be something nobler than a "mere dues-collecting agency," that it should express "a way of life with vision and a soul."

They lived in a state of chronic exaltation over the Class-Conscious Worker and the Toiling Masses. Naturally these rank-and-file Jeanne d'Arcs scorned the bureaucracy, by which they meant nearly every leader in the union. For years they had made life miserable for Rosenberg and Dyche, and now they were closing in on Ben Schlesinger. To all this trancendentalism of the girls the trade union bureaucrats reacted with bored indifference, and the heavy humorists among them offered cynical advice on how to get it out of their systems.

THUNDER ON THE LEFT

The Current Events Committee was a romantic movement, and like all such movements in their early stages it soon became a hatchery for disaffection and rebellion. Within a year or two the Committee evaporated, but the opposition to the union bureaucracy kept on growing. And this opposition was in many ways justified. The girls were not too starry-eyed to lack insight into the ways of the union bureaucrat. Many of the officials— managers, business agents, organizers, secretaries of this or that —were old-timers who had gradually degenerated into smug routineers. The hotheaded rebels of a former day now banked their fires to keep their chairs warm, and the barricades of their youth had been remodeled into rolltop desks.

The voice of opposition in Local 25 soon found an echo in other unions of the International, particularly among the cloak-makers of Locals 1 and 9. Local 1 was the charter union of cloak operators, while Local 9 consisted of finishers, tailors who give the finishing touches to a garment. These cloakmakers were by long habit devotees of grievances and cherished the memory of every factional dispute and union battle. A real cloakmaker always sounded like a Civil War veteran, endlessly recounting old campaigns. In their yarns the Sigman of the Wobbly days became a sort of Stonewall Jackson of the pressers, and the Hourwich affair assumed the proportions of the march through Georgia. In time these cloakmakers joined the dress-makers against the hierarchy.

The bureaucracy might have dismissed the "ravings" of the opposition but, alas, they could not laugh off history. By 1919 the Bolshevik Revolution was entrenched and, like the great American and French revolutions in their day, had unleashed global forces which no "pure and simple" trade unionist could handle. Leagues, groups and Jacobin clubs of all kinds sprang up overnight and gave the bureaucracy something real to worry about. The Soviet influence was all too clear in the very name of the most vociferous of these groups, the workers' councils which popped up in the various locals. The preamble to the constitution of these councils was taken word for word from that of the Soviet state.

Only one large group of garment workers was little affected by all this excitement. These were the Italian cloak- and dressmakers.

Originally the Italian cloakmakers in New York had been scattered among various unions—Locals 1, 9, 17 and 35—depending on whether they were operators, finishers, children's cloakmakers or pressers. The majority of them were rather recent immigrants and liked to flock together. Finally in 1916 all the Italian workers in the cloak trade formed Local 48—named with characteristically Latin romanticism in honor of the Italian revolutionary uprising of 1848. For many years the manager of this local was Salvatore Ninfo, a veteran leader of the International.

In 1919 the Italian dressmakers in turn formed a union of their own, Local 89—named in honor of the great French Revolution. From the very first their leader has been Luigi Antonini, now first vice-president of the ILGWU, and Local 89 has become the largest single union in the International. In those days Antonini tried hard to be a Communist, but was in constant hot water with the party because he refused to toe the line. It is hard to picture Antonini, who is full of folk humor and wisdom, as a revolutionary teetotaler.

The rank and file of these two Italian unions were never radical. Many of them had been Sicilian peasants a few years back, Catholic and tradition-bound. They did not consider themselves the victims of a stuffy and corrupt bureaucracy. They were not all lit up about having "a union with a soul" and they formed no Current Events Committee to let off steam in the faces of their leaders. The Russian Revolution did not affect them as it did the largely Russian Jewish locals among the cloak- and dressmakers. During the early stages of the civil war these Italian workers remained fairly tranquil. It was only when the struggle got desperate that they became involved. And then they sided with the Sigman administration and stuck to it through thick and thin.

By 1919 the insurgent groups in the various locals coalesced into a vague but ominous movement. It included left-wing socialists, IWWs, anarchists and Communists, each with a nondescript following. Their fellow travelers, who were all extreme radicals, called themselves nonpartisans. This motley opposition, led by the workers' councils, now dropped that Soviet label and launched the shop delegates' leagues, named after the more respectable shop steward movement then in vogue in Britain. The leagues attempted to transform the whole structure of the union after the Soviet pattern. Each shop was to elect its representatives to a soviet in the local, which in turn would elect the Council of Delegates, the supreme directorate for the entire International.

The various shop delegates' leagues agitated for a sweeping industrial, social and political program. They considered themselves revolutionary "cells." Originating among the waist- and dressmakers in Local 25, they spread to the cloakmakers and to other branches of the industry. Their members incessantly badgered the union officials, they proposed that the leagues take over union functions of various kinds, and even began to call unauthorized strikes. What the leagues really added up to was a dual union in the heart of the International.

But until 1921 the left-wingers were not formally connected with the Communist movement, which was still an underground affair in this country. In fact they were not dominated by any outside group. They were a genuine internal opposition, perpetually bombarding the "old leadership" for its alleged sins of omission, reaction, corruption and lack of social vision. They made the most of every blunder and peccadillo of the officialdom, and inflated them into "betrayals and sellouts of the masses."

Sooner or later these malcontents were bound to fall prey to the fanatic and the demagogue. And indeed prominent Communists such as Ben Gitlow, Louis Fraina, Alex Bittelman, Nicholas

Hourwich, the son of Dr. Hourwich, began negotiating with the left-wing dressmakers and cloakmakers. They even tried to get them to walk out in sympathy with the Seattle general strike of 1919, which the Communists advertised as a sample social revolution, the harbinger of the American Soviet State. The Bolshevik drums had begun their tattoo in the International.

THE ISSUE IS JOINED

As the war clouds thickened President Schlesinger, who looked so much like Lincoln, acted more and more like Buchanan. Buchanan is a much-maligned figure in American history. He was shrewd and competent, a master of diplomacy and a man of the world. The only trouble with him was that he couldn't save the Union. It just wasn't in him. And in the same way Schlesinger couldn't face the breakup of *his* union. He was an old-time socialist who in his day had gone through a good many factional and schismatic rows, but the Communists threatened to blow his whole familiar world to hell and back. And so the job of fighting the growing left opposition devolved more and more upon Vice-President Sigman, who wasn't afraid of anything that might come up.

Early in 1921 the General Executive Board of the International declared the shop delegates' leagues unconstitutional. And it cut Local 25 in two. The shirtwaist makers remained in Local 25 while the dressmakers were organized into a new union, Local 22. There was a definite strategy behind this move. Sigman believed that the left-wing opposition was largely confined to the shirtwaist makers, whose traditions went back to the Uprising of the Twenty Thousand. The dressmakers, on the other hand, were comparative newcomers to the industry. The GEB figured that the radical waistmakers were bound to dwindle in numbers with the decline of their trade, and might be allowed to stew in their own juice, while the dressmakers, in a separate local, would be isolated from the Communist virus.

Despite bitter resistance the operation was carried through and Local 25 was sundered. But the effect was quite different from what had been expected. The left opposition, including the shop delegate system, was soon as firmly rooted in the new local as in the old. Moreover, the infection spread to the cloakmakers as well. The attempt to quarantine Communism only hastened a red epidemic all through the International. For by 1921 the left-wing movement was no longer just a progressive opposition within the union. It had become the tool of the Communist party in its attempt to rule or ruin American labor.

From 1919–21 the Communist International (Comintern) was inspired by the hope of imminent world revolution, and set out to "smash" all capitalist institutions everywhere, including the dominant trade union movements. This involved the formation in each country of dual "revolutionary trade unions."

But in 1921 the Comintern, at its Third Congress in Moscow, reversed this dual union policy and adopted the slower process of "boring from within" the established labor movements. In the United States this meant a Trojan horse maneuver within the AFL. It was the old De Leon strategy of the nineties all over again, only this time Lenin was running the show. In short, the policy of violent overthrow—not only of labor but of all "bourgeois" institutions—was now replaced by the technique of the termite. And that could be everywhere attempted within the law.

Accordingly the American Communists fused various underground organizations into the open and legal Workers party * which embarked on a program of "winning the masses" within the AFL and discrediting its leadership. This maneuver was called in the Communist jargon "the united front from below." William Z. Foster, who had been the leader of the Great Steel Strike, went to Moscow in the summer of 1921 and received orders to revive his Trade Union Educational League, one of his many red trial balloons in the labor movement. This League was now affiliated with the Red International of Trade Unions

* In 1925 this became the Workers (Communist) party, and in 1929 the name was again changed into the Communist Party of the United States. We shall disregard these permutations and speak throughout of the Communist party.

(Profintern) and was ordered to get control of all the left-wing movements both within and outside the AFL.

From the first the trade union activities of the Communist party in the United States were financed and directed by Moscow. And the direction was not merely by remote control. Moscow sent over as its first commissar for trade union work in this country Carl E. Johnson, a Lett who had lived for years in Massachusetts, and who now used the pseudonym of Scott. He was followed by Boris Reinstein, an old De Leonite who had been a druggist in Buffalo until he went to Russia in 1917. At the height of the civil war in the International the commissars were Josef Pogany, who went under the name of John Pepper, and Gussev, an old friend of Lenin's, who called himself P. Green.

By the end of 1921 most of the left-wing leaders in the International were either Communists or very close to the party. They were not merely under its influence but took their orders from it; they believed in "revolutionary discipline." None of these leaders was well known at the time. They were young rebels, ardent and sacrificial. The most effective was Charles S. Zimmerman, who is today one of the outstanding leaders of the International. Another prominent left-winger was the late Joseph Boruchowitz, who later became a business agent of the cloakmakers, and one of the very few Communist officials in the union after the civil war was over. Other active left-wingers were Isidore Stenzor, now an organizer for the International in Montreal; Julius Portnoy, a cloakmaker; Rose Wortis, then a dressmaker and today a functionary of the Communist party; and Joseph Zack, a dressmaker, who became a Comintern agent in South America but who eventually broke with the party.

Many of these leaders—those who had a bona fide trade union background—often disagreed with the Communist party directorate and criticized it for failing to understand trade union problems. But they always ended by knuckling down to the party line. As for the left-wing rank and file, most of them were deeply discontented and excited by revolutionary phrases, and understood little or nothing of the shifts and rivalries in the Communist oligarchy. Their Communism was a form of superstition, at once a millenarian faith and a nostrum for their troubles. The constant changes in Comintern policies were too swift and mysterious for the average worker to follow; he could only parrot the alibis and explanations his leaders gave for their dizzy turns. And the leaders had their own troubles, because they had to follow orders from Moscow, which made as much sense in America as if they had been thought up by the Grand Lama of Tibet. For these orders were entirely determined by the struggle for power within the Kremlin walls.

Late in 1922 a serious crisis developed in the radical wing of the ILGWU. The non-Communist lefts, especially the anarchists, who had played a leading role in the opposition movement from the beginning, at last realized that the Communists had captured the whole left flank. The anarchists in the union had always been motivated by a sense of moral values and they were incapable of playing totalitarian politics. Among them were such veteran trade unionists as Louis Levy, today vice-president in charge of the Far Western department of the union; Rose Pesotta, now the only woman vice-president, who alternates between work as an organizer and a job in a dressmaking shop; Nicholas Kirtzman, now an organizer for the International; and Max Bluestein and Rose Mirsky, today officials on the New York dressmakers' Joint Board. They and their followers made a clean break with the Communists and lined up firmly with Sigman.

The left-wing socialists, who then had less influence among the workers than the anarchists, were split in two by the growing crisis. Some of them joined the Communists and others went over to the Sigman administration. Thus the Communist party came into absolute control of the left wing, which was at last free to follow the party line openly and to use the party press in the campaign to capture the union.

By the end of 1922 the lines were drawn up. The pure and simple trade unionists and the right-wing socialists were in control of the International machine; the anarchists, under the seasoned leadership of Saul Yanovsky, sided with Sigman but cautiously maintained their usual moral independence; and finally, the left-wing opposition was directly controlled by the Communist party and run by the Trade Union Educational League, or rather by the agents of the Kremlin. All three groups had their own clubs, circles and leagues. The stage was set for real war.

This was the indicated moment for Schlesinger's exit, as he himself realized. But he couldn't bear to relinquish his leadership. For years he had been threatening to resign because of his health and even more because he was not "appreciated." But no one had taken his threats seriously. At a GEB meeting on January 12, 1923, he became irritated as usual at the criticisms of the Board members and as usual threatened to resign from the presidency. Instantly Joseph Breslaw, who was sick and tired of the prima donna, took him up. "Put it in writing," he challenged. Schlesinger wrote out his resignation and it was immediately accepted; Dubinsky was the only member who voted against it. Salvatore Ninfo became acting president, and a few weeks later at a special convention in Baltimore Morris Sigman was elected president.

MORRIS SIGMAN

Morris Sigman was almost the exact opposite of Benjamin Schlesinger. Both had strength, integrity, personal dignity and devotion to the union. But it is amazing how differently these qualities expressed themselves in the two men. Schlesinger's virtues, like everything else about him, were bound up with his inordinate self-esteem. He was his own hero, an idealized figure who lived on a diet of limelight and approbation. His essential integrity sprang from this ideal conception of himself, which would not admit of anything low or soridd. He was often incredibly petty, with the pettiness of a spoiled celebrity, but he was never cheap.

Sigman's virtues, on the other hand, were direct and healthy. They were not, like Schlesinger's, a tribute to his ego, but simple functions of his nature. For that matter, so were his failings, which were not deformities but limitations of character. His bitterest critics recognized his tenacity of principle. They called him obstinate, pigheaded, unreasonable—always with an undertone of grudging admiration. What they really meant was that, unlike most politicians, he lacked the useful art of rising above his principles. He had no talent for compromising with his own faith. He sometimes had to compromise, as all leaders must, but he could make concessions only to those whose motives he respected. And he was too ingenuous to be capable of cynicism. At one stage of the civil war the Communists were expelled from the union. Sigman insisted that they could be readmitted only if they "swore an oath" that they were no longer connected with any Communist organization. His friends pointed out to him how meaningless this condition was. But he just couldn't believe that a man would "perjure his soul" to play a political trick.

In their personal dignity the two men differed in this same basic way. Schlesinger was finicky and snobbish; again his dignity was an expression of his idealized self. Sigman's dignity came out of his simplicity. There was nothing theoretical in his democracy, nothing neurotic in his self-respect, and there was no self-consciousness in his bearing. Schlesinger's dignity was purely personal, while Sigman's dignity was purely human. And this same temperamental contrast holds for their devotion to the union. Schlesinger was an opportunist and a schemer; he never did anything directly which might be accomplished obliquely. He was primarily a gifted public relations man. Sigman was loyal to the union for the simple reason that it was his home and his life.

A real proletarian, a type rare among labor leaders, Sigman was a good deal like Andrew Furuseth. Furuseth, for years president of the seamen's union and one of the powers in the AFL, lived most of his life in dingy hotel rooms and ate in cheap diners. When Sigman was president of the International he and his wife lived in a furnished room with the barest standards of comfort. The great and mighty of this world had no allure for him as they did for Schlesinger. During lunch hour he liked to walk over to Union Square where the pressers always foregathered, and chin with his old cronies in the pressers' local. They reciprocated his sense of solidarity by visiting his office every payday and "borrowing" most of his salary. One of Sigman's closest friends told me: "Every payday a dozen pressers would line up in front of Sigman's office, ready with their hard-luck stories. Sigman could never refuse them. Finally it got so bad that we arranged to pay him outside the office."

Sigman had the tailor's vice of listening to gossip. He liked the *shooshke*—the inimitable name coined by the garment workers for the whispering talebearer. To Sigman the gossip of the rank and file was the voice of the people. He might come back to the office from lunch and order an immediate investigation of a high union official merely because some presser had *shooshked* into his ear that the official was a stool pigeon, a sellout, a thief and a wife beater. Max Danish, who followed Yanovsky as editor of *Justice*, and who cherishes the memory of Sigman, thinks that this was his besetting sin. "Some low-life," says Max, "would *shooshke* a horrible slander to Sigman, with the sole idea of softening him up for a touch. Sigman would be fool enough to take it seriously, and then there would be hell to pay."

In appearance Sigman was unimpressive and quite homely. His right eye looked straight at you and his left was walleyed. The effect was rather startling, especially when he was angry. He was of medium height and build, and it was only close to that one got a sense of his personal and physical force. On the platform he made a poor showing. He was an ineffective speaker and his complete lack of personal culture hampered him. Sigman had almost no formal education. His range of interests was extremely limited and his reading was confined entirely to labor news and trade publications.

He was, however, very effective in a small group. He was lucid and logical in presenting a problem—in fact, he was apt to oversimplify it. An excellent organizer, he had great ability to plan a campaign and to execute it to the last detail. In this respect he was such a perfectionist that it interfered with his efficiency. In his long career he made many blunders, because he was a poor psychologist and because he could not grasp a complex situation in all its ramifications. He lacked subtlety and astuteness; he had a first-rate second-class mind.

Sigman was born in 1880 near Akkerman in southern Bessarabia. His father was an overseer of lumber gangs for a big landowner, and until he was grown up Morris was a lumberjack. This background was unique among the Jewish leaders of the garment workers, most of whom came from town and village ghettos. It no doubt had a great deal to do with his lifelong sympathy for the IWW, whose base was in migratory labor, especially among the lumberjacks of the Northwest.

When he was twenty-one Sigman went to England, where he worked in a men's clothing factory for over a year. In 1903 he arrived in New York and got a job as a cloak presser. The other pressers in the shop had refused to join the International, then only three years in existence. They considered its leadership "corrupt" because the initiation fee was five dollars, which seemed to them an outrageous holdup. They tried to get the Joint Board of the cloakmakers to admit them for a dollar, but were refused. Sigman was horrified by such "exploitation," and started the Independent Cloak Pressers Union, charging ten cents initiation fee.

Several hundred pressers joined Sigman's union and it attracted the attention of the Socialist Labor party. A representative of Daniel De Leon persuaded Sigman to bring his pressers into the Socialist Trade and Labor Alliance. That was in June 1904. The following year the De Leonites helped to found the IWW, Sigman enthusiastically joined up and became the organizer of the IWW among the New York garment workers. In time, however, he realized that the International was the logical home for all these workers. He liquidated the IWW unions he had organized and in 1907 took his following into the International.

But Sigman never lost his affection for the Wobblies. They paid their secretary the wages of a "working stiff" and to prevent his entrenchment never allowed him to serve for more than a year. While Sigman appreciated that this was no way to build a movement, he liked the idea. For he sincerely believed that power and soft living corrupt men, and that even the best bureaucracy is a necessary evil to be watched and pruned incessantly.

Sigman's role in the International was always a militant one. In 1900 he was tireless in helping the shirtwaist makers in the Uprising of the Twenty Thousand. Unlike so many leaders in the AFL, Sigman was incapable of sex prejudice. To him women workers were like any other workers in need of organization. But he really came into his own the next year in the cloakmakers' strike. He had the front-line job of chairman of the picket committee, and to him that meant going into the thick of the fight. He was a typical Wobbly in this respect; he had plenty of guts. He could always be counted on to come to the aid of a worker attacked by cops or thugs, and a number of times he was severely beaten up. He had great physical strength, and his battles on the picket line are still a legend among the cloakmakers. After the strike he became director of the New York cloakmakers' Joint Board, and in 1913 the manager of the cloak pressers, Local 35.

Sigman was against Dr. Hourwich in the famous affair, though the majority of his followers were rooting for the doctor. He recognized Dr. Hourwich as a man of parts, but thought of him as a brilliant fool and an apoplectic intellectual. His own radicalism was far too proletarian to fit in with the doctor's volcanic nature. On the other hand, he considered the Dyche-Rosenberg leadership lacking in drive and imagination. Being an opponent of both Dr. Hourwich and the Rosenberg-Dyche machine, he found himself in an odd alliance with the socialists, and especially with Abraham Cahan. And when the socialists managed to elect their own man, Schlesinger, to the presidency in 1914, Sigman became secretary-treasurer.

The new team did not pull together very well. This is not surprising, given their complete divergence of temperament and outlook. Besides, Sigman was too active to enjoy his sedentary life as secretary-treasurer. He was much happier in his next big job as manager of the Joint Board of the cloakmakers, which he held from 1917–21. In 1920 he was elected first vice-president of the

International, and when the civil war against the Communists
threatened to disrupt the union he was called to the presidency.

Schlesinger loved power for its glory and prestige. Sigman, of
course, also wanted power, for no one who hates it ever gets to
the top. And yet it was to him more of a duty than a triumph.
One is tempted to say that he put up with power in order to
accomplish the reforms close to his heart. He was by nature a
trouble shooter. The presidency came to him at a critical moment
in the life of the union when his unusual combination of toughness of fiber and personal disinterestedness made him the one
man for the job. When the union was out of danger Sigman was
no longer essential and Schlesinger came back.

Then Sigman was free to run off to his ten-acre farm near
Storm Lake, Iowa, which seemed the only place where he was
really happy. The farm was no great shakes; it was mortgaged
to the hilt, it was small and the soil was poor. He eked out a
living by turning part of it into a tourist camp, complete with a
merry-go-round and hot dog stand. But even in Iowa he kept in
close touch with his friends in the International. Every once in a
while he was called East to straighten out some snarl in union
affairs. He was the Cincinnatus of the garment workers who
would leave his potato patch to take on the cares of state. In 1930
he came to New York for several months and worked at his trade
as a presser. Then he went back to his farm and died there quite
suddenly on July 29, 1931. He was only fifty-one years old.

During his years of leadership Sigman suffered from the
dilemma of the born libertarian in a place of power. This is an
unusual predicament for a leader. The natural freeman either
wants no power or when he gets it is quickly disillusioned. This
dilemma was especially galling to Sigman, who was a convinced
anarchist and therefore was against the whole bureaucratic business—and yet was part of it. He always retained his emotional
preference for the rebel as against the bureaucrat. But ironically
enough, the situation often forced him into the position of the
bureaucraft fighting the rebels.

"At one time," Yanovsky reminisced in *Justice* after Sigman's death, "Sigman reproved me for . . . indulging in meaningless praise of the leadership, [which] he said was unconstructive, and moreover was not rendering the union any service. He was very much displeased with me when I replied that I wouldn't last long as the editor of *Justice* if I were to follow his counsel."

But in time Sigman came to distrust the rebels too. He discovered that most of the "revolutionary" leaders were merely radical phrasemongers, demagogues and politicians, avid for power, or else ineffective fanatics who were afraid of power.

And so he always had to fight on two fronts. During the civil war he fought Communist disruption on the left and at the same time undertook to clean up some of the political machines on his own side of the fence. In fact, under Sigman's leadership any serious conflict in the union always developed a number of fronts. For whatever issues emerged in the course of a struggle, he was impelled to track them down, even though it meant crossing all the battle lines. This relentless honesty was one of his great drawbacks as a leader, and the root of his tragic career.

ACTION ON TWO FRONTS

The election of Sigman signalized all-out war against the Communists. On August 16, 1923, the GEB ordered the disbanding of all the left-wing groups within the union, since they were nothing but cells of the Communist party. Sigman also determined to get rid of the Communists in control of Local 22. They had managed to elect nineteen members to the executive board of the local, which gave them a majority. The International now accused these nineteen officers of having met in secret caucuses with Bert Miller, a prominent Communist party functionary in no way connected with the union. They were tried before the GEB and convicted of conspiracy, removed from office and barred from holding any union office for five years. In Chicago thirteen leading left-wingers were removed on similar grounds. In Philadelphia the International supervised all elections and two local unions were deprived of their charters and reorganized to eliminate all Communists from office. Equally hard-boiled measures were taken in Boston and in a number of smaller centers.

But Sigman's election also meant a big drive in his program of reform, a program which had nothing to do with the fight against the Communists. To him reform spelled two things: a push toward industrial unionism and the cleansing of what he called the Tammany machines in the union.

The International has always been an industrial union: its jurisdiction covered all the women's garment trades. But unlike the United Mine Workers, which lumps all its crafts together into local units, the ILGWU is a federation of largely autonomous unions, each one of which usually represents a separate craft. Sigman, the old IWW, wanted the International to pattern itself after the miners' union, the purest type of industrial unionism. Soon after his election he merged the Joint Boards of the cloakmakers and dressmakers in New York. The following year he amalgamated Locals 1 and 17, the cloakmakers and the reefer makers, into a new union, Local 2, and also fused two smaller groups, Locals 3 and 11.

Amalgamation of separate bodies in organized labor touches the most sensitive nerve of the bureaucratic organism. It upsets the status quo, reshuffles leadership, disorganizes personal machines, and pulls chairs out from under comfortably ensconced job holders. In merging the Joint Boards of the cloak- and dressmakers no big jobs were abolished because the setup in the local unions was left intact. But the fusion of Locals 1 and 17 was really painful. In this case Jacob Heller, a strong personality and a member of the GEB, lost his place as manager of Local 17. He obtained an injunction against the International, but that got him nowhere. He then left the union altogether and went into business as an accountant. He did not return to the union until 1929, but his machine in Local 17 continued to function. His followers called themselves the Friends Forever of Local 17 and fought Sigman at every turn. Still, Sigman temporarily strengthened his position by these amalgamations, for in the reshuffling his adherents came out on top.

While all this excitement was going on Sigman was also fight-

ing for good government in the union. Long before he became
president he had opposed what he considered unsavory and
reactionary machines in the International. And now he went
after them in earnest. His particular targets were Joseph Breslaw,
manager of the cloak pressers, Local 35, and then as now one
of the big figures in the union, and Louis Langer, secretary
of the Joint Board. Sigman started a campaign against these
men, accusing them of having built up a corrupt machine among
the cloakmakers. Breslaw, Langer and friends countercharged
that Sigman was reforming everything in sight simply to build up
his own power, and that his tactics were irresponsible and fratricidal, endangering unity in the anti-Communist campaign. But
Sigman was relentless and by 1925 both Breslaw and Langer had
to retire from the fray. Breslaw became an insurance agent and
Langer went to work as a presser. But, like Jacob Heller, they
never lost their hold on their following, and when the fury of the
civil war was over they went back to their old posts.

DUAL UNIONISM

When the 1924 convention of the International met in Boston
the tension between the rights and lefts was near the breaking
point. It took twelve days to seat the delegates. The credentials
committee, headed by David Dubinsky and Joseph Breslaw,
steadfastly refused to seat any Communists or fellow travelers on
the ground that they were the agents of the Profintern. The convention also refused to reinstate the left-wingers who had been
expelled from office in various parts of the country. And the constitution of the International was amended to penalize any union
member who belonged to an outside group which attempted to
dictate union policy.

But all this careful locking of the doors against the Communists proved ineffective; they just oozed back in. After the convention the local unions held their elections as usual. Sigman
insisted that all left-wing candidates had to take an oath that they
did not belong to the Trade Union Educational League or similar Communist organizations. This was, of course, a worthless

precaution, for in the totalitarian faith all means are justified, and in the pursuit of the party line perjury is not only a duty but a pleasure. The left-wing candidates cheerfully swore that they had no connection whatsoever with the Communist party or any of its works, and when the ballots were counted they were in control of Locals 2, 9 and 22—in other words, of the bulk of the cloak- and dressmakers in New York City.

Naturally the International couldn't tolerate Moscow control at the very center of the union's life. It simply had to get rid of this fifth column in its midst. And Sigman soon found an excuse for throwing the comrades out of office. In 1925 the left-wing locals held a May Day demonstration in the Metropolitan Opera House and invited as the chief speaker the late Dr. Moissaye J. Olgin, one of the worst intellectual turncoats in the radical movement, who was then editor of the *Freiheit*, the Yiddish Communist daily. Sigman used this meeting as grounds for removing the officers of the left-wing locals. Luigi Antonini, Julius Hochman and other administration chiefs advised strongly against such summary action. They were all for getting rid of the Communists but they felt that Sigman's procedure was unwise and constitutionally questionable. But Sigman was adamant. In his eyes the left-wing leaders had broken their pledge to have no truck with the Communists, and obviously the Communist party had arranged the Olgin meeting.

After purging the unions of their left-wing leaders the International took over the Joint Board and called for new elections to be held in August. But the disbarred officials refused to recognize their removal and simply went on acting in their official capacity. And to fortify their stand they formed the famous Joint Action Committee, a militant alliance of all the left-wing locals against the parent body. It was organized in the spirit of the Committee of Public Safety in the French Revolution, to protect the left wing in its drive for power. Louis Hyman, manager of Local 9, and the best-known fellow traveler in the International, became the chairman of the Joint Action Committee and the secretary was Charles S. Zimmerman, the brilliant young leader of Local 22.

LOUIS HYMAN

Louis Hyman is still one of the most popular figures among the New York cloakmakers. Tall, lean and impressive-looking, he has an air of Dantonesque audacity—which is precisely the quality he lacks. He is a typical cloakmaker—cocky, witty, bold in his kibitzing but good-natured and obliging otherwise. On the platform he is inimitable: he has the great gift of intimacy with an audience of thousands. He is what the Jews call a *Volksmench,* a folk type. His knowledge of his own Local 9, the finishers, is amazing. He seems to know all 5000 of them personally and is always delighted to chew the rag with any one of them.

Hyman was born in a small village in White Russia in 1887, the youngest of twelve children. "My mother," he told me, "ran the village store and made the living for all of us." "And your father?" I asked. "My father was a very religious man," Hyman explained. "He hung around the synagogue all day with his cronies, praying and gossiping and enjoying himself. It was a happy family arrangement. Mother did the work and Father did the praying. The only time she got mad at him was when he tried to tell her how to run the store."

In 1903 Hyman went to Manchester, England, and worked in a men's clothing factory. He joined the British socialist movement, and became quite a figure in the Manchester trade union world. "I used to speak on the same platform with Keir Hardie, MacDonald, Snowden, Ben Tillett, all of them," he says. In 1911 he came to America, and on the day he landed he joined Local 9. He soon became a business agent, then a member of the executive board of the local, then its president and a perennial delegate to the cloakmakers' Joint Board.

In his politics he was always radical. In the Socialist party he belonged to the left wing, and when it split over the Communist issue, he walked out. But he never joined the Communist party, though he became a fellow traveler of the most dependable sort. When the Joint Action Committee was formed he was the natural choice for chairman: he was very popular among the rank and file, he had a fine presence, and the fact that he was not a party

member made him a perfect front. He was a magnificent stooge
for the party, honest yet pliable, who might put up a terrific
argument but in the end was sure to toe the line.

After the civil war Hyman became president of the Communist Needle Trades Workers Industrial Union, the dual union
which the party set up in all the major needle trades. Then he
became a writer on the *Freiheit*. He didn't break with the party
until the Stalin-Hitler pact in 1939. A year later President Dubinsky, who appreciated Hyman's abilities as a general factotum
among the cloakmakers, took him back into the union, and in
1942 he was once more elected manager of his beloved Local 9.

Today his hero is David Dubinsky. "There's a man for you,"
he told me. "After all the years I fought him and abused him, he
took me back into the union. Here's what happened. I sneaked
into the back of Carnegie Hall during the convention of the
International in 1940. I just wanted to look around. Dubinsky
was making a speech, but when he saw me he stopped dead and
said, 'I want Brother Hyman right up here on the platform.' "
When he gets to this point of the story Louis is too choked up to
go on. And that's how Brother Hyman hit the sawdust trail for
union and democracy.

THE JOINT ACTION COMMITTEE

The Joint Action Committee was a flagrant dual union. It
functioned as a rival Joint Board, it issued membership cards,
it instituted its own shop control. It called upon its followers to
refuse to pay dues to the International and to ignore all its
instructions. It called strikes. It informed the manufacturers that
it was the only legitimate body representing the workers in the
cloak and dress industries in New York.

In July 1925, in order to display its control over these workers,
the Committee called a mass meeting at the Yankee Stadium,
which was attended by over 40,000 excited garment workers.
They roared their approval of a plan for a "demonstration stoppage" to take place on August 10 from three to five-thirty in the
afternoon. This stoppage was to show Messrs. Sigman and

Dubinsky just where the rank and file stood. On the appointed hour tens of thousands left their machines and filled seventeen halls throughout the city, where they were addressed by the left-wing leaders and Communist party orators.

Obviously the vast majority of the workers were with the left wing and not with the International. But that didn't seem to faze Morris Sigman. He calmly proceeded to reorganize the rebel locals and to reconstitute the Joint Board. Then the International took physical possession of the offices of the Joint Board and of the cloakmakers' Locals 2 and 9. Next it tried to storm the headquarters of the dressmakers' Local 22, which had a building of its own. But they were forewarned and resisted invasion. The Communist party mobilized its "mass support"—its Praetorian guard of Bronx housewives, students from the various city colleges, members of the Young Communist League, and other such would-be revolutionary shock troops, to swell the ranks of the beleaguered dressmakers. They camped in Local 22 day and night and finally the International gave up.

But in spite of all the turmoil and the intransigeance on both sides, a tentative truce was arranged between Sigman on the one hand and Zimmerman and Hyman on the other. Much as Sigman abhorred Communism, he had a strong affinity for young rebels like Zimmerman who opposed the old bureaucratic machines in the International. Conversations between Sigman and Zimmerman began about a month after the great demonstration stoppage and a modus vivendi was sketched out. It was agreed that the International was to "tolerate political differences"; the charges against the expelled left-wing officials in the local unions were to be "reviewed," which in effect meant rescinded, and they were to be allowed to run for office in new elections; and the left-wing delegates on the Joint Board were to be reinstated.

With these points out of the way, Zimmerman and Hyman demanded a system of proportional representation in the election of delegates to the various joint boards and of course to the conventions of the International. This was a crucial demand, for Sigman's power rested—much against his own democratic convictions—on the rotten borough system which still prevailed in the union. A small local of a few hundred buttonhole makers, for instance, had five delegates on the Joint Board and so did the huge dressmakers' Local 22. In the same way the small local unions had a disproportionately large number of delegates in the national conventions. Since most of them were mainly right-wing, they made up a Sigman majority in the conventions. In spite of this Sigman was heartily in favor of reforming this rotten borough system, and in his truce with Zimmerman he agreed that the question of proportional representation should be referred to a special convention and then submitted to the membership in a referendum. He also agreed to withdraw the two leading officials of the Joint Board, Israel Feinberg and Meyer Perlstein, in the interests of unity. Both men were given other posts in the International.

On the basis of the armistice special elections were held. Needless to say, the left-wing leaders were returned to office. Louis Hyman became the general manager of the New York Joint Board and Zimmerman the manager of its dressmakers' department. The armistice terms were plainly a great victory for the left wing. And yet the truce did not mean that Sigman intended to yield to the Communist party. He was hoping to pry Zimmerman and other young trade unionists loose from their Communist moorings and enlist them in his reform program.

He hoped for the impossible. The armistice terms only showed Sigman's guilelessness as a politician. His naïveté often played havoc with his stubborness.

THE SPECIAL CONVENTION OF 1925

The emergency convention of 1925, which began in Philadelphia on November 30, is still remembered by the women's garment workers as the most fateful in their history.

The Communists undoubtedly dominated the vast majority of the workers in New York City, and they were strong in other centers as well. Their battle cry was "Proportional Representation." It was an effective slogan, though everyone knew that the Communist party had adopted it not to advance union democracy but to fasten its own hold on the International. The Communists had another advantage. The left wing was one solid bloc; there were no arguments about leadership and no lost motion in tactics.

The Sigman administration had about 60 per cent of the delegates in the convention, but they were by no means united. Though Sigman had defeated Breslaw, Langer and Heller in his "cleanup" campaign their machines were still intact. The alliance between Sigman and the followers of Breslaw and Heller was merely one of dire necessity, and they made uncomfortable bedfellows.

However, Sigman could always count on the Italian locals. Salvatore Ninfo, manager of the cloakmakers' Local 48, and then the first vice-president of the International, sided with the administration as a matter of course. And Luigi Antonini, manager of the dressmakers' Local 89, had broken with the Communists completely and was now a staunch progressive. The Italian leaders had in fact no great problem about Communism in their unions. "The Communists in our local had enormous mass meetings," Antonini remembers, "in a room half the size of my office. We Italians were always with Sigman, and we're still with him." "But Sigman is dead," I reminded him. "Sure, he's dead," said Antonini. "So are Mazzini and Garibaldi, and we are still for them too." In the convention the Italian delegates simply voted *en bloc* on Sigman's side. Without their support the International would have been lost. They, together with the out-of-town locals, were the Solid South of the administration.

But the elite guard in the fight against the left wing were David Dubinsky and his cutters. Dubinsky held the real balance of power between all the forces lined up against the Communists. As the struggle intensified, the role of Dubinsky and his Local 10 became paramount. The cutters were strategically placed in the industry, and they used their influence with the employers for recognition of the Sigman forces in collective bargaining agreements.

Local 10 had a solid membership of over 6000 union aristocrats who were held together by high wages and firm discipline.

Its finances were in excellent shape, and its leaders as well as its members were overwhelmingly anti-Bolshevik, not only as a matter of union politics, but from a deeply rooted craft interest and a pretty consistent middle-class outlook on life. Their leadership, centering around Dubinsky, was competent, intelligent and coolheaded. It was during this period that Dubinsky's star began to rise. And when the civil war was over he was as well known to the rank and file of the International as Schlesinger and Sigman.

The truce between Sigman and the left wing was parked outside the convention hall. Neither side could keep up a state of suspended animosity in an atmosphere of irreconcilable conflict. On the one hand, the leaders around Sigman realized that a truce with the janizaries of Moscow was no truce at all, for they had used the armistice simply to strengthen their own position. On the other hand, the high commissars of the Communist party were also anxious to break the truce at the earliest possible moment. For the armistice had become a political football in the scrimmage for power among the big shots of the American Communist party. Each one of them tried to curry favor with Moscow by being redder than the next fellow. And so W. Z. Foster and Ben Gitlow, the party's trade union commissars, who cordially hated each other, were obliged to outdo one another in denouncing all appeasement of the "class enemy"—the class enemy being Sigman, Dubinsky, Ninfo, Antonini and friends.

The atmosphere in the convention was surcharged with hostility. What the left-wingers lacked in voting power they made up in sheer noise and nastiness. For the first time in the history of the union the galleries were packed with "visitors," the typical Communist claque of fanaticized viragoes, students, insurance agents and what not. They organized themselves into booing, hissing and clapping squads and did their stuff with venomous enthusiasm.

The two sides clashed at every point, important or trivial. It was a catch-as-catch-can fight with no holds barred. The left strategy was guided by William Foster as head of the Trade Union Educational League. The Communist party chiefs insisted that the fight must be conducted on the lowest possible level and that the morale of the whole International must be broken down so that the Communists could capture it.

William Z. Foster has all the deviousness of an ambitious but weak nature, screened by a mild and reasonable manner. He joined the Socialist party in 1900 and was expelled from it in 1909, whereupon he joined the IWW. The Wobblies got rid of him two years later and then he formed the Syndicalist League of North America, the first of his personal ventures in carving out a career for himself in organized labor. In 1916 his Syndicalist League became the International Trade Union Educational League, which again failed to catch on. During the Great Steel Strike of 1919, of which he was in charge, he posed as an orthodox AFL trade unionist. At the same time he was playing with the various Communist underground factions.

In 1921 he went to Moscow and got into the big time as the trade union commissar for the United States. Once in the Communist party itself, he continued to play the same game for personal power, hatching his little plots and knifing his rivals. He is cordially disliked by his fellow commissars—but Moscow keeps him on as chairman of the Communist party of the United States.

When the convention opened, the left-wingers began a campaign of character assassination against the leaders of the International, which was broadcast and amplified in the Communist party press. The whole idea was to rouse the mob spirit against them. The labor editor of the *Freiheit* was one Yuditz, whose columns reeked with the coarseness of an East Side saloon. No term of abuse was too low for the leaders of the International— crooks, gangsters, gunmen, stool pigeons, yellows, mobsters, police agents were among the more printable epithets. The chief victim was Morris Sigman. In Dubinsky's opinion this campaign— which kept on for years—was really responsible for Sigman's early death. "Most of us in the International just took it," he said. "But Sigman was so pure that it made him sick at heart. And that scum on the *Freiheit* and the *Daily Worker* knew it."

As soon as the convention opened the lefts insisted on a general amnesty for their "political victims," as they called the Communists who had been disciplined in one way or another by the union. The administration refused to dignify these disrupters as political offenders, but in the interests of peace it did grant a blanket amnesty. Then the real fight started, on the issue of proportional representation. If the lefts had carried the day they would have gotten control of the union. Naturally the administration fought them tooth and nail. Moreover, Sigman and Dubinsky did not favor scientific proportional representation because it always tends toward parliamentary anarchy and plays directly into the hands of those who are least interested in democracy. But they did believe in reforming the rotten borough system, and introduced a resolution of their own.

This plan provided for a more equitable system of representation which would enable the larger unions to carry their due weight on the joint boards and in the conventions of the International. And in order to keep the large locals from swamping the small ones their delegates were limited to a certain maximum. It was not scientific proportional representation, but it was a fair and practical solution of the difficulty.

Louis Hyman attacked this proposal as "inadequate and hypocritical." And Zimmerman quite correctly pointed out that in the preconvention truce Sigman had agreed to refer the question to the membership in a referendum. But Dubinsky, who was in the chair, ruled that the convention had final authority to adopt any form of representation it saw fit. He proposed to put to a vote the administration's own resolution on this matter. The lefts, declaring that this ruling repudiated the truce, staged a dramatic walkout under Louis Hyman. Whereupon the Communist party ordered them to return; it wanted to capture and not split the International. Bill Dunne, a member of the Central Committee of the Communist party, told the left-wingers: "You're going back in there if you have to crawl on your bellies." And back they went.

The administration's measure for correcting the rotten borough system was adopted. Once this was settled no major issues—

beyond the irreconcilable conflict itself—remained. There was no other business before the convention but the election of officers. Hyman ran for president against Sigman, and Zimmerman for secretary-treasurer against the incumbent Abraham Baroff. Sigman and Baroff were re-elected by a vote of 158 to 110. Everybody went home to prepare for the next battle. And that was the calamitous New York cloakmakers' strike of 1926.

THE STRIKE OF 1926

War or no war, the industry had to go on. The American woman couldn't walk around in tatters while the International was trying to shake off the grip of the Comintern.

When Sigman came to power in 1923 the Harding depression was gradually lifting. He felt that the time had come to press for long overdue reforms in the cloak market, and advanced what he called the New Program of fourteen points, which was widely discussed by the employers as well as the workers. This program called for greater industrial efficiency, for higher standards of competition, for week work on a 40-hour week basis, and for an annual minimum of thirty-two weeks' employment. But the central plank in his program was to make the jobber, the wholesale merchant, responsible for maintaining union standards in the shops of his contractors and submanufacturers. Sigman wanted to restrict the number of contractors any one jobber could employ. This "limitation of contractors" was designed to eliminate once and for all the sweatshop which still flourished in the lower depths where the marginal fly-by-night contractor was constantly shaving his price to the jobber. Unless that chronic mess was cleaned up the industry could not be rationalized either for the manufacturer or the worker.

The employers were not enthusiastic about the New Program. And indeed they had something on their side. The contracting curse is not entirely the fault of the manufacturer. It is a vicious circle in which both the union and the bosses are caught. Whenever the union and the manufacturers between them managed to abate the contracting evil, the manufacturer began to profit by having the work done more efficiently under his own eyes. Whereupon the union would raise its demands; the manufacturer would feel himself penalized and would once more farm out most of his production.

No agreement on the New Program could be reached and Governor Smith appointed a Special Advisory Commission to suggest a way out of the impasse. The Commission was composed of the usual assortment of dignitaries—George Gordon Battle, a prominent New York lawyer; Herbert H. Lehman, then head of the family banking house; Arthur D. Wolf, another well-known banker; Professor Lindsay Rogers of Columbia; and the New York State Industrial Commissioner, Bernard L. Shientag, one of Al Smith's closest advisers. The Commission's report, which came out in June 1924, was decidedly in favor of Sigman's reforms. It was given wide publicity and under public pressure the employers had to give in. But gradually conditions slid back to their normal disorder, especially since the union was too preoccupied with its internal battles to supervise the enforcement of the new contract.

The Governor's Commission was revived, it studied the situation all over again, and reported once more early in 1926. Again it sustained Sigman's program, especially his desire for greater efficiency. But that involved better management, and better management involved allowing the manufacturer greater freedom in hiring and firing. Rationalization of industry doesn't go with a categorical "right to the job." Accordingly the Commission conceded to the employer the privilege of "reorganizing" his shop, by which was meant the privilege of discharging up to 10 per cent of his working force in the course of any one year.

Sigman advised that the Commission's report be accepted as a basis for negotiations. The inside manufacturers were willing to co-operate, but the jobbers refused. So did the left-wingers in the union. They rejected the report on orders from the Communist party, which saw a wonderful chance to fish in troubled waters. The party ordered the Joint Board to issue a call for a general strike in the New York cloak market. The left-wing unionists, notably Zimmerman and Hyman, were by no means enthusiastic about this ukase. They knew that the union could not afford the enormous expense of a general strike and that the workers were not psychologically prepared for a long struggle. But the Central Committee of the Communist party insisted, and as always the left-wing trade unionists came to heel.

The strike was called on July 1, 1926, and it lasted for twenty-eight weeks. Over 30,000 cloakmakers quit their jobs. When the strike was over the International was almost wiped out.

The Communists sublimated the strike into a "revolutionary struggle." To the left-wing leaders it suggested the classic revolutionary ordeal of fighting on two fronts, internally and against the outside world, just like the French and Russian revolutions. Zimmerman, Hyman, Boruchowitz fancied themselves as regular Dantons and Trotskys, and issued calls and manifestoes to the embattled cloakmakers, accusing the International leaders of sabotaging their struggle.

The tradition in the International has always been for the president himself to act as the chairman of a general strike committee. But the Joint Board appointed Hyman to that post and named exclusively left-wingers with very little strike experience to head the various committees. Only David Dubinsky was allowed to come into the picture, as secretary of the strike settlement committee, an unimportant job during the struggle itself; then when the left-wingers were ready to settle, he was frozen out.

The picket committee, run by one Elias Marks, a complete nonentity, spent nearly $250,000, only half of which was ever accounted for. The other half was supposedly spent on bribes to the police and other such items which could not be listed. All the other committees spent hundreds of thousands which were so scantily accounted for that it became a scandal. The entire strike cost about $3,500,000, of which only $1,500,000 went for strike benefits. One of the most disgraceful features of this orgy of mismanagement and corruption was the misappropriation by the Joint Board of $800,000 of the employers' money, deposited with the Board as security for their contracts.

Such well-known trade unionists as Hyman, Zimmerman,

Boruchowitz were, of course, not corrupt. And no one thought of accusing them of any such thing. The same goes for scores of minor officials. And yet corruption was rife. Questionable characters of all sorts muscled into the strike by the simple device of joining the Communist bandwagon. All a cheap little racketeer had to do was to become an enthusiastic red pro tem, and he would be welcomed and trusted as a collaborator by the Communist party functionaries who were really running the strike. What was worse, these functionaries siphoned off thousands of dollars of union funds into the party coffers.

Seldom in the history of American labor has a strike been so incompetently, wastefully and irresponsibly conducted. Scabbing was rampant. The employers, as usual in those days, had their full complements of gangsters, and the Joint Board fought back with professional gorillas. The employers hired the Legs Diamond gang and the Communists hired Little Augie, the Brooklyn mobster. Later it was discovered that both gangsters were working for Arnold Rothstein, czar of the New York underworld.

When a union calls in the underworld the gangsters are apt to muscle in and terrorize the leadership. In "unions" such as "Tootsie" Herbert's poultry wagon drivers or "Socks" Lanza's seafood workers, the whole organization is a racket. In a bona fide union like the International the gangsters, of course, cannot get control. But they can do plenty of damage before they are thrown out. The ILGWU leaders appreciated this danger and objected strenuously to the use of gorillas, feeling that picket duty should be left to a few husky and devoted union men. But their protests were ignored.

In the old days, say before 1920, gangsters were often hired in industrial disputes, but only for the duration. During the prohibition era, however, when the gangster invaded our whole social order, it wasn't so easy to show him the door. By the 1930s, indeed, he was able to dominate a great many metropolitan industries. This gradual industrial entrenchment of the racketeer was already beginning in the mid-twenties. In their efforts to get together with the employers to settle the strike the leaders of the Joint Board soon discovered that many manufacturers and jobbers were doing business directly or indirectly with Arnold Roth-stein, the leading underworld figure in New York. Rothstein in turn was in touch with the Communist party, which dealt with him precisely because of his great power in the industrial under-world. In short, since the Communist party leaders wished to settle with the employers over the heads of the International ad-ministration, the whole setup forced them to deal through under-world channels.

FATHER AND SON

For years one of the great figures in the New York cloak indus-try was A. E. Rothstein, a manufacturer who by 1926 was retired. He was considered by everyone who knew him a man of rare integrity and generosity of nature. He was one of those unusual American-born Jews who was strictly orthodox in his religion, and what was even more unusual for a native-born Jew and businessman, he was a serious Hebrew scholar.

Rothstein gave away a great part of his fortune to various charities and was chairman of the board of the Beth Israel Hos-pital, one of the best in America. After his wife died he moved into an apartment in the hospital, devoting his entire time to his philanthropies. Such a saint sounds too good to be true, and in a skeptical spirit I questioned a number of people who knew him. The reaction was always the same: A. E. Rothstein was a splen-did character.

But he had a deep tragedy in his life. One of his sons was the greatest criminal of the 1920s. Arnold Rothstein first came to national attention when he bribed the White Sox of Chicago to throw the World Series to the Cincinnati Reds in 1919. He quickly rose to the position of financier of the New York under-world. There was nothing of the typical criminal about him. He was a polished Mephisto, not a Caliban like Capone. He con-trolled gambling, prostitution and the drug traffic in New York, and as financier of the narcotics ring, bootlegging and the white slave traffic his activities covered the country. He bought judges, owned hotels and night clubs, and kept a retinue of skilled shyster

lawyers. He was shot in November 1928 at the Park Central
Hotel in New York City. His murderer was never found but the
underworld suspected George McManus, a gambler and an intimate of Jimmy Hines, the Tammany leader whom Tom Dewey
finally sent to prison.

Arnold's brothers and sisters would have nothing to do with
him. But after his mother's death his father would let him come
now and then to his apartment. The old man couldn't bear to
cut his son out of his life entirely, and hoped that in some miraculous way Arnold might be regenerated. And the strangest part of
this strange tale is the fact that Arnold craved his father's affection. As one man put it to me, "He slipped in and out like a
shadow. He just wanted to see the old man."

When the strike was going against the cloakmakers the Communist leaders approached the elder Rothstein, thinking he might
persuade the employers' associations to settle. In the past he had
often acted as a conciliating influence in labor troubles. But the
old man was by this time pretty much out of touch with the
industry, and he called in a large cloak manufacturer who knew
the ins and outs of the trade. And this gentleman promptly and
quite realistically told the strike leaders that the man they needed
to see was not the father but the son. A meeting with Arnold was
arranged, and the famous criminal graciously inquired what he
might do for them. The first thing he was asked to do was to call
off the Legs Diamond mob, which was acting for the employers.
A telephone call fixed that.

The Legs Diamond mob now vanished from the picket line,
and the Joint Board thought it could very well dispense with the
services of Little Augie. But Little Augie thought otherwise—
until he too received a telephone call from Arnold Rothstein.
Little Augie then vanished as quickly as his opposite number,
Legs Diamond, and that's how it became known that Arnold
Rothstein controlled both mobs. Then he got the Joint Board
leaders in touch with the employers—and that revealed his influence in the industry.

Some people think that one of the reasons Rothstein consented
to intervene in this rather open way was a desire to please his

father, who felt that helping to settle the strike would give Arnold a touch of respectability. But the real reason undoubtedly was that he wanted to muscle into metropolitan industry in a big way—as indeed his lieutenants, Lepke and Gurrah, were to do in the 1930s after his murder.

THE STRIKE COLLAPSES

During the first eight weeks of the strike, all through July and August, the Joint Board kept making haphazard settlements with individual contractors and submanufacturers on terms far below those recommended by the Governor's Commission. These were the very groups against which the strike had been called. The result of these piecemeal settlements was disastrous. About 12,000 cloakmakers filtered back to work and began producing for the jobbers, in effect sabotaging the strike as a whole. It was at this point that the left-wing leaders got in touch with Arnold Rothstein. And they reached a tentative agreement with the Industrial Council, the organization of big manufacturers which covered about a third of the industry. This tentative agreement provided for an average wage increase of 10 per cent, for the 40-hour week, a 32-week employment guarantee, and the right of the employers to discharge 5 per cent of their help in reorganizing their shops. Zimmerman and Hyman were anxious to settle at once on these generous terms, but the leaders of the Communist party—Foster and Gitlow and William Weinstone, the district organizer of the party in New York—insisted that the terms be rejected and that the strike go on.

This rejection of the favorable moment was the greatest calamity the International had ever suffered. And the rejection was motivated by the personal rivalry between the high muckamucks of the party who were vying with each other for an extreme "revolutionary" position, then the Comintern line.

The strike went on—from bad to worse. Not until two months later, on November 12, was an agreement reached with the Industrial Council. This time the inside manufacturers insisted on the right of cutting their working force by 30 per cent in the next two years. The union received no increase in wages except for 800 out of 8000 workers. It did win a guarantee of thirty-two weeks' employment a year, with a 42-hour week. But since the average work year in the large shops was about thirty-eight weeks, this gain was largely metaphysical. And finally, the union had to relinquish its demand for the "limitation of contractors." The Communist press hailed this settlement as "a great victory for the masses." It was the worst defeat the International had experienced in its entire history, and a major disaster for the cloakmakers.

On December 1 the submanufacturers' association demanded an identical agreement. And the jobbers, who were the main enemy, wouldn't even talk of settling.

On December 13 the International formally took over the management of the Joint Board to salvage what was left of the wreckage. Within a month Sigman wound up the strike. He could do nothing about the big inside manufacturers, for they had already settled with the left wing. And he couldn't get anywhere with the contractors and submanufacturers, but he submitted the dispute with them to a subcommittee of the Governor's Commission, which granted the contractors what they wanted—virtually the same terms as those arranged with the inside manufacturers. Finally, on January 12, 1927, Sigman renewed the old agreement with the jobbers, the one against which the strike had been called in the first place.

The International assumed the debt of $800,000 which the Joint Board had misappropriated from the manufacturers' security funds. Altogether $3,500,000 had been wasted or worse, a busy season had been lost, and the union was a wreck.

THE RIGHTS INHERIT CHAOS

The International now established a provisional Joint Board and ordered the cloakmakers to register anew and to receive new union books. This meant a complete reorganization of several of the most important local unions in the New York cloak industry. The ousted left-wing leaders branded this reorganization as unconstitutional. They urged their followers not to register and continued as a dual Joint Board. Many cloakmakers stuck to the left wing, refused to register and paid their dues to the outlawed Joint Board.

Yet the International's registry office did a fair amount of recruiting, and new charters were issued to the reconstituted unions. Members who failed to register were dropped. The rightwingers had, of course, the tremendous advantage that the employers recognized them as representing the workers. Within a few months the new Joint Board and the reorganized locals began to function in a convalescent fashion.

As soon as possible substantially the same measures were taken against the left-wingers in Chicago and in other centers where the civil war had raged. In 1926 the Communists had captured all the posts on the Chicago Joint Board except that of secretary-treasurer. Sigman went out to Chicago early in 1927, but found that the time was not ripe for the International to take over. Sigman had, however, valuable allies in John Fitzpatrick and Ed Nockels, the president and secretary of the Chicago Federation of Labor. John Fitzpatrick, for decades one of the most progressive labor leaders of the Middle West, was violently against the Communists. He had been in close alliance with Foster before the latter went over to Moscow, and he had sold Gompers the idea of putting Foster in charge of the Great Steel Strike—an idea both of them were to regret bitterly.

In August 1927 the Chicago Federation of Labor and the International together put the leaders of the Joint Board on trial, found them guilty of taking orders from the Communist party and of wrecking the union, and expelled them from the AFL. The International then ousted them from office. The left-wing leaders set up a dual union and had to be restrained by court order from using the name of the ILGWU. But their dual union didn't last very long.

The civil war played havoc with the cloakmakers in a number of other centers. But in all these cities—Montreal, Boston, Baltimore, Los Angeles and San Francisco—the Communists were eventually weeded out. The real battlefield of the civil war, from beginning to end, was New York. In the rest of the country the struggle was largely a reflection of the conflict in the heart of the trade.

MOSCOW'S THIRD PERIOD

Late in 1927 the winds of doctrine in Moscow once more veered sharply. Stalin had just won his historic struggle against the "left opportunism" of Trotsky, and now it was time for him to attack the "right opportunism" of Nicolai Bukharin and his friends. History knows no other technique of establishing a personal dictatorship: the dictator constantly selects and develops issues inherent in a great revolution, issues which are bound to divide his opponents to the right and the left of him; then by stealing the thunder first from one side and then the other he kills off his opponents in the social thunderstorm he has created. In all history there is no more brilliant example of this zigzag technique of usurpation than Stalin's conquest of power.

Stalin had now stolen the thunder of Trotsky's international Permanent Revolution with which to attack Bukharin's more conservative policy. Bukharin's "right opportunism" advocated slowing down the revolution at home and taking into consideration the indigenous problems of each country in spreading the revolution abroad. Stalin's victory over Bukharin meant, therefore, a decisive shift of the whole Comintern and Profintern to the left. The second period of the Comintern—the period of boring from within all democratic institutions—was now replaced by the third period, which called for a frontal attack on these institutions and especially on the dominant labor movements the world over. The Trojan horse technique was dropped. Arnold Lozovsky, then the head of the Profintern, launched a bitter attack on the American Communist party for "dancing quadrilles around the AFL," and ordered it to "organize the unorganized" into a rival labor movement.

Finally, at the Sixth Congress of the Communist Intertional, held in midsummer, 1928, the third period was officially launched. Moscow directed the American Communists to start agitation for a Labor party, and ordered the Trade Union Educational League to replace the AFL, as a federation of dual unions. Foster quickly fell in line with the new orientation, changed the name of his outfit to the Trade Union Unity League, and set to work. To justify this sudden reversal in policy the Comintern needed American "Bukharinites" to denounce as "right opportunists." Jay Lovestone, secretary of the American Communist party, and Ben Gitlow, his chief lieutenant in the trade unions, made satisfactory scapegoats. For one thing, they had been in power all during the second period and could be blamed for its supposed reactionary "deviations"; and for another, they had genuine difficulty in making a quick volte-face. They had been identified too long with the Trojan horse policy and were not too happy about the new one. They felt that a frontal attack on the AFL would merely isolate the Communist party from American labor.

Even more opposed to the new party line were the leaders of the expelled left-wing locals, especially Zimmerman. They were, after all, trade unionists first and Communists after that. They had insisted that their outlawed Joint Board was *not* a dual union, but a legitimate opposition within the International, and they knew that the rank and file would never follow them into an open dual union movement. But they found it impossible to oppose anything the party ordered. They were out on a limb— outlawed by the International and at the same time in disharmony with the Stalinist line to which they were tied. On party orders they formed a National Organization Committee, with Louis Hyman as chairman, for the murky maneuver of demanding admission to the International and then using the expected refusal as an excuse for forming a dual union. Their battle cry was "Build the Union"; their strategy was to tear it down.

Late in 1929 the National Organization Committee, which comprised left-wing leaders from all the needle trades, was ready to form a dual industrial union, including the furriers, the milli-

ners and the men's and women's clothing trades. The backbone
of this new organization were the furriers under their president,
Ben Gold, then as now an open Communist party member. The
new organization, the Needle Trades Workers Industrial Union,
was, of course, affiliated with the Trade Union Unity League
and the Profintern. Its chairman was Louis Hyman, and its secretary was Ben Gold.

But even before the formation of the NTWIU Lovestone and
Gitlow were expelled from the Communist party and formed a
heretical sect of their own which became known as the Love-
stonite movement. Zimmerman and many other left-wing leaders, with the exception of Louis Hyman, now joined the Love-
stonites. They broke with the party and with the NTWIU, and
began to work definitely for readmission to the International.
This time they weren't riding inside a Trojan horse; they wanted
to get back to the union openly and aboveboard. Zimmerman
and his group now put up a tremendous fight against all dual
unionism, opposed every effort to sabotage the union, and in the
struggle against the Communist party sought alliances with every
progressive group in the International.

It took them a long time to get back. Finally, in May 1931,
Zimmerman and his followers submitted to the ritual of regis-
tration and returned to the fold. Within a few weeks they were
once more active leaders in their local unions. In 1932 Zimmerman was elected to the executive board of the dressmakers',
Local 22, and in March 1933 he became its manager, which
office he still holds. After his long Moscow detour he was once
more back on the highroad of the International.

"SASHA" ZIMMERMAN

Charles S. Zimmerman is today a vice-president of the International and among its half-dozen most effective leaders. He
went into the Communist party because as a youth he had believed in revolutionary socialism, and Communism seemed to
him the logical conclusion of the socialist faith. His beliefs and
his loyalties were so bound up with the Communist movement

that he couldn't give it up without a long and painful inner struggle. But finally he turned against Bolshevism as being totally destructive of the very libertarian and democratic ideas which had originally impelled him. It has been my observation that a sincerely reconstructed Bolshevik is apt to be far more devoted and certainly more sophisticated in his appreciation of democracy than those who have never gone through this Machiavellian school. The graduates of the inner councils of Communism are never naïve about social politics. And anyone who has been a power in the party and then has broken with it on principle is also a brave man.

Zimmerman shows his schooling. He knows the answers in dealing with political groups. He knows his colleagues and the rank and file, and what to expect of them. He is an executive of the modern type—his intelligence is realistic, alert and efficient. And his leadership has the rare quality of style; he satisfies the leader image in the collective mind of his union. The dressmakers, with their romantic radical background, want élan and idealism in their top leadership—the last qualities one associates with the typical bureaucrat. But they also want realism. And Zimmerman's combination of dash and efficiency, of imagination and common sense, insures his popularity in the union.

Born near Kiev in 1897, "Sasha" went to a Russian school and had the equivalent of about two years' high school. In 1913 he came to New York and got a job as a knee-pants worker. Soon after, his shop, where the operators were mostly youngsters under twenty, went on strike, and after it was settled they joined the United Garment Workers, the old AFL union in the men's clothing trade. The boys discovered that the business agent who had organized them had stolen $5.00 out of every initiation fee of $7.25. With Zimmerman as ringleader they made such a row, ignoring union protocol, that the agent had to be fired, an unprecedented event in the stodgy old United Garment Workers of those days. Sasha later joined the Amalgamated Clothing Workers, which was formed in 1914 as a dual union to the United Garment Workers. In 1916 he got a job as a waistmaker and became a member of the International.

In the Socialist party he gravitated to the left, then joined the Communist movement in its early days. He remained in it for a decade. During his Bolshevik days he met Rose Prepstein, another radical member of his local, who is now his wife. She is still in the trade as a highly skilled dressmaker, and a member of Local 22. "What a crazy life we led in the party," says Rose Zimmerman. "It was like being lost in a fog."

THE CONVENTION OF 1928

The civil war in the International had really passed its crisis when the Sigman administration took over the left-wing unions and joint boards in the various centers of the industry. By 1928 the Communists had all been driven out and there was peace in the union—peace without victory. The membership had fallen to 40,000 members, of whom thousands were behind in their dues. And every effort to get the International on its feet again was sabotaged from the outside by the Communist dual unions and joint boards.

This exhausted condition was bound to emphasize the tensions in the top leadership of the International itself. Appeasement of the Communist party was out of the question, but even some of Sigman's staunchest supporters believed that it was time to re-shuffle the cards. Sigman, it was felt on all sides, was fine on the battlefield but not the man to rebuild. He symbolized civil war, not reconstruction. Moreover, everybody knew that in the coming period of convalescence Sigman would be temperamentally less interested in healing the wounds of battle than in fighting for his old reform program against the "Tammany machines" in the union. Suddenly there was a vivid nostalgia for the days of splendid opportunism under Schlesinger. His virtues were remembered—his flexibility, his flair for favorable public relations, his skill at collective and political bargaining. But the most important thing was that he was relatively unscarred by the mudslinging and hatreds of the civil war.

Sigman or Schlesinger—that was the issue which faced the Boston convention of 1928. And this issue somehow had to be settled without stirring up old animosities and creating new resentments. And so a group of Sigman's friends and enemies agreed to call in Morris Hillquit as moderator. His loyalty to both Sigman and Schlesinger was beyond question and his moral prestige in the union was unassailable.

President Sigman still had a nominal majority. His main support came from the unions outside of New York, from the Italian workers in New York City, and from many individuals to whom he was the peerless leader. But the minority had more real power. It included the strongest leaders in the International aside from Sigman himself. Three months before the convention Dubinsky had told Sigman that Schlesinger had to come back. Dubinsky felt that the union needed a change. He knew that to the thousands of left-wing sympathizers in the union Sigman was the symbol of civil war and a perpetual source of antagonism. During this whole delicate transition period, from 1929–31, while the left-wing progressives were trying to find their way back into the union, Dubinsky was to represent their interests almost as much as he represented his own cutters. Somebody had to. And in his desire to bring Schlesinger back Dubinsky could count on right-wing leaders such as Breslaw who had been traditionally against Sigman.

The right-wingers demanded a constitutional amendment to elect the officers of the International by referendum instead of in convention. The proposal was put forward in the name of democracy, but it was obviously aimed against Sigman, for if it passed it would be in effect a vote of no confidence in his administration. The majority, of course, realized that the move for a referendum was merely a ruse to oust Sigman, and they defeated it. And yet the demand for Schlesinger's return was too strong to ignore. Dubinsky knew that he and his group could swing the convention behind Schlesinger, provided it was done without stirring up added antagonisms.

The maneuver had to be carried through with great diplomacy, and the man for this task was Morris Hillquit. Acting as master of ceremonies, he made a speech eulogizing Sigman's leadership during the civil war, and urged the convention to re-elect him by acclamation. But he also suggested that a new office be created, that of first vice-president of the International in charge of New York City, and that Schlesinger be unanimously drafted for this post.

All this time Schlesinger had been hovering in the background, eager but coy. Sigman was persuaded to yield to the new arrangement, though he knew it was only a matter of time before some issue would arise on which he would have to resign. The truth is that he was thoroughly tired out and anxious to get back to his farm. The convention did exactly as Hillquit proposed. The delegates unanimously re-elected Sigman to the presidency and put Schlesinger into the newly created and most strategic office of vice-president in charge of New York.

As everybody expected, a few months after the convention Sigman resigned. At a meeting of the GEB in October it was decided to redivide Local 2 into its original Locals 1 and 17— to separate once more the cloakmakers from the reefer makers. This meant that Sigman's whole fight for industrial unionism within the International was lost, and that Jacob Heller would come back as the official leader of the children's cloakmakers. Dubinsky voted for the restoration of Local 17. He believed in reform, but only with the consent of those to be reformed. The fact is that the children's cloakmakers wanted to have their old local restored, and that was enough for Dubinsky. Then and there Sigman resigned, and Schlesinger stepped into his place.

RECONSTRUCTION: THE RETURN OF BENJAMIN SCHLESINGER

The International did not really recover from the havoc of the civil war, followed by the national economic collapse, until the NRA enabled it to organize the industry once more. The union was so prostrated that anybody who could keep it going at all was performing a miracle. And the Schlesinger administration did work this miracle. When there was no mortal feud to paralyze Schlesinger's energies he was an incomparable promoter. With strong enough backing his initiative and audacity functioned superbly.

The International's most pressing problem was financial. It was over $2,000,000 in debt. Schlesinger went out and raised enough money to get the machinery running again. In December 1928 he floated a bond issue among the membership which he called the Reconstruction Bond Loan, and raised $250,000 in cash. Then he got Julius Rosenwald to lend the union $50,000 and Herbert Lehman and Felix Warburg another $25,000 apiece. As one of the vice-presidents of the International, who knew Schlesinger intimately, remarked, "I don't know how he did it. Only Schlesinger could have gone to some of the biggest financiers in the country and got them to invest in a bankrupt union. I'll bet he even made them feel that he was letting them in on something pretty damn good."

In 1929 Baroff had retired as secretary-treasurer and Dubinsky was named as his successor. He was an ideal man for the job. He loves sound and thrifty administration, and can be awfully tough about it. He enforced a policy of drastic retrenchment. The official publications of the International were all put on a monthly basis. The number of organizers was reduced to a minimum, and salaries, from president to office boy, were slashed—on paper. Actually most of the officers and a great many of the employees of the union—stenographers, bookkeepers, elevator men—volunteered to forego most of their wages until things got better. They lived on their relatives and friends or borrowed money or ran up bills, but somehow they scraped through. Later they were paid their back wages. But these amazing sacrifices went on for a long time and created a spirit of fellowship among the officials and staff members which survives to this day.

These heroic measures might have succeeded in putting the union back on its feet had it not been for the national crash in October 1929. Now the union had plenty of company in its financial misery. In December, at the Cleveland convention, the delegates voted a ten-dollar per capita tax, which brought in $350,000. During the next year and a half the union used most of this money, plus what dues came in, to whittle down its indebtedness. But in August 1931 the union received another staggering blow. The International-Madison Bank and Trust Company, to which the union owed $140,000, was taken over by the State Banking Department, and all loans were called. There was nothing to do but impose another per capita tax, and by levying $3.75 the union hoped to be able to pay 50 per cent of its debt to the bank.

The old left-wing unions, Locals 1, 9 and 22, refused to pay this levy. They were against Schlesinger and had no scruples about exploiting the predicament of his administration. And they managed to work up some dissatisfaction among other local unions when the International announced that the Reconstruction Bond Loan, floated among the membership, could not be redeemed for several years, and that the bondholders would have to be satisfied with the interest. (These bonds were finally redeemed to the last penny.)

The financial situation was still pretty desperate when the Philadelphia convention met in May 1932. But Secretary-Treasurer Dubinsky could report that in the last eighteen months he had been able to reduce the International's debts by nearly $1,000,000. The union had actually paid out only a little over $470,000. The rest was adjusted with the creditors. Even so the International was still deep in the red, and the convention had to vote another ten-dollar per capita tax.

On the industrial front, too, the International began a slow convalescence. In July 1929 there was a brief general strike in the New York cloak market, with fair results. The next February the New York dressmakers also went on strike. Through the intervention of Governor Roosevelt and Lieutenant Governor Lehman the walkout was settled in a few days. The most significant feature of this settlement was the introduction of an arbitration system with a full-time impartial chairman in the New York dress industry, a system which is today a model of its kind. Aside from this the dressmakers gained nothing.

There were a good many other strikes through the country

between 1929 and the advent of the NRA, most of them pretty feeble and ineffectual. For by 1930 the general depression began to tell heavily in all the apparel trades. And all along the Needle Trades Workers Industrial Union, the Communist dual union, had to be reckoned with. It called strikes, it scabbed on the strikes of the International, it did everything possible to sabotage, to hinder and to obstruct. The avowed purpose of the Communist party was to destroy "the company union," as it called the International.

Schlesinger did his utmost to win back the workers who had gone over to the Communist union, and the even larger number who had dropped out altogether, for one of the invariable results of dual unionism is to discourage a great many workers with unionism of any kind. The International drastically lowered initiation fees, and even offered to reinstate without fee those who had joined the NTWIU. When Zimmerman and the other expelled left-wing leaders finally returned to the International they brought a couple of hundred followers with them. This was quite an accretion. Nothing illustrates more dramatically the low point to which the International had fallen than the fact that the dressmakers' Local 22, which now has a membership of about 26,000, then had no more than about 1500 members. In 1931 the whole International had about 40,000 members, and many of these could not pay their dues.

The return of Zimmerman and his group served to stimulate the various dress- and cloakmakers' locals. They brought energy and enterprise into the union. They immediately formed a Committee of Twenty-five, with Zimmerman as chairman, this time not as a Communist caucus but as a progressive vanguard, which went out to organize shops, to collect dues, to preach optimism.

Schlesinger, having come into office in opposition to Sigman, considered it part of his mandate to cancel some of Sigman's pet reforms. In January 1929 the decision of the GEB to redivide Local 2 into its original components was carried out. Locals 1 and 17 were rechartered and Jacob Heller resumed his old post as manager of the children's cloakmakers (Local 17). A few months later the merged Joint Board of dress- and cloakmakers was also resolved into its original bodies—a separate Joint Board was set up for each trade as before.

This liquidation of Sigman's whole reform program roused a storm of protest from his followers—the Italian dressmakers, the anarchists and syndicalists, and other die-hard Sigmanites, who deeply resented this "counterrevolution." They formed a loose federation and called themselves the Progressives. The Zimmerman contingent, of course, made common cause with them. The old left-wing locals—1, 9 and 22—formed a "triple alliance" in opposition to the Schlesinger administration. And for a brief moment the antagonism between the Progressives and the Schlesinger machine flared up in the Philadelphia convention of 1932.

Local 22 had elected Zimmerman and Louis Nelson to its executive board, although they lacked the constitutional requirement of one year's continuous membership in good standing. Their election was challenged at the convention and a brisk fight developed around that issue. But Dubinsky, now the real power in the union, adopted a conciliatory attitude and succeeded in getting the election of Zimmerman and Nelson confirmed. Dubinsky was hell-bent on peace. Moreover, he was essentially a progressive himself. He was glad to have people like Zimmerman and Nelson back in the union as a counterbalance to the old right wingers who surrounded Schlesinger.

The Progressives in the convention were now ready to air their grievances. They urged the immediate reamalgamation of the dress- and cloakmakers' Joint Boards in New York, the re-merger of Locals 1 and 17—in fact, they came out for complete industrial unionism. They proposed the abolition of all separate craft locals, which they declared were anachronistic, wasteful and "bulwarks of reaction." They were defeated on all points. For not only were Schlesinger and the right wing against them, but Dubinsky as well. However, the Progressives accepted their defeat with good grace. They too were anxious for peace, and they felt that in the long run they could work with Dubinsky. And when the convention voted the new ten-dollar assessment

Locals 1, 9 and 22, which the year before had refused to pay the levy of only $3.75, loyally fell into line.

Schlesinger was a mortally sick man. Ever since his return to the presidency he had lived on his nerves, and indeed part of the time Dubinsky had served as acting president. In the convention Schlesinger was so ill that for hours he had to lie on a couch in a little room off the platform. But he couldn't let go. He wanted to be re-elected, he wanted to be recognized as the savior of the International. The natural candidate was Dubinsky—young, powerful, progressive—who could have had the presidency for the asking. But Dubinsky didn't want it. For one thing, he wanted the old man to die happy; it was plain that Schlesinger's days were numbered. And for another thing Dubinsky, as he puts it, "didn't feel big enough for the job." Schlesinger was nominated, and to please him a little scene dear to his heart was enacted, for the last time. Morris Hillquit begged him to accept, and Schlesinger, with many protests, finally allowed himself to be persuaded.

A few weeks later, on June 6, Schlesinger died in a sanatorium in Colorado Springs. And on June 15 the General Executive Board named David Dubinsky to succeed him.

VIII

Shrewd but Honest: David Dubinsky

I<small>N THE LAST</small> thirty years the International has had three outstanding leaders—Schlesinger, Sigman and Dubinsky.

Schlesinger represented the immigrant past of the garment workers when this past was still part of their outlook. He himself was the seasoned but never completely assimilated immigrant, a man who lived between two cultures, in whom the Old and the New Worlds were always straining for mutual adaptation. In his own twisted way he expressed some of the great values of the immigrant tradition—the romantic humanitarianism of the early socialist movement, the struggle to adjust to American life, the longing to improve our democracy. His neurotic personality fused the American dream and the Marxian apocalypse into a luminous mirage—and he fashioned this illusion into a halo for himself.

Sigman represented the American tradition within the union, labor's anarcho-syndicalist heritage which reached back to Reconstruction days and the Knights of Labor. In his attitude Sigman was no immigrant at all; he might as well have been a native of the IWW Northwest. As a younger man he was far closer in spirit to Bill Haywood, and in his maturity to Sam Gompers, than he was at any time to Schlesinger or Cahan or the United Hebrew Trades. Sigman reflected the assimilation of the immigrant tailors to the persistent voluntarism of American labor: the desire, as Gompers put it, for "more and more of the good things of life, with the least possible interference by the state."

Until the New Deal our dominant labor movement was always animated by this spirit of Jeffersonian democracy in industrial relations. The garment workers, for all their socialist ties, were not Americanized by the socialist movement or its fellow travelers among the settlement workers and reformers. They were Americanized in the melting pot of their own union, which burned out many isms and in the end produced an essentially progressive trade unionism based on the philosophy of free economic enterprise. The victory of these voluntaristic forces under Sigman during the civil war showed how thoroughly democratized the masses in the International had become.

But the New Deal signalized a drastic reorientation in our society. It marked a real break with the past. The old voluntaristic drives, the "rugged individualism" of both capital and labor, had lost their momentum. Today the whole world must bear the socialist cross. In its original impulses the New Deal was an American variant of European collectivisms—trying to function within our traditional system.

Labor is at the very center of this social revolution. It furnished the mass base for the New Deal. But within organized labor the same fight goes on—how to reconcile traditional democracy with the onrush towards statism. In this struggle the International, because of its long history in this very type of doctrinal conflict, is far more conscious of the issues than is the rest of labor. Consciousness may, of course, only deepen the quandary; it is not necessarily the best guide to action. Be that as it may, it is this awareness of our times which characterizes the International and explains its adherence to the politics of the middle way. The International is a *right-wing progressive union.* It would bring about even the most far-reaching changes only within our democratic framework. And David Dubinsky is the natural exponent of this policy. He is a congenital centrist. Unlike Sigman he was brought up in the socialist and not in the anarcho-syndicalist tradition. But his socialist outlook, unlike Schlesinger's, has never been parochially immigrant. He is all for the "social gains" of the New Deal—without totalitarian undertows. Dubinsky represents the upsurge of the International under the Roosevelt regime and the epoch which it symbolizes.

THE GREAT TRADITION

Dubinsky grew to leadership under his two predecessors. In the Schlesinger era he was coming into his own as the head of the New York cutters. And he matured in the hard school of the civil war under Sigman. Few men in organized labor have had such a thorough grounding. Dubinsky is the heir of the great tradition in the International—great because it recapitulated in its own history all the moods and currents which shaped our labor movement—the tradition which came down through the Knights of Labor, the Socialist Labor party, the various schools of anarchism, the AFL, the Socialist party, the IWW, the varieties of Communism—each of them playing upon and molding and enriching the basic drive for collective bargaining.

This conscious heritage explains Dubinsky's range and sophistication as a leader. He knows his way through the mazes of radical politics, which is the best school for the understanding of our revolutionary day. And yet the wealth of his background does not tie him to past ideologies. He plays his role and his politics in the present tense. He is a pragmatic leader—shrewd, buoyant and ultracontemporary. Meeting or avoiding issues as they arise, he is a skillful opportunist, the effective leader for a period of union expansion in a day of social turmoil.

Dubinsky is not only of the great tradition in the International, but he belongs to the elite of the labor movement: he began his career way on the left. Personal prestige in organized labor derives in a peculiar degree from an early record of rebellion. The line for labor leadership always forms on the left.

The reasons for this should be obvious. Leadership is not a normal human occupation. Power is like a pearl—a disease which may be of great value. The exercise of power involves a continuous moral predicament for the simple reason that private ethics and social politics are rarely in harmony. The leader cannot often afford to indulge his better nature since he is not an individual but the "servant" of a cause. And yet if he is a mere opportunist he ends by being corrupted as a person—and as a leader.

In a labor leader this predicament is especially acute. For a man cannot rise to leadership of underprivileged masses unless he begins by representing their social protest. He has to start his career as a critic of society in general and as the champion of the rank and file against their entrenched officialdom. Even conservative leaders, therefore—such men as Gompers, Green, Woll—all started out as rebels. But once a labor leader becomes part of the oligarchy the reverse process sets in. One can't sign collective agreements on the picket line or attend to union business by keeping the rank and file in a constant ferment. Moreover, once in power the quondam rebel has to fight the leaders of the new left wing. Such is the mechanism of power in the trade union world, a mechanism which keeps the leader in the difficult position of having to reconcile his radical promise with his official performance, his rebellious beginnings with bureaucratic necessity. It is this tension which demoralizes so many labor leaders into cynical job holders or bosses and sometimes into plain racketeers. Men of character, on the other hand, grow in stature in this evolution from left to right. They are capable of maturing into power without serious moral rupture. They learn to discipline their convictions by the demands of responsibility.

But in this evolution the leader must retain the confidence of the rank and file. And his prestige with them rests to a great extent on his early record. His baptism of fire in the labor struggle is his original patent of leadership. It is always harder to defy the politician who began as a hero. I have known some labor leaders who have invented for themselves a glorious revolutionary youth just to impress their followers and to combat left-wing attacks.

Of all the top-flight labor leaders today Dubinsky has probably the most radical early history. Nobody in labor's Who's Who can match his pure unadulterated 100 per cent revolutionary youth. At fourteen he was a local union official in czarist

Poland, at fifteen a revolutionary conspirator, at sixteen an inmate of a czarist prison—rats, lice, beatings and all. At eighteen he escaped from Siberian exile, and at nineteen he was soapboxing for the Socialist party in New York, when the party was still considered a very subversive affair.

BOY AGAINST CZAR

David Dubinsky was born in Brest-Litovsk in Russian Poland on February 22, 1892, the youngest of six children. His mother died when he was seven. His father, Bezallel Dubinsky, ran a bakery in Lodz, where the family moved when David was a child. He went to a Zionist school, which was different from an orthodox *Kheder*. It was a secular school where Russian and Polish were part of the curriculum. But by the time he was eleven he went to work in his father's shop. At fourteen he became a master baker and immediately joined the bakers' union.

The Jewish Socialist party of Poland, known as the *Bund,* was the most active agency in organizing the workers in the various Jewish communities. The bakers' union of Lodz was affiliated directly with the local *Bund,* and David joined both organizations the year after the abortive revolution of 1905. Under the reaction and its terror which now set in, the socialist and trade union movements were virtually outlawed. After a few weeks in the union David was elected assistant secretary. "Believe it or not," Dubinsky told me, "I was elected because I was considered quite a scholar. Most of the members were illiterate, but I could read and write and keep books. And keeping books was just as important to the bakers in Lodz as it is in the International today." David did most of the routine work because the secretary of the union, known only by his revolutionary name of Ivan, spent most of his time in *Bund* activities.

In 1907 the czarist reaction was at its darkest and there was a wave of mass arrests. David was caught in the dragnet, and spent two weeks in jail. When he got out he ran into Ivan on the street and greeted him with happy excitement. But Ivan pretended not to know him. "I realized what had happened," said Dubinsky. "He was through. We never saw him again. Hundreds of good men were broken like that almost overnight."

The next day fifteen-year-old David succeeded Ivan as secretary of the union. "Everything looked so black and the workers were so discouraged," Dubinsky told me, "that we had to do something to keep up morale. So we decided to call a strike of all the bakers in Lodz." David organized the strike and with typical adolescent dramatics picketed his father's shop. "Was your father against the strike?" I asked. "Good Lord, no!" Dubinsky exclaimed. "The strike was really a demonstration against the system, and my father was certainly with us." Father and son were devoted to each other. "He was all right," is Dubinsky's characteristic way of understating his affection. In his study at home there is a reproduction in color of an old photograph of his father which shows a round-faced, friendly old man with a wisp of gray beard and a skullcap, smiling down benignly at his youngest, who, minus skullcap and beard, is his spitting image.

The authorities knew that young David was the ringleader of the Lodz bakers. He was arrested in the dead of night and put in jail. And then the typical czarist police racket went into operation. The chief of police got his expected bribe from David's father, and after two weeks the boy was released with the understanding that he was to leave town. He went to his native Brest-Litovsk, but by the end of the year he came back to Lodz and soon called a meeting of his union. On January 8, 1908, eighty members met in secret—with the inevitable provocateur among them. Every one of them was arrested and eleven of them, including David, were sentenced to Siberia. But he had to spend the next year and a half in the Lodz prison waiting until he was legally old enough for exile.

Again old Bezallel dug into his pocket and gave the warden three rubles a month to make life easier for his son. "That didn't mean," Dubinsky said, "that I was pampered or that I escaped the terrible beatings which all of us had to take. It simply meant that I was allowed to act as the contact man between the political prisoners and the outside world, to smuggle letters and messages back and forth and all that sort of thing. Naturally, as 'political commissar,' I enjoyed a key position among the prisoners, and I made some lasting friendships in jail."

One of his prison comrades was B. Charney Vladeck, who later became the manager of the *Jewish Daily Forward,* the first Socialist alderman in New York City, a city councilman and a pillar of the early La Guardia administration. Vladeck was a man of great personal culture and charm, a smooth politician but also a good deal of a humanitarian. He developed into one of the leaders of American Jewry, and when the Nazis came into power he was instrumental in getting tens of thousands of dollars into Europe for anti-Nazi activities and refugee aid. Some of that money came from Dubinsky's union. As long as Vladeck lived, Dubinsky was one of his closest friends and collaborators; and the *Forward,* which is still a power among the Jewish workers, has never deviated in its support of the International, especially in the fight against the Communists.

By the middle of 1909 David was old enough to begin the long trek to Siberia. He was banished to the Orenburg province just beyond the Urals. The czarist government paid the penal authorities nine kopecks a day for the maintenance of each convict. The officials often abetted the escape of prisoners in order to pocket this allowance, which explains why so many revolutionary figures made seemingly miraculous escapes from Siberia in the days of the Czar. Once across the Urals the prisoners were no longer entrained but were marched along by mounted guards and spent the night at wayside camps. Some distance beyond Chelyabinsk, the capital of Orenburg, David presented one of the guards with all his spare clothing and was allowed to disappear. He started back toward Chelyabinsk, walking nights and sleeping in the daytime in ditches or haystacks.

"You weren't apt to run into anybody but peasants," Dubinsky told me, "and they were very friendly to us political prisoners. Early one morning a peasant found me asleep in a ditch. He gave me food and a gun, and even bought me a railroad ticket to Chelyabinsk. It was a pleasant little town and I worked there for several months as a baker. Father helped out by sending me twenty-five rubles. He worked hard to get me released, and early in 1910 I was amnestied. But I was forbidden to come back to Lodz."

Once more Dubinsky went to Brest-Litovsk, but after a few months he slipped back to Lodz under an assumed name and got a job with an express company. He tried to reorganize his old bakers' union. However, he found that life in the revolutionary underground had no longer any allure for him. He was too normal and friendly to enjoy the role of a conspirator. And he had set his heart on going to America. To the Jewish communities in the czarist pales America was the promised land. Almost every family had someone in this country who sent home glowing and often boastful reports about life under freedom. David's oldest brother Jacob had been in New York for some years and was the business agent for the bakers' union. David saved up his money and again with some aid from his father he was able to buy passage for New York, where he landed on New Year's Day, 1911.

FROM BAKER TO CUTTER

Within two weeks after landing Dubinsky took out his first papers, joined the Socialist party, registered at night school and got himself a job as a dishwasher. He soon found a better job as a knee-pants operator in a small shop. His ambition was to be a doctor and he decided that the quickest way to save money for his education was to become a cutter.

It was about as easy for an inexperienced greenhorn to crash the cutters' unions as it would be for a hillbilly to crash the Racquet Club. Like most highly skilled crafts, Local 10 was an exclusive outfit. Dubinsky's brother got Abraham Rosenberg and Ben Schlesinger to recommend David for membership, but his application was turned down. Finally Saul Metz, one of the officials of the Cloak Joint Board, called up his crony Jesse Cohen and wangled an examination in the trade for Dubinsky. Jesse Cohen, the manager of Local 10, was a typical Tammany politician who loved to oblige the right people. Dubinsky was given a somewhat nominal test which he passed with flying colors and thus he made the select fraternity of Local 10.

Later, when Dubinsky became the leader of the opposition in the union, Cohen was one of his main targets. "I always felt bad about fighting Jesse," Dubinsky told me. "He was a good fellow, but we had to get rid of the old crowd who had turned the local into a little Tammany both politically and industrially." Dubinsky has a temperamental liking for the typical politician. He is drawn to the good fellow, the poker player, the amiable fixer. On a higher plane he is that sort of person himself. Though he has always fought for political and social reforms both in and outside the labor movement, he has none of the reformer's cant. He is essentially a politician, a man's man who can sit up till all hours in a smoke-filled room and can hold his own in liquor and in language.

Equipped with his union card, Dubinsky went to see a *Landsman* from Poland who was a foreman in a big cloak shop. For fifty dollars, to be paid in installments, this bighearted soul gave him a job. He worked a month without pay, and after that he got only three dollars a week as a helper until the foreman was paid his split. But he mastered the trade and by the end of the year he was a first-rate mechanic and ready to work as an experienced cutter.

In those days there was a curbstone "hiring hall" for cutters at the corner of Twenty-fifth Street and Sixth Avenue. The mark of a successful cutter was a diamond ring, and Dubinsky borrowed one from a friend and let the jewel sparkle in the sunshine. He promptly got a job. For almost a decade he worked steadily at his trade. He became one of the highest paid cutters in the city, making as much as eighty dollars a week when the standard scale was around forty-five. He is still proud of his craftsmanship.

For about six years he worked for two large houses and then

he got a job with Aaron Levine, who was a cutter himself and ran a small cloak and suit shop. Levine was quite a character—a flashy dresser, a devout poker player and a follower of the horses. Every now and then he would have to borrow the pay roll from Dubinsky—"just a couple of hundred for a day or two." "Under my expert guidance," Mr. Levine informed me, "Dave became a wonderful mechanic. Next to myself he was the fastest and surest cutter I've ever known. And he was such a nice young fellow, bright and clean-looking, full of fun and the life of the shop. But I never could get him to work overtime. He was full of meetings and socialism and all that. I wanted him to settle down and would have taken him in as a partner. But I guess he did better at the union business. Did you see his picture in the papers lunching with Rockefeller? But Dave is still the old Dave. He hasn't gone high-hat on his old friends. I bet you he'd introduce me to Rockefeller in a minute. . . ." Mr. Levine can go on like that for hours.

Dubinsky stayed with Levine until 1921, when he became the manager of Local 10. In the midst of the civil war in 1926 Levine was approached by a former business agent of Local 10, a tough character who had joined the Communist party. He offered Levine five hundred dollars if he would sign a statement to the effect that Dubinsky had a record as a scab and a stool pigeon.

"I grabbed a chair," Mr. Levine said, "and broke it over his head. And while they were taking the bum to the hospital I called up Dave and told him what I'd done for him."

Dubinsky's version is milder. "Well, Aaron didn't exactly send that lowlife to the hospital, but he certainly got rid of him in a hurry."

Still, Dubinsky and his old friend don't always see eye to eye.

"I must say," Mr. Levine confided, "that sometimes Dave is terribly unreasonable."

"How is that?" I wanted to know.

"Well, a certain lady of my acquaintance, the wife of a friend of mine who is a cutter, helped herself to a fur coat in a department store. So she got into trouble with the police, and my friend wanted me to go and see what Dave could do about it. So I asked Dave to call up the captain of the precinct and fix things up. Dave practically threw me out of his office. I explained that this lady is not a thief, but suffers from what the doctors call kleptomania, the stealing sickness. 'Aaron,' Dave yelled, 'get out of here. A union man's wife can't afford such a sickness, and I can't afford to help her.' "

In time Mr. Levine's loyalty was rewarded. "In 1931," he said, "I was completely broke. I lost my shop and I couldn't get on my feet again, so I went to Dave. 'I am downhearted and in bad shape,' I told him, 'and I don't feel so good.' So Dave sent me to the Union Health Center and loaned me a couple of hundred dollars. And he paid forty-seven dollars out of his own pocket for my union book and got me a job as a cutter."

Levine is still a cutter, still a member of the union, though not precisely a "class-conscious" worker, still follows the horses, and still thinks that Dubinsky is "the swellest guy on earth."

There are many people in the International who feel the same way about "D.D." He is no doubt the most popular leader in the union. His enormous vitality draws people to him, and he is emotionally accessible. No one feels the compulsion to be at his best with Dubinsky, because he takes people as they are. Union officials often come to him with their problems, especially in union politics; his advice is apt to be shrewd and practical and he is free from intellectual or moral superiority.

In his relations with the employers Dubinsky is a capable businessman—friendly and reasonable. He is not given to driving hard bargains. Far more than either Schlesinger or Sigman, he tends to consider the good of the industry as a whole. Indeed in collective bargaining procedures he often acts as a sort of umpire between union officials and manufacturers.

Ordinary rank-and-filers can see him easily, but people must have a reason for taking up his time. He has none of that inverted democracy which considers every worker one of God's noblemen. He is not a professional democrat, and this is one reason for his popularity with the membership. Conversely, he will neither snub important people nor cater to them. He makes distinctions between individuals, which are based on his judgment of them.

The office staff loves to tell about the visit of Albert Einstein to International headquarters. During the early refulgent days of the New Deal a big clothing jobber had the bright idea of colonizing a group of contracting shops in New Jersey. Three hundred families were to live in a "garden city," the Hightstown project of the National Housing Authority. The jobber went to Washington and sold the idea to Mrs. Roosevelt, Rexford Tugwell and other enthusiasts. Of course the motive behind this scheme was to evade the union in New York, and Dubinsky's answer was a resounding no.

The jobber then went to Einstein and appealed to him on racial grounds. It would be wonderful, he said, to demonstrate that Jews were not inveterately urban, but could live happily in the countryside. Einstein too thought it was wonderful, and promised to plead with Dubinsky. With his usual instinct for modestly backing into the limelight the great scientist notified the press. On the appointed day reporters and photographers piled into Dubinsky's offices to witness the encounter between Science and Labor. Flanked by a group of jobbers, Einstein led off with a speech on the joys of country life for weary tailors. Dubinsky thereupon explained to him the real motives behind the scheme. But Einstein persisted in his idyll. Finally Dubinsky brought things to a head.

"My dear Dr. Einstein," he said, "when it comes to physics you're the professor. But when it comes to tailoring I'm the professor."

Everybody laughed, and the scheme blew up then and there.

EMERGENCE OF A UNION TACTICIAN

Until 1916 Dubinsky was not very active in the union. He was a successful and well-paid craftsman and his free time was taken up with the Socialist party and the co-operative movement. He is naturally efficient with nothing of the dilettante about him and cannot get interested in something without assuming and exploiting the responsibilities it offers. Having promptly joined the Socialist party on his arrival in this country, he gave his energies to it. In 1912, a year after he got here, he was soap-boxing all over the East Side for Meyer London in his success-ful campaign for Congress. He was busy as a beaver in the party, doing everything from writing and distributing leaflets to run-ning committee meetings. His socialist activities led him into the co-operative movement. For the co-operative movement, espe-cially in those days, was very closely allied to the left-wing politi-cal groups. It attracted idealists of all kinds, who regarded it as a modest sample of the future co-operative commonwealth. It was a social outlet for the young folks and an ideal kibitzing ground for the serious-minded night owls.

Many of the co-operative fans were vegetarians of the deepest dye. One of them was Julius Hochman. Hochman loves to re-member his vegetarian days when there were burning discus-sions on whether or not it was right to wear leather shoes and bone buttons. After this question had created a right and left wing—the left-wingers wearing sneakers and non-animal buttons —Hochman thought up a really irreducible moral dilemma: may a true vegetarian eat bread, which cannot be produced without first plowing a field, and plowing a field means killing innocent worms? "That had us stopped," said Julius.

Dubinsky never indulged in such high-minded scholasticisms. He was a moving spirit in organizing the Industrial Co-operative, which ran two restaurants, two boardinghouses and a grocery. His love of management soon made him a sort of efficiency engi-neer for these enterprises. He pored over invoices, checked ac-counts and kept the machinery oiled. It was in the co-operative movement that he met Emma Goldberg, a member of Local 62 of the underwear workers. They were married in 1914 and have a daughter, Jean, who is now the wife of a physician.

By 1916 Dubinsky suddenly became very active in Local 10. His co-operative phase was over. His sense of reality told him that consumers' co-operation had no dynamic role in economic

EUGENE V. DEBS

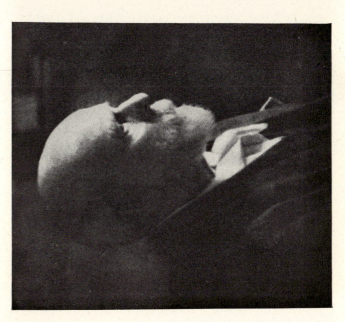

DANIEL DE LEON

SAMUEL GOMPERS

ABRAHAM CAHAN

HERMAN GROSSMAN

JAMES McCAULEY

ABRAHAM ROSENBERG

JOHN DYCHE

MORRIS HILLQUIT

MEYER LONDON

ABRAHAM BISNO

JOSEPH BARONDESS

DR. ISAAC A. HOURWICH

Acme

LOUIS D. BRANDEIS

MORRIS SIGMAN

BENJAMIN SCHLESINGER

DAVID DUBINSKY

Maurice Seymour

WILLIAM GREEN

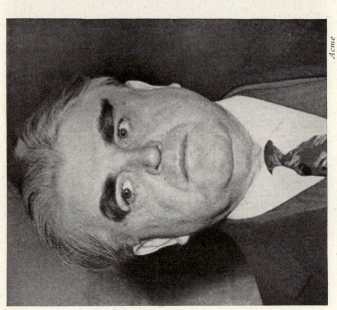

Acme

JOHN L. LEWIS

The late DR. GEORGE M. PRICE, founder and director of the ILGWU Health Center

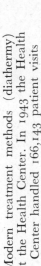

Modern treatment methods (diathermy) at the Health Center. In 1943 the Health Center handled 166,143 patient visits

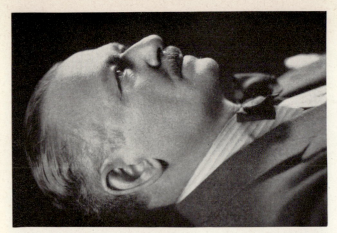

MAX D. DANISH

LUIGI ANTONINI

FREDERICK F. UMHEY

Vandamm Studio

Two scenes from *Pins and Needles*

PRESIDENT ROOSEVELT and DAVID DUBINSKY at
a "command" performance of *Pins and Needles* at the
White House

GENERAL EXECUTIVE BOARD ILGWU

Top Row: Anthony Cottone, Meyer Perlstein, Charles S. Zimmerman, Abraham W. Katovsky, Samuel Otto, Louis Levy. *Center Row:* Morris Bialis, Samuel Shore, Elias Reisberg, Max Cohen, Jacob J. Heller, George Rubin, Charles Kreindler, Harry Wander, Harry Greenberg. *Bottom Row:* Philip Kramer, Rose Pesotta, Julius Hochman, Luigi Antonini, *First Vice-President;* David Dubinsky, *President;* Frederick F. Umhey, *Executive Secretary;* Israel Feinberg, Isidore Nagler, Joseph Breslaw.

UNITY HOUSE

life. Trade unionism was the right field for him, and the situation in Local 10 gave him plenty of scope for his energies.

The cutters' union had been changing rapidly in the composition of its membership. Beginning with the great cloakmakers' strike of 1910, a new element had been pouring into Local 10. Many of these were newly arrived European Jews who were close to the socialist or some other left-wing movement. The control of the local, however, was still in the hands of the old-timers—Scotch-Irish or Jews or Irish of an older immigration. Many of the leaders were Tammany Hall braves and had the social outlook of chiefs on an Indian reservation. They were "pure and simple" trade unionists of the most gnarled variety.

The newcomers were mostly in the waist and dress trades, which was the new and expanding part of the industry. These dress cutters were less highly skilled than the coat and suit cutters and naturally were paid less. And yet a waist and dress cutter might easily have shifted to the higher grades of work had it not been for the entrenched opposition of the union bureaucracy, who had a vested interest in keeping the choice jobs for the old-timers. All in all these new members of the union, who by 1913 outnumbered the veterans by almost four to one, were given slim pickings. They were sent to the more seasonal jobs, hired last and fired first. Though the local had no recognized apprentice system many of the newer workers were classified as "helpers" and given miserable wages. They felt that they were being pushed down to a sweatshop level by their own union leaders.

By 1912 the tension between the Old-Timers and the Newcomers—as the factions were called—became acute. The situation was absurd. The great majority of the members were discriminated against by a little group of die-hards who refused to recognize either the transformation which was occurring in their industry or what was happening in the country at large. In spite of their shorter experience in this country the Newcomers were much closer to the spirit of the day. In 1912 the Socialist party polled a million votes; La Follettism had become as popu-

lar in the labor movement as it was among the Midwestern progressives; Wilson's New Freedom was in the air.

Late in 1913 the Newcomers formed a Committee of Fifty to
promote the candidacy of Elmer Rosenberg for president of the
executive board against John C. Ryan, one of the ancient pillars.
Rosenberg was a leading progressive whose main assets were
personal decency and a gift for oratory. To everybody's surprise
he was swept into office by a vote of 742 to 425. But the rest of
the offices went to the Old-Timers. Their most effective leader
was Isadore Epstein, a native of New York, a tall and handsome
man who was honest in his views, which were standpat and long
since out of date. The Newcomers seemed to him a completely
wild and un-Americanized lot who were destroying the "very
foundations" of pure and simple craft unionism.

Exhilarated by the election of Rosenberg, the Newcomers decided to create a permanent progressive nucleus, the Welfare
League—popularly known as the Good and Welfare League.
They kept up a running fire against the old guard—such hardy
perennials as Epstein, Ryan, Jesse Cohen, Edward Fruisen, John
Pierce, Alexander Bloch and Jesse Greenberger. The "Good and
Welfare" was supported by voluntary contributions and put out
a great quantity of literature, surprisingly temperate in tone. It
concentrated on its reform program and avoided personal vilifi-
cation, a good-natured restraint rather rare in union politics.
There were many reasons for such moderation. For one thing,
Elmer Rosenberg, who was editor of the *Ladies' Garment Cutter*
from 1914–17, and the people around him, realized that with a
few exceptions the Old-Timers were not so much corrupt as
superannuated. A more important reason was that the progressives had to watch their step: the AFL, the ILGWU administration, and the Socialist party naturally watched the development
of any intraunion group with anxiety as a potential dual union
movement. Even Meyer London, whose progressivism could not
be questioned, was very critical of the Good and Welfare League.

Rosenberg was the type of leader who accumulates honors
without building power. He held office of one kind or another in
Local ﹖﹖ until ﹖919. In 1917 he was elected to the State Assem-

bly, and from 1917 to 1920 he was the first vice-president of the International. But the fact is that after his first year or two as the leader of the progressives in Local 10 he petered out. Amiable and lazy, he lacked the sustained power for political application which a leader must possess to hold a new movement together. From 1914–17 the real moving spirits of the progressives were Charles Margulies, who was active in the Socialist party and is now a well-known manufacturer, and Harry Berlin, who later joined the Communists but is now back in the union fold.

Dubinsky was a member of the Good and Welfare League from its beginning. But it was not until 1916 that he threw himself into union politics. He quickly became one of the rank-and-file leaders though he held no office until 1918, when he was elected to the executive board of the local. From the first he showed great skill in avoiding factional bitterness without over-compromising his position. Then as now he steered clear of anything which might leave deep and incurable resentments, and he tried to get all but the most hopelessly intransigeant Old-Timers to accept the world around them. When the United States entered the war in 1917 the Old-Timers had a flurry of hope that the Newcomers, many of whom were socialists, would discredit themselves by an outright anti-war stand. Dubinsky took the wind out of their sails by staunchly backing the war effort. As Isadore Epstein told me, "Our crowd had expected Dave to come out against the war. Instead, he went around selling Liberty bonds to the members and made patriotic speeches. We could hardly stop that. Anyway, it was useless for us to fight him. He was energetic, effective, what I would now call a conservative progressive. And he deserves all the opportunities he's made for himself."

By 1919 the old guard was making its last stand. It formed the American Benevolent Association, which launched a super-patriotic drive against the "Bolsheviks." But it soon fizzled out. Isadore Epstein was defeated as secretary of the executive board, and with him went the last of the Mohicans. The leaders of the Benevolent Association were brought before the executive board,

now consisting mostly of progressives, on charges of union dis-
loyalty and sabotage. They were convicted and disciplined. Most
of their followers dropped away. Within a year the great bulk of
the Old-Timers reconciled themselves to the situation and some
of their leaders were successfully absorbed by the new ruling
group.

Dubinsky was now in the saddle. He had a good deal to do
with the peaceful liquidation of the old order in Local 10, and
was enormously popular with both the old and the new membership. In 1919 he was elected vice-president of the local and
a year later president. Under his leadership the entire policy
and atmosphere of the union changed. The cutters got a shorter
work week, the union really enforced penalties when agreements
were violated, favoritism was ended in the distribution of jobs
and the administration of the local was markedly improved.

As president of the local Dubinsky was giving so much time
to union affairs that he had to choose between continuing at his
trade or becoming a union official. The local then had three
departments—one for the coat and suit trade, another for the
waist and dress trade and a third for the miscellaneous division.
The executive board decided to merge these three branches and
to put one general manager in charge; and the new post was
offered to Dubinsky at sixty-five dollars a week, about fifteen
dollars less than he was making as a cutter.

"I wanted the job," he told me, "because there was so much
to be done. And yet I hesitated—I was afraid that I was not
big enough."

But he accepted, and in 1921 he became the general manager
of Local 10. It was his first big job in the International. In 1924
he got the local to combine the offices of general manager and
secretary-treasurer. He has always felt that control of the purse
strings is essential to sound administration.

Soon after Dubinsky was firmly established as the head of the
cutters the rifts which led to the civil war in the International
became apparent. The conflict, from its first rumblings to its
aftermath, lasted a decade. Straight through these ten years

Dubinsky was a tower of strength to both Sigman and Schlesinger. The civil war developed him as the potential leader of the International and as a rising figure in American labor. And with his usual luck he became president just before the New Deal opened up the greatest opportunities to organized labor in our history.

PORTRAIT OF A LABOR LEADER

It has been part of my job to know a good many labor leaders. One of them was truly great. Samuel Gompers was all character, strong and narrow, a man who knew exactly what he thought and wanted—the archetype of the prophet and the founder. He was the chieftain of the trade union tribes, whom he led through the wilderness of a primitive monopoly capitalism.

William Green is the inheritor and hierarch. He has the baffling faculty of surviving many issues which one might think he ought to face. But his seeming weakness is a variety of strength which is hard to beat. He has implicit faith in the cohesive power of the traditions of the AFL, which his long career really embodies. The last half century of American labor is, after all, his personal experience—and what is research to other men is reminiscence to Brother Green. His habit is to let well enough alone, to let issues resolve themselves. Even in the civil war with the CIO, which threatened the very life of the AFL, Green let the authority and weight of the Federation do the fighting. After all is said and done, it was the almighty Lewis who had to come to Canossa in asking for readmission to the fold. Like Gregory VII, Green had the Church behind him.

John Lewis is tough and massive, a superb tactician, especially when in danger, for he has the power of being dangerous himself. He is a virtuoso of power politics, and in playing it he can ring every change from the most ingratiating charm to utter ruthlessness. And he never knows when he is licked, which means he never is. To Lewis even Canossa is not a place where one submits but where one goes to make the next move in the game for power.

Matthew Woll is "the brains" of the AFL. And indeed his outstanding quality is his social intelligence. Calm, steadfast and informed, he is a spokesman and interpreter rather than a fighter.

Each one of these men is a leader, not merely a high official. Each has some one outstanding quality that dominates and integrates his entire personality. One cannot imagine waking any of them out of a sound sleep in the middle of the night and finding him a different man than he was that afternoon. In Gompers the central trait was his great moral force; in Green it is his ponderous patience; in Lewis it is the colossal toughness of his ego; in Woll, his unfailing intellectual balance. For all their vast experience, these men have changed very little as personalities. Half a century ago, when he was the leader of a miners' local in Ohio, Green was very much the same sort of person he is today. And that is true of the others.

Dubinsky is a very different type of leader. His is a complex and protean nature. He has no one predominant trait; instead he has a useful assortment of talents and some of their corresponding failings. His qualities now balance and reinforce each other, now cancel each other out.

The comparative anatomy of leadership makes this clearer. There is a good deal of the pioneer in Dubinsky, as his record of the last twenty years shows. But while Gompers built a movement to fit his times, Dubinsky is forever adapting himself to social pressures and opportunities. Gompers led by carrying the torch ahead; Dubinsky maintains his leadership, like a veteran congressman, by following his constituents whenever necessary. He has a ruthless streak and an enormous drive for power, but unlike Lewis he is hampered by being too conscious of the power of others, which partly explains his emotional need for conciliation. He has great social intelligence, but **he** is apt to tie it up with immediate considerations.

He is a natural born opportunist, but in the good sense—that is, he is actuated not only by expediency but also by a sense of social decency. And he is a shrewd tactician. For one thing, he never makes a move before he is thoroughly informed about all the factors involved. And he plays these factors with great skill, though now and then in a gust of excitement he will do or say something rash that he is bound to regret. But on the whole he is such an excellent politician that he is always on guard against his own shenanigans. He is conscious of the shadowy dividing line between decent and cynical opportunism, between sound expediency and inner capitulation. Aware of his susceptibility to the fleshpots of opportunism, he watches his politics as a man might watch his diet. One of the most attractive qualities about Dubinsky is his genuine desire, occasionally thwarted by circumstances or ambition, to be morally as right as possible, no matter how clever he may be.

But his great forte is his sheer intelligence. He is shrewd about men and movements and understands how they interact. And because of his rich personal experience in the various ideological drives behind the labor movement, his political orientation is sensitive and knowing. For instance, although he is all out for the New Deal, he wouldn't start a purely theoretical discussion of its merits, knowing only too well the odds and ends which have gone into its making.

In fact theoretical discussions rather bore him. He is not interested in social abstractions. And this fools a great many people, especially highbrows, who are apt to think of Dubinsky as a rough-and-ready type. To them a man like Sidney Hillman who talks like an article in the *Survey Graphic* or the *New Republic,* is an "intellectual." The exact opposite is true; Hillman has no background in social theory, and merely dishes out the patter of so-called industrial statesmanship. It is people like Lewis and Woll and Dubinsky who are saturated with knowledge of the labor movement as it has evolved in our society. And even a cursory discussion with any of these men brings out the wealth of their background.

Fortified by this background, Dubinsky's flair for social politics makes him a superb commentator. He can tell you not only what happened at the President's labor conference in Washington the day before, but why. He knows who said what, and from what motives. What will Lewis do next? Why did Phil

Murray line up with the left wing? How about the War Labor Board and wage freezing? What is the politics behind the Little Steel formula? To such questions Dubinsky can give you an analysis of men and events which is canny and convincing. To the intelligent reporter he is an invaluable off-the-record guide and gossip—an almost perfect guide, for his gossip is purely social and never private. His perceptions are quick, sardonic without being cynical, realistic, and very much from the inside. Dubinsky reflects more elements and facets in the current relations of labor to the rest of society, and reflects them with more speed and sensitiveness, than any other labor leader I can think of, with the possible exception of John Lewis. If you want to know the story of American labor since the New Deal, Dubinsky is probably the most illuminating man to watch.

One of Dubinsky's chief attractions is his perennial youthfulness. He is forever evolving, which is both an asset and a handicap. It is an asset because it keeps the union in step with the experimental mood of a revolutionary period. The danger is that in such a period it is sometimes hard to tell where experiment ends and confusion begins. And the life of an organization cannot always be experimental, a chronic laboratory of trial and error. Dubinsky understands much better what is going on than he can look into the future. Hence he is given to such fluidity of policy that some of his policies have no time to cool.

Much of Dubinsky's temperament can be explained by the inner struggle between his drive for power and his feeling of inadequacy. In the convention of 1932, for instance, he could easily have had the presidency of the International. "I didn't want it," he told me, "because I didn't think I was big enough." This sense of inferiority, which his more positive qualities turn into a genuine humility, is another expression of his youthfulness. But this diffidence also helps to explain his democracy. He runs the union without the least touch of usurpation. His power has been achieved by flexibility, not authoritarianism.

The occupational disease of all leaders—their only common denominator—is egotism. For without it no man can rise to the top and stay there. Dubinsky has his due share of egotism, but it is checked by his shrewd sense of proportion. Hillman, his opposite number in the men's garment trades, is the perfect example of a labor leader whose yen for being a great public figure is all out of proportion to the realities of his personal background and capacities, and when he went to Washington as our leading labor statesman his ultimate failure was a foregone conclusion. Dubinsky never victimizes himself in that way. Wild horses couldn't drag him off his base, which is the union, and into a spotlight so powerful as to blot out his real figure. He is too smart. "Not me," he says.

The fascinating interplay of Dubinsky's temperament—his great experience and his youthful eagerness for more, his expansiveness tempered by his shrewdness, his active intelligence—are all expressed in his appearance. Short, stocky, full of energy, he is of the round-faced Churchill-Hoover type who at first glance look like babies and on second glance decidedly do not. His face is expressive, merry rather than humorous, full of vitality and character. Dubinsky is handsome as people are apt to be who not only retain their youthfulness but reveal registered experience, the secret of distinction. In repose his face looks rather abstracted and curiously burdened, somehow suggesting a deep and almost unconscious frustration under all his solid accomplishment and ebullient temper. His success has been the steady overcoming of a sense of insecurity which may have come from a half-orphaned childhood and the brutalities of prison and exile when he was still a youngster.

UNION DEMOCRAT

Dubinsky pays more attention to his job than most top-flight labor leaders. He functions so much through the union that it is difficult to think of him apart from it. Wherever he is, he is Dubinsky of the International. He doesn't think of himself, as so many labor leaders do, as a public figure by the grace of his own achievement, but as a representative of labor. When time and good judgment permit, he is glad to act on public boards and committees or to attend public functions. But it is always understood that labor's interests must somehow be served by these activities.

His picture of American labor is objective. He knows all its weaknesses and dark spots. But he believes, or acts as if he believes, that labor is the most progressive force in modern society. He is the kind of person who would think so from sheer self-respect. If he is talking to someone he trusts, he is perfectly frank about corruption in the labor movement. But in his presence one doesn't make fun of graft and racketeering in the labor move-ment any more than one tells dirty stories to a self-respecting minister. His objectivity is not corroded into cynicism. Dubinsky creates this atmosphere precisely because he thinks of himself as less than the International. And his attitude gives the tone to the whole union. Cynicism is not considered smart, corruption is not considered funny, and even bureaucratic entrenchment, the bane of all organizations, is not regarded as a God-given right.

Dubinsky's loyalty to the union is loyalty to its democratic heritage. He himself is the product of this tradition; he rose on it and feels at home in it. If he didn't he wouldn't be where he is. For the International is so steeped in this tradition that it wouldn't put up with a dictator. Even Schlesinger, who always had to have his own way, had to get it like a spoiled child, not like a tyrant. It is, of course, understood that Dubinsky, or for that matter other high executives, must have broad discretion-ary powers. But it is equally well understood that any official body in the union can at any time raise hell if it seems indicated. And when Dubinsky boasts that the union is bigger than any leader in it, he is merely stating the truth.

And it all plays in with his temperament. He loves the politi-cian's art, and though he prefers to win he doesn't care to play the dictator. "Usurpation is the exact opposite of leadership," he once remarked. To him the fun of leadership is in persuading or outsmarting the opposition, not in trampling it to death.

In many unions even the top leaders are so many bellhops who run the errands of the president. Dubinsky could not be happy in such an environment. Yes-men bore him. His General

Executive Board includes a number of assorted prima donnas, three or four powerful and realistic politicians, a few veteran administrators, and, of course, some superannuated bureaucrats—altogether twenty-three vice-presidents. But even the small number of ineffectives on the Board aren't there as Dubinsky's stooges.

Some time ago I was invited to sit through a quarterly meeting of the GEB which lasted for a week. A number of important issues came up, and on most of them Dubinsky's position was finally endorsed. But he got his way by persuading, bringing out and developing the facts, in short by winning a majority. And the two or three matters on which he lost did not hurt his prestige. Each session was a process of give and take, lively, argumentative and good-natured. Nothing was fixed beforehand; there was no ganging up or knifing.

Of course there is plenty of politics in the conventions of the International. And there Dubinsky has built up and balanced his power in the course of years through canny and sometimes amusingly oblique devices. He is adept in the art of playing men off against each other without leaving scars. I have heard some of his victims laugh rather sourly at his cleverness in defeating them.

The story of how Dubinsky came to retain the office of secretary-treasurer after he became president still tickles the union politicians. When Schlesinger died the GEB named Dubinsky to succeed him until the next convention. It was a foregone conclusion that the convention two years later would elect him president. But Dubinsky insisted that he would not accept the presidency unless he knew exactly who his secretary-treasurer was to be. As he put it, "I won't work with someone I can't work with."

Two leading aspirants, Heller and Breslaw, began electioneering for the job. During the convention Dubinsky called in Heller, then manager of Local 17, and "confidentially"—in the presence of half a dozen vice-presidents—"made him a proposition." He told Heller, "If you will agree to permit the merger of Locals 1 and 17, and get through with this everlasting jurisdictional fight, I'll support you for secretary-treasurer." Brother Heller was willing. Naturally, when word of the deal got around, Breslaw hit the ceiling and accused Heller of trying to cut him out of the running. The two men killed each other off, and finally Morris Hillquit suggested that Dubinsky keep both offices "for the time being." That was in 1932 and Dubinsky is still president and secretary-treasurer.

In 1934 he persuaded Frederick F. Umhey, who had been Hillquit's partner, to take on the administrative work of the secretary-treasurership. Umhey's father was a Czech who came to this country in the eighties. He was the typical socialist paterfamilias, and was very active in the Yorkville *Krankenkasse,* the sick-benefit society of the Bohemian and German workers in New York City, for which Hillquit was counsel. When Fred left grammar school he went to work for Hillquit as an office boy, and in the course of years became his business associate. The firm was prosperous, and as Hillquit's health declined the prosperity was increasingly due to Umhey's gifts as a businessman. Soon after Hillquit died Dubinsky got Umhey to move over to the International. Though he is not an elected officer, he holds, next to Dubinsky, the most strenuous and responsible job at headquarters. Today he is to all intents and purposes the business manager of the union, and has made himself both invaluable and enormously popular. The whole arrangement has worked out so well that no one thinks of upsetting it; and at every convention Dubinsky is re-elected secretary-treasurer as a twin job to the presidency.

Astonishingly enough Dubinsky has no personal machine. This is a matter not so much of principle as of a deep temperamental twist. For all his friendliness and accessibility he has no gift for intimacy. The politician who can build machines (and machines are not bad as such) must be capable of those intimate friendships which unite people in a personal loyalty, not merely in a common loyalty to an institution. The best example of this type of politician is Jim Farley. But behind all his zest and fun Dubinsky is intangibly aloof. No one can get really close to him. People come to him with their problems but not with their personal

troubles. And unless a leader has a capacity for personal intimacy he can never have a political machine.

The two people in the International who are closest to Dubinsky, partly by virtue of sharing a grueling working pace, are
Hannah Haskel and Max Danish.

Hannah Haskel, who is the wife of Vice-President Charles
Kreindler, is as much part and parcel of the International as
anybody in it. Her father, a silk weaver in her native New Jersey, was blacklisted for his union activities, and she went to
work at the age of twelve. Somehow she got herself through high
school. In 1924 she started her career in the union as secretary
to the manager of the New York Cloak Joint Board; two years
later she became secretary to President Sigman. And she has
served both Schlesinger and Dubinsky in the same capacity.

Miss Haskel has the details of the union machinery at her
finger tips, and she is an encyclopedia of International life and
policies. Her efficiency is a bit overwhelming and at times chills
the more leisurely kibitzers who wander in and out of the office
In spite of her fidelity to Dubinsky she distinctly has a mind of
her own—and a good one.

Once I happened to ask her what she thought about the American Labor party.

"Not much," she said firmly.

This astonished me, because Dubinsky was then the big shot in
the ALP, and I asked her why she felt that way.

"Because," she said, "after all the deals have been made, there
is nothing in it for labor."

Max Danish, besides being the editor of *Justice,* is also the
director of publicity for the International. He is a graduate of
the New York University Law School, but never practiced; he
was born to be a newspaperman. For over thirty years he has
been with the International and is probably the outstanding labor
editor in the country today.

Way back in the summer of 1910, when he was still in law
school, Schlesinger asked him to do the publicity for the great

cloakmakers' strike. And when in 1914 Schlesinger became president, he made Danish the director of publicity of the International and editor of the *Ladies Garment Worker,* then the monthly union organ. In 1918 he became the managing editor of *Justice,* when the various ILGWU publications were merged into this semimonthly; and in 1925 he succeeded Saul Yanovsky as editor in chief.

Today *Justice* is the model for the intelligent trade union press in the country. Nearly all the better union journals have followed its style in layout and coverage. Danish has successfully avoided the deadly dull type of official organs such as the building trades or railway brotherhoods turn out. But he has also steered clear of the "socially conscious" type of journalism fancied by high-brow labor editors, who pattern themselves after the liberal weeklies. *Justice* is first of all a journal for the membership, giving the union news and discussing the world from the point of view of the labor movement.

Above all, Danish is an able publicity man, who hasn't worked with wizards in public relations like Schlesinger and Dubinsky for nothing. By his sheer expertness in handling public relations for three long decades, Danish has had as much influence as anyone in getting the big newspapers of the country to raise their standards of labor reporting, in many cases training their own men in this field.

Like so many newspapermen, Danish is hard-boiled enough to cover up his essential friendliness and his almost sentimental devotion to the union. His capacity for work is endless. More than once I have left Dubinsky's apartment toward midnight to find Max just coming in "to do a little work with the boss."

Dubinsky's machine is the International as a whole. His power rests on the fact that during the last ten years of tremendous expansion he has led the union with such skill and has represented it so effectively that no one has a chance to step into his shoes—for quite a while to come. And knowing this, nobody tries. Dubinsky functions on authority, not bossism. He has

entrenched himself by getting public opinion in the union behind
him.

Now, how is public opinion in a large and free organization
kept alive?

With his usual common sense Dubinsky has clarified in his
own mind what trade union democracy means in function.
Obviously the ideal can be only approximated. He knows that
the rank and file cannot participate constantly and fully in
union affairs. They have to make a living, they have their own
personal lives, their opportunities are limited, and besides, most
human beings like to be led. There is nothing wrong with delegation of power provided the checks on power are in good working order.

In other words, trade union democracy is not a matter of
perpetual and total participation by everybody—it is a thing of
tradition, atmosphere, approximation. But while the union public cannot be expert, its interest in the basic policies and program
of the union can be kept alive. This is Dubinsky's whole conception of union democracy. There is one important addition: the
roster of leadership must not be closed; the rank-and-filer who
wants to rise must be given a chance. Unfortunately, within a
bureaucracy it is so difficult to keep the green light of opportunity
functioning properly that even in the most democratic organizations the traffic of leadership is often clogged.

Essentially Dubinsky bases his own power in the union on the
intelligent public opinion of its membership. If he has to fight
a local machine in the International, as he has had to on occasion, he can appeal to a comparatively enlightened rank and
file. His technique is to let the membership know as quickly and
clearly as possible what it is the administration wants—and why.
More than any other union the International is in the habit of
calling special meetings, issuing special literature, keeping the
membership interested in the broad questions which concern
them. The administration uses *Justice* to present the basic issues
of union policy and those public questions which affect the
International. Max Danish can turn out an article in a few hours

that will clarify some major issue in the dress industry or some important political situation—and start a buzz of discussion throughout the union. The administration's point of view may be right or wrong but it is sure to be presented clearly and honestly to the membership, so that they can discuss it and if need be vote on it.

The rank and file really understood why the International left the AFL for the CIO and why it returned. To make sure that they understood the issues involved, Dubinsky prepared a well-documented pamphlet which told the whole story. Moreover, union members are required to attend important policy-making meetings of their locals. The idea is to get a really representative vote.

But to keep tens of thousands of people interested in their union requires education. It is characteristic of Dubinsky that he has infused considerable realism into workers' education, which is one of the slushiest subjects on earth. To him the union is not a "way of life" as the addlepated yearners use the phrase. To any realist the only way of life for an American is American society; and a union cannot furnish a microcosm of that society to its dues-paying membership. It is not the union's job to train good citizens or to give its workers a moral or a formal education. It cannot take on the functions of the home, the university or the church.

Under Dubinsky's watchful eye the International has learned to give its members what they really want—amusement, sports, such services as health and vacation centers, and courses to train officers in union administration. It has cut down on formal classroom work, which the interested individual can get better elsewhere. The emphasis is on sound public relations within the union and with the outside world. This emphasis gives the average member a feeling of participation in the social life of the union. A worker who is proud of the national success of *Pins and Needles* is far more apt to come to an important meeting to settle a strike than a member who has taken a hand-me-down course in English literature.

Late one evening I dropped in at Dubinsky's home and found Max Danish there. Somehow we got on the subject of leadership and after a drink or two I became quite eloquent about the inevitable lag between leaders and followers. I maintained that leaders develop interests, associations, standards of living which are bound to separate them from the masses; leaders evolve into an oligarchy and in the long run they cannot help but betray the the best interests of the rank and file. In short, I repeated all the familiar arguments of the "degradation of the democratic dogma."

Danish, whose loyalty to the International is second nature, objected strenuously. "Why, you're crazy," he protested. "In the International we know our people. We know their minds and their needs and problems, and the idea that the interests of the leadership are opposed to those of the membership is ridiculous."

Dubinsky just listened while we carried on, and finally we asked him what he thought about it.

"I think Stolberg is letting his argument run away with him," he said. "After only two drinks he's ready to call me a labor faker. Still, there's a good deal to what he says. I honestly believe that we in the International succeed pretty well in keeping close to our membership. But the gap is always there. The most difficult job in the world is to keep this gap as narrow as possible. Take the difference in pay, and especially the difference in economic security, between a high union official and a dress operator—or a hod carrier. I get $10,000 a year. Some union leaders pull down $20,000 and $25,000. But the latest figures show that the average wage of the garment worker is still less than $1500 a year. Do cloakmakers live like this?" And he looked around his comfortable living room.

"Of course there are reasons why I get more than a cloakmaker. The point is that such a contrast in income is bound to make all kinds of differences. But even so, the economic difference isn't the whole story.

"The real difference is in the way we lead our lives. The average worker has a very limited contact with the world. Unless he's an unusual person his private life is all he has. Public life is practically closed to him. His education is limited, and I don't mean only his schooling. I mean his daily contacts. His existence is all routine and headaches, and it's apt to contribute very little to personal growth.

"In my job I meet all sorts of people—government officials, labor leaders from every corner of the world, politicians, businessmen, journalists. That's what opportunity is all about—being able to touch the world at many points.

"The job of democracy as I see it—not only in the union but everywhere—is to open up more opportunities for people so that they can really live in the society in which they make their living. In such a democracy it would be a damn sight harder to exploit people. But that's quite a job—and now I'd better get some sleep."

Dubinsky is one of the lowest-paid presidents of a large union in the country. But he still doesn't feel right about his $10,000 a year. Being an exuberant spender, he's always looking forward to the next payday; he's not a hair-shirt type like Andy Furuseth or Sigman, who were proud of their proletarian standards and always looked like respectable lodgers at a Mills Hotel. However, he is bent on keeping the economic gap between the officialdom and the rank and file as narrow as possible.

Since salaries in any organization are graded, Dubinsky's comparatively modest pay brings down the wage scale all through the officialdom. To be sure, joint boards and local unions decide the pay of their own officers, but they feel obliged to follow the example of the International. Thus Julius Hochman, who is the general manager of the New York Dress Joint Board, and undoubtedly the most influential personality in the national dress industry, gets $100 a week. Zimmerman, who is the head of 26,000 dressmakers, draws $75. In the ILGWU the business agent, who in the public mind is a flashy gent with a fat cigar, gets between $50 and $60 a week after years of service; most of the organizers are paid around $35 or $40. There is considerable griping about these wages. As one business agent put it to me, "Dubinsky is so hipped on keeping the union clean that he leans over backward and puts temptation in our way by under-paying us. I think we ought to have a CIO union of business agents and picket the International." One of the high officials of the union had a more brilliant explanation: "Dubinsky is an old socialist. He was in a czarist prison and so I have to support my family on seventy-five bucks a week."

There is probably no labor union in the country in which the common garden variety of honesty—plain money honesty—is more rigidly enforced than in the International. Dubinsky feels that Westbrook Pegler's exposures of graft in the labor move-ment have been "a good thing," in spite of the fact that he has come to consider Pegler an "enemy of labor."

Dubinsky is very frank about discussing the problem of cor-ruption in the unions.

"There is always some corruption in an organization as large as ours," he said. "But one thing I'm sure of. There is no graft *within* the union itself. Naturally, I can never be certain about the relations between union officials and employers. We have hundreds of officials who deal with employers and there is no way of checking absolutely the interplay of graft and favoritism in such relations. But in my opinion these relations in our indus-try are as clean as possible. If you know how to watch for graft you can keep it down to the minimum compatible with human nature. In the ten years I've been president I have gotten rid of some twenty business agents or managers. And in most cases it was not obvious graft. It was merely well-founded suspicion.

"For instance, a couple of years ago I learned that the mana-ger of a small out-of-town local was accepting 'Christmas pres-ents' from employers. This was no friendly and open exchange of holiday gifts. I called him in. He was a young man with a family, and after I talked with him I felt it was only fair to give him another chance. But later I had to let him go. I decided that he could not be trusted.

"The best way to keep a union clean is to be everlastingly sure where every penny goes. We are fussy about our expense accounts. The managers of important unions, some of them vice-presidents of the International, have a weekly expense account ranging from ten to twenty dollars. They have to treat and take cabs and all that. Nobody watches how they spend it—they wouldn't be where they are if they needed such petty watching—but if they go over their allowance for three or four weeks running I want to know why, even if I trust the man as well as I trust myself. And don't forget that their wages and expense accounts are paid by the locals and not by the International. But I'm responsible for the good name of the union as a whole. My own expense account is also an open book.

"But there's one form of handout in the union which is very difficult to control. That is the business of banquets and so-called appreciations for union officials which has grown up in the course of years and which has become a real nuisance. The members of a local will give some union official a banquet to celebrate his tenth anniversary in office, or maybe his silver wedding. Or the union will present him with a car, or even with a house, in gratitude for his long and selfless services. It got so that for a while the International seemed to be primarily a banquet bureau, throwing five-dollar-a-plate dinners to Brother So-and-So. Now, I know damn well that the workers don't crave to honor Brother So-and-So every time some pal of his whips up a banquet. But they don't like to refuse. Finally I decided to create a precedent. After a year or two in the presidency I announced that there were to be no banquets for me, nor would I go to any such banquets, unless there was a genuine reason for honoring a man—let us say for twenty-five years of loyal service.

"But on the tenth anniversary of my presidency I made a bad mistake. As you remember, the GEB gave me a banquet at the time, attended by about a hundred people. The union officials presented me with a $3750 war bond. I was pleased and touched, and I accepted it. Besides, the government and me, we both could use the money. And that's where I made my mistake. For within the next few weeks there was a small epidemic of gifts of smaller war bonds to various overwhelmed officials from a grateful membership. We'll have to do something about it, but at the moment it's got me floored."

PRESIDENT DUBINSKY

When Dubinsky became president of the International the union was at its lowest point. The wits among the cloakmakers congratulated him on his election as "undertaker." The membership was down to 45,000, the treasury was deep in the red, the future looked dark and almost hopeless. But Dubinsky's optimism and his dogged efficiency infused a new morale into the organization. And of course when the New Deal came into power in 1933 this rising morale turned into a fever of elated activity. In another year the union grew to a membership of almost 200,000 and most of the industry was organized.

To be sure, the NRA was behind this miracle. And yet this same miracle did not happen in most AFL unions. The International was prepared to take advantage of the NRA because, like the United Mine Workers and the Amalgamated Clothing Workers, it was an industrial union and could go ahead full steam in its organization drive without the jurisdictional disputes which stymied the craft unions. Dubinsky's fighting energy supplied the steam. He saw the NRA coming and was ready for it. Strikes or stoppages were called in strategic points to strengthen the International's bargaining position vis-à-vis the employers before the prospective code hearings. In every great market the workers rushed into the union.

The vast majority of these new members had to learn the ABC of union life. It was Dubinsky's leadership which saw to it that this job was done.

For a generation the immigrant garment workers had wanted one of their leaders on the Executive Council of the AFL. This recognition had been blocked by the presence on the Council of Tom Rickert, the late president of the United Garment Workers, who in a general way represented the clothing industry. As a matter of fact Rickert's union was reduced to about 20,000 overall workers because most of the men's tailors had been drained off into the Amalgamated Clothing Workers, started in 1914 as a dual union and hence outside the pale of the AFL.

The garment workers had always felt that they were excluded from the Executive Council because they were "immigrant workers" and because of their socialist background. And there was something to that feeling, especially on the second score. No AFL union with a long socialist history could boast a member on the Council. The International was, moreover, an industrial union. Most of the members of the Executive Council represented tight conservative crafts; John Lewis, as head of an industrial union, was a conspicuous exception. In short, the case-hardened craft chiefs on the Council were not anxious to admit another large industrial union which in addition was full of "radicals and foreigners."

But in 1934 Dubinsky was elected to the Council. This was a milestone. It signified that the old fight between the pure and simple trade unionists and the right-wing socialists was over, that old-fashioned socialism was no longer an issue in the AFL. The leaders of the International and the AFL hierarchy had fought side by side against Communist disruption. But beyond this shift in sentiment Dubinsky's election was a personal triumph. By all the canons of the Council the perfect representative of the needle trades would have been somebody like Max Zaritsky. Zaritsky, president of the hat and millinery workers, is a socialist, a conservative, a very fine man, and speaks for a small skilled craft. The fact that the Council elected Dubinsky, who represented the largest and most articulate group in the needle trades, was a tribute to his personality—his gift for winning and keeping confidence, his friendliness, his balance.

In 1935 he was re-elected to the Council. The next year he served as treasurer of the Labor Chest, organized by the AFL to combat Nazism, and was sent by the AFL as its first delegate to the International Labor Office of the League of Nations.

In August of that year, however, he resigned from the Executive Council because of his stand on the CIO.

We shall discuss in a separate chapter the role of the International in the struggle between the AFL and the CIO. Dubinsky's leadership of the International during this profound convulsion in American labor displayed his strategic acumen at its best. The International helped to found the CIO, then it became an independent union for the first time in its history, and finally returned to the AFL. Throughout this complicated maneuver Dubinsky followed a consistent line. He was for industrial unionism because our basic industries could not be organized on a craft basis; but he insisted that there must be no secession, no rival federation. When the Executive Council of the AFL suspended the dozen unions which had formed the CIO, Dubinsky opposed the Council and resigned from it. He was for peace. When later it became obvious that Lewis and the Communists in the CIO were in fact setting up a rival federation, he took the International out of the CIO. For two years the International was an independent union. During that time and ever since its return to the AFL Dubinsky has been insisting that disunion jeopardizes the whole future of American labor. And he does not exaggerate.

His stand on the CIO also required great tactical skill in handling the various forces within his own union. On the one hand the International had a long tradition of industrial unionism and on the other hand it was one of the citadels of the AFL. Both traditions had to be satisfied. When the International joined the CIO the GEB was evenly divided and it was Dubinsky's vote that tipped the scale. All along he had to carry his people with him in his double policy. Finally he got the union solidly behind him. Today the International, more than any other union, symbolizes the hope of unity in American labor.

Peace within the labor movement has always been a passion with Dubinsky. Even in the darkest days of the civil war he never failed to use his influence for conciliation. He took advantage of the NRA upswing to sublimate the old factional hostilities into enthusiasm for the New Deal. The moment was, of course, propitious. Everybody in the hierarchy, whether he considered himself a right-wing socialist or an ordinary liberal or a radical, was now a Roosevelt progressive.

In 1936 Dubinsky ended his lifelong association with the Socialist party. In the campaign of that year he was a Democratic presidential elector. The Socialist party had just split in two: the left wing under the leadership of Norman Thomas retained the party label, while the right wing reorganized itself into the Social. Democratic Federation. Neither group amounted to very much. The New Deal had stolen all the socialist thunder; the influence of orthodox socialism in American labor was over.

But though the New Deal had weakened the old political line-ups in the International this did not mean that the garment workers would register en masse in the Democratic party. They were for the New Deal but against Tammany. In New York, where the great majority of them live, they were used to the device of fusion, which cuts across all parties. Mayor La Guardia had shown what could be done by mixing all sorts of political factions in the name of roaring progress. Dubinsky and other New Deal labor leaders decided to combine those trade union and "good government" forces which had been the backbone of the fusion movement in New York into a labor party. They felt that the socialist traditions of the workers could thus be canalized into support of the New Deal, which would give them a good deal of political power. The American Labor party was to be that strangest of all animals—a non-partisan political party.

The ALP is the only labor party in our history which has not collapsed after one or two elections. In the course of eight years it has deeply affected politics in New York State, indeed has affected the balance between the two great parties in national politics. And, until 1944, Dubinsky was the most influential leader in the ALP.

In the last chapter we are going to discuss the pros and cons of an American labor party. There are many reasons why American labor should not form a class party in this period of international class conflicts. But quite apart from these, the ALP was doomed from its very birth. For it began as a political Popular Front in which the Communists were an important element. They immediately set out to capture the party and by 1943 they had seized control of four of the five boroughs of New York City. In the long run—and no one should have known it better than Dubinsky—the Communists were bound to win out. The Popular Front is merely a cover behind which they operate as a fifth column. One of the reasons the right-wingers continued to stay in the ALP was that the New Deal wanted them there. Without them there could have been no ALP and the politicians in the New Deal needed such a party in New York State.

But for all his solicitude for the New Deal, Dubinsky will not side with the New Dealers when they get a hate on a legitimate trade union. When, after his break with President Roosevelt, John L. Lewis was attacked from all sides, especially by the New Dealers, Dubinsky made it a point to come to his defense. And this in spite of the fact that of late years he and the miners' chief have seldom agreed on basic issues. Lewis had been Dubinsky's main opponent while the International was in the CIO; he had supported Willkie in 1940; he was a leader in the isolationist camp before Pearl Harbor; he had become the leading opponent of the Roosevelt Administration. But to Dubinsky he represented 600,000 miners.

He knows Lewis and he has his own ideas of his powers for good and bad. "But nothing is more ridiculous," he told me, "than the notion that Lewis is some sort of fascist. No one whose power rests on the trade union movement can be a fascist. All totalitarian leaders without exception grew out of political party life, where demagogues can flourish. Whom can Lewis lead toward fascism—half a million coal diggers?"

Knowing the strategic importance of the miners in American labor, Dubinsky has been careful never to break irremediably with Lewis. Taking advantage of Lewis's letter of congratulation to him on his tenth anniversary as president of the International.

Dubinsky sent a long reply on June 24, 1942, in which he reveals a good deal of his attitude on the labor movement in general.

Your letter offers me an occasion [he wrote] to say something which I have long felt should be said. It has recently become the fashion in certain quarters to declare the current period as open season on John L. Lewis—to disparage your efforts in behalf of labor, and to belittle your accomplishments. Despite my own disagreements with you in the past and our differences in outlook today on some questions, I never have and never will join this unseemly exhibition of stone-throwing. There are many among us who cannot forget the great contribution which you have made to the welfare of the miners and to the general labor movement, particularly your ingenuity in undertaking the organization of the great mass production industries which has redounded to the everlasting benefit of the American workers. This unmatched achievement will fill some of the brightest pages of American labor history.

In recent years, I sharply disagreed with you on paramount issues involving labor policy and strategy. Many among us were deeply grieved by your failure to support President Roosevelt, by your views on American foreign policy until December 7, as well as by your position with respect to labor unity. We particularly disliked the clique (Communists) by which you were surrounded at that time, the very same hypocritical coterie which is so vociferously belaboring you now, ostensibly for the very views which they themselves had so fanatically espoused but a short time ago. Today, these political fanatics, who as late as the CIO convention of November, 1940, urged you not to carry out your pledge to resign as president (their shouts 'We Want Lewis' still ring in our ears)—are waging a campaign to smear you as an enemy of our country and as a traitor to the labor movement for opinions you held at that time and which they supported and publicly endorsed, although the record shows that since December 7 you have given public support to the war effort, even to the extent of offering the treasury of the United Mine Workers to the government in this emergency.

I do not like to sound as being all-wise, nor do I presume to offer any lessons in labor history. But I do say from long and distasteful experience we have learned the treachery and unscrupulous tactics of those fanatics, which eventually must recoil upon those who place any trust in them. In your fight with the American Federation of

Labor, you made use of the Communists as allies by making it possible for them to attain certain positions of influence, depending, in
all likelihood, on your ability to get rid of them when you might
deem it necessary. Today, in the crusade that is directed against you,
there is the parallel situation of the Communists being again in the
thick of the fight—this time against you, with one essential difference: in the clash with the AFL, the Communists had made use of
your prestige to climb to certain places of vantage in the movement,
but you too had used them to the limit, while today, as the Communists are rapidly entrenching themselves in the CIO, the nominal
leaders of the CIO actually have become prisoners in their hands.

It is my earnest hope that the growing sense of unity among all
elements of the American people, brought about by the catastrophe
of war, will mold us closer together and that the disagreements of
the past will be dissolved in a united effort to create a bigger and
greater labor movement within the framework of a greater democracy.

A year later, in the summer of 1943, Dubinsky was sympathetic with Lewis's demand for a raise for the miners. And he
supported vigorously, as a matter of course, Lewis' bid to return
to the AFL.

Dubinsky never asks for trouble, but on sufficient provocation,
when his sense of decency is outraged, he will even court it. Early
in 1943 William Green was informed by Ambassador Litvinov
that Henryk Ehrlich and Victor Alter, the two great leaders of
the Polish workers, had been executed by the Kremlin in December 1942 as "Nazi agents." Green and Woll and a number of
other outstanding labor leaders the world over had intervened
in behalf of these two men as soon as it was known that they
were Soviet prisoners. So had Mrs. Roosevelt. So had Wendell
Willkie, when he visited Stalin. Actually, most of these pleas
were made after the men had been murdered, for they were
shot in December 1941. The horror of this crime, and especially
the fantastic accusation that these two Jewish socialist leaders
were Nazi agents, swept the labor movements of the democracies.

Dubinsky, who had begun his political life as a boy in the
Polish socialist movement and who was a personal friend of

Ehrlich's, went to work and organized a mass meeting of protest. At that time public sentiment in America was markedly pro-Russian—and rightly so, for the Russian people were putting up a magnificent fight on the Eastern Front. It took a lot of courage to call the meeting. Dubinsky got William Green, Mayor La Guardia, Senator Mead, James Carey of the CIO and other notables to speak.

In his own address Dubinsky called the executions "a black crime." "As free American citizens," he said, "as workers and as democrats, in registering our fiery protests against these executions we shall assert and reassert to the end of time our unshakable belief in their innocence and their stainless idealism. Ehrlich and Alter died as martyrs. They died because even at the price of life itself they would not renounce their convictions, the principles of a free democratic world."

The Communists and some of their most influential fellow travelers had moved heaven and earth to prevent the meeting. And after it took place they began a campaign of hysterical slander against Dubinsky which defies belief. The *Daily Worker* accused him of being "especially guilty" of the fall of Kharkov, which happened to occur soon after the meeting. He was called the leader "of a gang of unscrupulous fascist agents" and a traitor to our war effort. In an article on anti-Semitism in the *New Masses* Earl Browder accused Dubinsky of being the kingpin of the anti-Semitic movement in the United States. In a single issue of the *Daily Worker* Dubinsky was mentioned scurrilously fifty-four times. This campaign of slander was kept up straight through the fight for control of the ALP and through every major issue which concerned American labor: Dubinsky was pictured as a Hitler agent—no less.

When Dubinsky called the meeting he was quite aware of the torrent of abuse he would suffer at the hands of the Communists. But he went through with it because he felt it was essential to clarify the public mind on the issue of the Soviet Union as an ally; to make it plain that to help Russia with lend-lease and other military aid is one thing, but that to let the Soviet dictatorship pass for an enlightened democracy is quite another.

PHILOSOPHY

Some trade union leaders—and they are rare—have such a clear philosophy of labor that it shines through everything they say and do. You could always tell where Gompers stood, not only as a man of action but also as a man of faith. Other leaders have no philosophy at all; they function as administrators and politicians. To such men organized labor is more a magnetic pole than a system of ideas. Bill Hutcheson of the carpenters and Dan Tobin of the teamsters are typical of this kind of leader.

Then there is a third type, such as Dubinsky. One may know him for years without thinking it pertinent to ask him—or oneself —just what his attitude on the labor movement and its place in society might be. And yet one has a strong impression that he has an integrated outlook, that he has thought things through.

One evening I called him up. "I want to talk to you about your philosophy of labor," I said.

"About my what?"

"About your philosophy of labor," I repeated.

"Say," came the slow reply, "it *would* be interesting to know. Come over, and we'll find out."

To pin down any man's philosophy, especially that of a political personality, is somehow an unreal proceeding. Fortunately Dubinsky and I happen to disagree on certain basic ideas, and disagreement is a good catalytic agent. It precipitates points of view rather than cloudy generalizations.

"Do you believe in capitalism?" was my first question.

"What do you mean by capitalism?" Dubinsky inquired cautiously.

"Just go ahead," I said, "and think aloud about it."

"As you know, I was a socialist for many years. When I resigned from the Socialist party in 1936 it was for purely political reasons. We believed in the New Deal and wanted Roosevelt re-elected. But since that time I have come to the conclusion that socialism, certainly the orthodox variety, will never work. Trade unionism needs capitalism like a fish needs water. De-

mocracy is possible only in a society of free enterprise, and trade
unionism can live only in a democracy. Look what's happened
to the trade union movement in the totalitarian countries.

"But capitalism is an awfully big word. We all know today
that if we're going to keep free enterprise it must be made responsible. It must function in the public interest. Nobody but a
lunatic could believe in a system—or rather a lack of system—
that produces violent business cycles, mass unemployment and
misery for millions of people.

"The big question is, and has been for a long time, where does
freedom of enterprise become license to exploit? Where do we
draw the line in a society as infinitely complicated as the modern
industrial world? History will take a long time, I suspect, to work
this out. I'm for the New Deal, with all its faults, because it's
an American attempt to make capitalism work in terms of industrial democracy, to harness capitalism so it won't run away
with itself."

At this point I suggested that labor might have to pay, and
pay heavily, for its gains under the New Deal, which had developed into a tremendous hydra-headed bureaucracy.

"Yes, of course," Dubinsky said. "That may be so. Just the
same, the New Deal has given labor a tremendous chance. And
I don't think that we in America are in danger of a European
kind of statism. Once Hitler is licked fascism is licked all over
the world. And the Communists won't go places in this country.
The traditions of democracy are too deeply rooted here. Our real
danger after the war is a terrific old-fashioned reaction."

"Next," I said, "what is labor's place in politics?"

"Well, its first consideration should be—no class government
of any kind. Labor, as you once remarked, should be a social
pressure group, pushing its views on great social questions, lobby-
ing for progressive legislation, keeping our society in balance.
Labor must be in social politics, not in party politics."

"Then why in the world are you in the ALP?"

"The ALP," he stormed, "is a purely local affair. I am against
its becoming a national party. And, of course, I am against its
domination by the Communists. But our people wanted the ALP.

We founded it not merely to safeguard the social gains of the New Deal and of our progressive state administrations, but to keep Tammany from ever coming back to power. If they need a labor party in any other state, let them start an ALP of their own."

I could not agree with this analysis of the ALP. But any real analysis of the ALP makes Dubinsky very mad. He insists on believing that it is not fundamentally a political party, but an up-to-date expression in an organized form of Gompers' old theory of non-partisanship. The man of action in Dubinsky is apt to rationalize his outlook to fit his tactics, and he dislikes to have his rationalizations broken down.

My last question was, "What, if anything, is wrong with labor?"

"The worst thing that has ever happened to American labor is the failure to reunite the AFL and the CIO. This great division is responsible for most of our troubles. If we had one movement we could get rid of the racketeers who infest some of the AFL unions and of the Communists who dominate some portions of the CIO. What is more, the rivalry between the two great federations prevents constructive leadership. The masses of American labor are in search of leadership, which a divided movement can't give them. And if after the war labor faces a militant reaction, there will be hell to pay for this lack of unity and leadership."

Like all congenital conciliators, Dubinsky is essentially a centrist. Being a progressive, he bears to the left, and a bit ahead. He instinctively knows where the center is going to be and usually manages to get there ahead of time. And so he often finds himself standing alone, though not for long.

He likes to think of himself as a "lone wolf." "In 1923," he said, "I was the only member of our GEB who voted against accepting Schlesinger's resignation. And I had no love for Schlesinger. My admiration had always been for Sigman, but I didn't want him in power before the Communist situation had fully developed. Sigman made too many enemies. In 1928 I was the first to begin agitating for Schlesinger's return. We needed peace after we had licked the Communists.

"In 1935 I was the only member of the Executive Council of the AFL who voted against expelling those unions which had formed the CIO. In the CIO I was the only one who opposed the admission of the radio and electrical workers. The AFL had a union which covered the field and there was no need to work up further jurisdictional bitterness. Back in the spring of 1938 it became clear that the CIO was to become an official rival federation to the AFL. And so I began preparing the ground for our withdrawal from the CIO. The International was the first big union to go back to the AFL. And all the time we are working for peace."

THE BIG SHOT

Of late years Dubinsky has received a great deal of recognition. He is today one of the half-dozen names in American labor familiar to the public. And he has won this prestige partly because he has avoided the mantrap of Washington. Even his excursion into the ALP is closely tied up with the problems of the International as he sees them. He has never been part of the Washington hurly-burly or the New Deal bureaucracy, which has caused some of the best reputations to collapse like pricked balloons. The New Deal has been rather like the famous Macy Thanksgiving Day parade of inflated Tony Sarg marionettes: the figures are enormous but they are soon deflated and put away. Dubinsky has stuck to his job and so he cannot be deflated.

He is now one of the outstanding civil leaders in New York. At most great public functions he is invited to represent labor. In this he is, of course, helped by the traditional participation of the International in public life and good works. Now that it is rich, its largesse is princely. When Mme. Chiang Kai-shek made her first appearance in New York, in Madison Square Garden, Dubinsky spoke for labor; and behind him was the union with a $100,000 check to establish a home for Chinese war orphans.

By now the snowballing of honors for "D.D." has reached a point where he is a close runner-up to Dr. Nicholas Murray Butler in Who's Who in America.

He is a member of the board of directors of the National War Fund; director of the Greater New York Fund; director of the executive of the Joint Distribution Committee (the great Jewish international philanthropy) ; treasurer of the Jewish Labor Committee; treasurer of the Labor League for Human Rights; New York treasurer of the AFL War Labor Chest; member of the AFL Postwar Planning Committee; vice-chairman of the American Labor Conference on International Affairs. He is also Cordell Hull's appointee to the Committee on Labor Standards and Social Security; Governor Dewey's appointee to the Hanes Committee to survey business and employment activities in New York City; sponsor of the Merchant Seamen's Club in London, for whose foundation the ILGWU gave $75,000; sponsor of 100 field hospital tents for Russia, to be financed by the International; and the list goes on.

The baker's apprentice from Lodz didn't do so badly in the land of his adoption. And be it said to his credit that he has come the whole way by always acting and thinking of himself as less than the movement which he leads. Like all the outstanding leaders of this union in the past he has kept the atmosphere of the institution spiritually bigger than any personality in it. That is really the best part of the contribution of Dyche and Rosenberg, of Schlesinger and Sigman and also of Dubinsky.

IX

The New Deal, 1933-1940

Fʀᴏᴍ 1910–26—from the great victory of the New York
cloakmakers which put the union on the map to their disastrous
defeat under Communist leadership—the International was forg-
ing ahead, turbulently but mightily. It was during those sixteen
years that it gained its reputation as one of the most progressive
unions in American labor. It established minimum wage scales,
reduced hours, civilized conditions in the shop, founded health
and vacation centers, pioneered in workers' education and public
relations. The Protocol of Peace, though historically premature,
introduced a new and lasting conception of self-government in
industry.

The civil war shattered all these gains and left the International utterly exhausted. In New York it was struggling for mere
survival. In the rest of the country local unions were disintegrat-
ing, disappearing. The old jungle of the sweatshop was once
more overruning the industrial clearings. Then, apparently out
of a clear sky, came the national catastrophe of October
1929.

The blow seemed fatal. To be sure, the depression did not hit
the clothing trades as quickly and violently as it hit the basic
industries. For the next year or two the American woman simply
bought cheaper clothes. But in 1931 the garment workers began
to join the ranks of the unemployed in droves. Collective bargaining agreements were disregarded, standards were shot to
pieces, dues were uncollectable. By 1932 the personnel of the
entire union, from coast to coast, had shrunk to seventy officers

and forty clerks who drew an occasional five or ten dollars when it was there to draw. At national headquarters the telephone service was sporadically discontinued and for days at a time one had to walk the stairs because the power was shut off. Visiting employers were told that the elevator was "out of order." The situation was as ludicrous as it was desperate.

The Philadelphia convention of 1932 marked the low point of the crisis. The GEB reported a membership of only 45,000, less than half the number of ten years before. And yet a new hopefulness crept into the proceedings. The union was weak but at least it was united. No copperheads were present. Zimmerman, Nelson and other expelled left-wing leaders had returned to the fold. The re-election of Schlesinger was not merely a gesture of sentiment toward a dying chief; it was also a reaffirmation of a long tradition. Above all Dubinsky, who brought new vitality to this tradition, was the coming man. And indeed two months later, when Schlesinger died, he took his place.

Dubinsky is primarily a man of action. His optimism and resourcefulness energized the whole organization. He regarded every failure as a problem to be solved and invested every defeat with the quality of a strategic retreat. And his gaiety made light even of payless weeks and unpaid bills, which were to last until the mad, glad days of the NRA.

THE NEW DEAL TO THE RESCUE

On March 4, 1933, Franklin Roosevelt moved into the White House. The new Administration had come in on a tidal wave of angry againstism—against Hoover, against Big Business, against the bankers and the speculators, whom the American people blamed severally and jointly for all their troubles. The new President was surrounded by a bevy of Brain Trusters who would revaluate all values without revolutionizing society. To the labor movement they were no new phenomenon; they were its intellectual fellow travelers in the liberal world. Now they were in power, excitedly experimental, and naturally labor was expectant.

The New Deal could not wait for the depression to run its course, the classic remedy under capitalism. Too many people were being mangled in the lower depths of the business cycle. Moreover, the heroic remedy of doing nothing was politically impossible: it would have been an invitation to chaos. The British, who understand not only the technology but also the philosophy of capitalism, went in heavily for the dole, which does not compete with private enterprise. But the New Deal considered the dole un-American; it had other ideas. It "primed the pump" to start up production; it built excellent public works; it also created mock work as complexly meaningless as a Goldberg cartoon; it set in motion a thousand and one projects—some constructive, others demoralizing; it plowed under millions of acres and millions of little pigs. It spent billions to revive private enterprise by competing with it and to initiate abundance by creating scarcity.

But the first thing the New Deal tried to do, after meeting the banking crisis, was to rationalize industry. This meant the lining up of capital so that it might plan production and the organization of labor so that it could force higher wages to give the workers increased purchasing power. The government was to be the coordinator and final authority. The NIRA was an American version of the world trend toward economic statism. Two years later it was declared unconstitutional by the Supreme Court for essentially this reason, but in the meantime it had helped tremendously to organize American labor. During the first half of the New Deal the greatest labor leader of them all was Franklin Delano Roosevelt.

Section 7A of the Recovery Act made it illegal for employers to oppose the organization of labor and outlawed the company union. And Section 7C empowered the President to fix "such maximum hours of labor, minimum rates of pay and other conditions of employment as he finds to be necessary . . ." for the purposes of the act.

This was easier said than done. The vast majority of the AFL unions were so craft-bound that they could not tackle the basic industries. The old-line crafts showed their impotence the moment the NRA tried to seduce them into a clinch with United Steel or General Motors. They simply could not rise to the occasion. All they could do was to get into one another's jurisdictional hair over unorganized workers whom they had neither the will nor the power to organize.

In the General Electric, for instance, some fifteen AFL unions claimed jurisdiction, though the industry is so highly automatic that 95 per cent of its employees are not craftsmen but robots. Gerard Swope, president of the company, naturally didn't want to see his working force torn apart by the conflicting claims of fifteen unions. And so he suggested to William Green that the AFL organize his plants into a single union—on an industrial and not a craft basis. As the AFL unions are neurotically autonomous, Green cautiously sounded out the fifteen interested union presidents and then sorrowfully reported to Mr. Swope that the AFL could not co-operate with him in unionizing the workers of the General Electric. Later, when under government pressure the AFL did try to organize the automobile industry in Detroit, it got into such difficulties with itself that it had to liquidate its efforts.

But those unions which were already organized on an industrial basis—such as the miners, the men's and women's garment workers—rushed ahead at the green light of Section 7A. They had no jurisdictional problems to paralyze them, they were able to regain what they had lost in the open-shop days of the twenties and during the depression, and they could conquer new fields without interference.

PRELIMINARY SKIRMISHES

Even before the Recovery Act was passed the International prepared its strategy. The first battle ground selected was the Philadelphia dress market, which for over two decades had been an open-shop stronghold. The Philadelphia union was a mere skeleton organization and for years some of its most devoted members, mostly women, had begged Dubinsky for permission to call a general strike. He always put them off with the promise,

"I owe you a strike." But now he was ready to act. In April 1933 the Philadelphia Joint Board gave the employers a 24-hour ultimatum, demanding a 5 per cent increase and union recognition. The employers refused and on May 3 the strike was called. Ninety-five per cent of the dressmakers walked out. In three days the whole thing was settled with a 10 per cent increase, a considerable improvement in conditions and, most important, with union recognition. The completeness of the victory surprised the workers no less than the bosses.

Just what the coming of the union meant to these Philadelphia dressmakers is best illustrated by the following incident. As Dubinsky was addressing them at the victory meeting after the strike, a girl from the balcony interrupted him. "Before the strike," she called out, "I made $6.00 a week. Now I'm going to get $6.60. Could *you* live on that?"

"For a minute she had me stumped," Dubinsky says. "But then I told her that the thing that mattered was the recognition of the union; that, with the union to fight for her, her wages would not long remain at $6.60."

Two years later Dubinsky addressed the same workers at the celebration of the renewal of the agreement. Their union had grown from 400 members to almost 5000. Suddenly he remembered the girl in the balcony and asked whether she was in the hall. She was. He reminded her of their little brush.

"And how much are you making now?" he asked.

"Eighteen dollars a week."

"And who got it for you?"

And the crowd roared back, "The union!"

The Philadelphia exploit electrified the whole International. And when the NIRA was enacted a few weeks later the ILGWU was psychologically prepared for an all-out offensive. The whole country was laid out like a strategic map and one trade after another went into action through the months of June, July and August. In some trades the organizing drive preceded the code hearings, in others it took place during or immediately after them. Clearly, strategy dictated that each trade be as well organized as possible when it came up before the NRA.

The campaign was a concerted movement covering over sixty cities throughout the United States and spilling over into Canada. It unrolled in three great waves—first in the coat and suit trade; next in the dress trade; and finally in the minor branches of the industry. Every officer and active member of the union was mobilized "to prepare for immediate strikes." Millions of circulars and leaflets were distributed and meetings held in every community where women's clothes were made. Nothing was left to chance.

THE BATTLE OF THE CLOAKMAKERS

The code hearings in the cloak and suit trade began on July 20. The union delegation was headed by President Dubinsky and Isidore Nagler, the general manager of the New York Cloak Joint Board. Morris Hillquit was counsel for the union. He was then a dying man, rising from his sickbed to represent his beloved cloakmakers. He was flown in an ambulance plane from New York to Washington to deliver the brilliant argument which was to be his last public appearance, the capstone of his long service to these workers whom he had helped to organize almost half a century before.

The New York manufacturers had submitted to General Hugh Johnson, NRA administrator, the draft of a code which provided for piecework and comparatively low wage rates, but was silent on the crucial issue of "jobber responsibility" and "limitation of contractors." The union protested vigorously against this draft and presented one of its own. Above all it insisted that the jobber must be recognized as the real employer of the workers in the contracting shops to which he farmed out his production; and that he must employ only as many contractors as he actually needed, so that he could no longer play them off against one another.

The hearings lasted only two days. On the whole the code embodied the suggestions of the union. It provided for the 35-hour week; for adequate minimum wage rates for each craft; and for piecework for everybody except cutters, sample makers and examiners. The union was opposed to piecework but accepted it in return for the far more important concessions of the limitation of contractors, jobber responsibility and the 35-hour week. The code quite rightly provided for a wage differential for the Eastern Area, which included the seaboard states from Maine to Maryland, and the Western Area, which covered the rest of the United States.

The Communists denounced the NRA as "fascism" and made a demagogic issue of the restoration of piecework. On this issue they had considerable support among the older workers who had fought under Sigman for week work and were loath to give it up. But otherwise the code was popular with the rank and file. And in a referendum held on August 9, the cloakmakers approved it by a vote of almost two to one.

Now that the code—which of course specified only the minimal conditions for collective bargaining—was in force, the Cloak Joint Board set out to enroll every cloakmaker in Greater New York before negotiating an agreement. The union called an "organizational stoppage"—a fancy term for a strike which, it was felt, must not be characterized by its right name so soon after the hearings. The stoppage began on August 14 and lasted two weeks. When it was over the cloakmakers had over 35,000 members in the metropolitan area. Thousands of workers who had dropped out during the civil war and the depression poured back into the union. Once more the Cloak Joint Board was a powerful organization, indeed far stronger than it had been before the fratricidal conflict in the twenties. In the matter of hours and wages the new agreement followed the provisions of the code, but in addition it guaranteed the "union shop"—a labor euphemism for the closed shop—which had become a dead letter, and renovated the broken-down arbitral machinery into an effective system with a responsible impartial chairman. At last the Protocol of Peace was beginning to bear fruit.

The other cloak markets, as was to be expected, followed the New York pattern. Organizational stoppages were called and quickly settled by agreements. Wages went up, the 35-hour week became general and the closed shop became a national institution in the trade.

THE BATTLE OF THE DRESSMAKERS

In the dress industry the sequence of events was reversed. Here a great general strike took place before and not after the NRA hearings and the resulting agreement became the actual model for the code. The dressmakers could boast, "We have written our code on the picket line."

Soon after the NRA was set up the New York dress manufacturers, like their brethren in the cloak and suit industry, rushed to Washington and tried to push through a code which they had drafted. It called for a 40-hour week and a weekly minimum of thirteen dollars. The Dress Joint Board, of course, denounced this "sweatshop code," demanded a 30-hour week, much higher minimum wage scales, and insisted that the jobber must be made responsible for conditions in the shops of his contractors.

The leaders of the International realized that, code or no code, they could never reorganize the dress market without a successful strike. And their feeling communicated itself to the rank and file. The dressmakers held mass meetings, paraded through the garment center and demanded an immediate walk-out. Even the request of President Roosevelt that labor refrain from striking before the code hearings took place failed to cool their ardor. They were convinced that public opinion was with them.

The hearings were set for August 10. But Dubinsky managed to have them postponed until August 22, and the strike was called for August 16. It was a critical moment. There was precious little time to waste. After all, less than 15 per cent of the New York dressmakers were in the union and, for all the excitement in the air, it was impossible to tell how many of the thousands of unorganized workers would actually walk out. But when the day came 70,000 of them quit cold. The entire industry came to a standstill, not only in New York City but in the whole "out-of-town" territory from New Haven down to the suburbs of Philadelphia.

Julius Hochman, the general manager of the New York Dress Joint Board, was in charge of the strike. He has a superb sense of publicity and knows how to combine the dramatics of audacity with the realism of astute negotiation. To the workers he seems a veritable Danton on the barricades; to the insiders he seems the patient and honest broker between clashing interests, more sorrowful than angry over the passionate follies of mankind.

On the eve of the strike he tried to persuade Grover Whalen, then the local NRA administrator, to head a committee of mediation. Whalen didn't think much of the idea. After all he was a government official and the Administration did not approve of strikes as a prelude to certification. But Hochman explained to him that the strike was essential for the organization of the union, without which no code could be enforced. And then he went into much detail about the great careers which men like Brandeis, Mayor Mitchel, Governor Smith and others had made by settling strikes at the right moment. "Why, Mr. Whalen," he said, "our union has launched a great many national figures that way. Why don't you come in and then we'll have you settle the strike? It won't last more than four days." Mr. Whalen immediately grasped the big idea.

And indeed the strike was settled in exactly four days. As the ink was drying on the agreement Whalen turned to Hochman and said, "Julius, when you told me it would be over in four days, I didn't believe you." "Grover," Hochman replied, "I didn't believe it myself." The two men liked each other—each thought the other quite a character, and both were right.

The agreement provided for a 35-hour week without overtime and for excellent minimum wage scales in the various crafts. The rusty arbitration machinery was streamlined and put under an impartial chairman. The closed shop was resuscitated. And the jobber became responsible for the conditions in the shops of his contractors. He had to register them with the Dress Joint Board so that their premises could be under constant union supervision.

On August 15, the day before the strike, the New York Dress Joint Board had less than 10,000 members. Two weeks later it had 70,000. The "out-of-town" locals—in Connecticut, New Jersey, near-by Pennsylvania—rose from a scattered membership of a couple of hundred to over 20,000. The metropolitan dress industry was now 95 per cent organized. This strike of 1933 was as memorable a victory in the history of the International as the famous Uprising of the Twenty Thousand in the same trade in 1909.

Now the dressmakers were ready for the code hearings, which were quickly over. The agreement just negotiated was simply codified. Ironically enough, the New York manufacturers argued in favor of it as enthusiastically as the union. For competitive reasons they wished to see all the dress markets bound by the same or similar standards.

The day before the code hearings began, the dressmakers of Chicago went on a strike which lasted for a week. Strikes took place in Boston, Cleveland, Los Angeles, St. Louis and elsewhere. They were all quickly settled with agreements based on the code, though of course wages differed regionally to conform with the local cost of living. But these wage differentials were not important. Unions half dead for years revived overnight. Probably the most spectacular comeback was that of the Chicago dressmakers, whose membership rose from a few hundred to over 6000.

Money poured into the local treasuries; the unions once more became a "way of life" to their members. Being incurable romantics, the dressmakers saw the New Deal as an economic picnic on the way to Zion, with F.D.R. and D.D. leading them on to ever greener pastures. The Blue Eagle was soaring in the sky. And even General Hugh (Iron Pants) Johnson, who looked like W. C. Fields after another beer, was to them another Angel Gabriel.

THE BATTLE OF THE MINOR TRADES

The third phase of the campaign was in the minor trades, in such "miscellaneous" industries as bathrobes and children's dresses, underwear and lingerie, corsets and brassières, raincoats, embroidery. The unions in these trades had always led a sort of twilight existence on the periphery of the labor movement. The workers, mostly young and semiskilled, were the Forgotten Women of the International.

In the summer of 1933 a series of strikes was called in these trades in metropolitan New York. The employers, the majority of whom were small-fry businessmen, could not resist the combined pressure of the International and the New Deal, and most of the strikes were settled before the code hearings began. The agreements signed seemed incredible victories to the rank and file.

Before the NRA these unions were mainly paper organizations, though some of them had a long and militant history. But the collapse of the International during the civil war had knocked them all out. They had no control in the shops; wages were between six and twelve dollars for a 50-hour week or more; there were no standards of any kind. After the strikes wages were almost doubled, hours reduced to 37½ or 40 a week and the closed shop was established.

Since the NRA these industries have changed unrecognizably. The employers no less than the unions have come into their own. A good many of the former sweatshop keepers have prospered into large and efficient manufacturers—who enjoy the shorter hours and the 5-day week no less than their employees. They have learned to deal with the union through a machinery of arbitration which protects the interests of both sides. Not only wages but profits have steadily increased, standards have risen, the unions are well run. And two of them—the children's dressmakers and the underwear workers—are among the largest and most solid organizations in the International.

PROBLEMS OF SUCCESS

The achievements of the International during the NRA period were phenomenal. Before the NRA the work week in the women's garment trades was supposedly 40 hours. But that had become pure fiction; most workers put in between 50 and 60 hours. Now over 90 per cent had a 35-hour week and none worked more than 40. Wages throughout the industry increased from 20 to 50 per cent. In some of the minor trades they increased as much as fourfold.

The financial report submitted to the Chicago convention in 1934 reflected this astonishing revival. In 1929, when the civil war was over, the ILGWU owed more than $2,000,000. This sum included deposits made by employers as security for the "faithful performance" of their contractual obligations—moneys which were squandered and never accounted for by the Communist leaders of the 1926 cloak strike. When the International took over the New York Cloak Joint Board in 1927, it assumed responsibility for all these debts, including the employers' security deposits. By 1932 the debts had been reduced to $1,000,000. The assets of the union, however, were largely imaginary and it had only $10,000 in cash.

At the 1934 convention Dubinsky could boast that indebtedness of the union had been practically liquidated, that the assets of the union were over $850,000, of which more than $520,000 was in cash. For the first time in years there was no need to levy an emergency tax in order to survive. "This great difference in our financial standing," said Dubinsky, ". . . represents the change in the union's strength between 1932 and the present. It represents the difference between inactivity, pessimism and apathy, on the one hand, and buoyancy of spirit and boundless hope on the other."

Best of all, it represented an increase in membership from 45,000 to over 200,000.

All this was most exhilarating. But the problem of assimilating these tens of thousands of new workers was appalling. The miners, too, under the leadership of John L. Lewis, had more than trebled their membership. But most of their new members were actually old-timers who had dropped out of the union in the twenties and during the depression or they belonged to the younger generation, brought up in the mining camps in the militant tradition of this greatest of American unions. Many if not most of the new members of the International, however, were more like the raw recruits in the brand-new unions of auto, radio or steel workers.

For the most part these new members were young girls and women—"NRA babies"—utterly innocent of trade unionism. They were first or second-generation Americans from every variety of regional and racial background. Thousands of them were old-stock Americans, especially in the small towns. Negroes from Harlem, Spanish-speaking Puerto Ricans, black West Indians with an Oxford accent came into the industry in New York; Mexicans entered it in the Southwest; Chinese on the West Coast. But the majority of newcomers were young Italian-American girls who poured into the dressmaking trade on the Eastern seaboard. They were usually of Sicilian descent from devout Catholic homes. The history of American labor, its factional struggles, its place in our society, the traditions of the International were a closed book to them.

The cloakmakers, cutters, pressers and other veterans were a bit contemptuous of these innocents flooding the union. Some of the officers, too, especially those in the lower ranks, were rather skeptical about them. A bureaucracy is alway apprehensive of the influx of new masses, whose moods and mores are an unknown quantity, who may develop a leadership of their own. But these doubts were soon resolved. The NRA babies, for all their youth and industrial callowness, quickly developed into good unionists and were absorbed into the life of their locals. Their very lack of trade union sophistication seemed to contribute to their union loyalty. They were as yet too naïve to question the established leaders or to raise factional issues. To these trade union freshmen the International was an Alma Mater, strange but wonderful.

Their hero was Dubinsky, who traveled all over the country visiting the revitalized and the new unions. His enthusiasm and energy, his whole platform personality, made them feel that they belonged to an organization which had at once a great tradition and a great future. Dubinsky considered the assimilation of these

new members a task in workers' education—the creation of an enlightened public opinion in the International. He geared the
whole officialdom to get hold of them and make them feel at
home. The newcomers were constantly kept in touch with the
exciting developments in the world of labor and particularly in
their own union.

The educational department, which had been skimped during
the lean years, was rapidly expanded. Local unions were encouraged to start programs of their own; some of them established
sick-benefit systems, credit societies and other practical services.
The International promoted sports events, musical and dramatic
clubs, and put on pageants and festivals. These various activities
became a cohesive force in the life of the union, developing a
spirit of freemasonry in its heterogeneous population.

THE OLIGARCHY AND THE NEW RANK AND FILE

By 1934 the ethnic composition of the International had un-
dergone a profound change. For half a century before the NRA
the vast majority of the garment workers were Jews. Thousands
of them had been tailors in the old country and naturally drifted
into the needle trades over here; and the thousands who followed
them, friends and relatives, joined them in the sweatshops. The
Jews almost monopolized the labor market in this field for the
same reason that for many years most of our miners were Welsh,
Scottish and English and the majority of our steel workers came
from Eastern and Southeastern Europe. This ethnic stratification
characterized much of American industry from the eighties until
the end of mass immigration during the first World War and
persisted to a considerable extent till the New Deal.

The New Deal revived an almost collapsed trade union movement after mass immigration with its characteristic industrial
clannishness had ceased. The new blood of the unions came from
every stock in the American community. But the composition of
the leadership did not change perceptibly.

The International re-emerged in 1934 with as diversified a

membership as any American union. The Jews had shrunk to a minority; today they constitute no more than 30 per cent of the rank and file. Forty per cent are of Italian origin. The rest represent almost every strain in our national life. Furthermore, the vast majority of the new members are women. But of the twenty-four highest elected officers of the International—the GEB, which consists of President Dubinsky and twenty-three vice-presidents —only three are Italian and only one is a woman. The rest of them are Jews of East European origin, most of whom were on the Board when the NRA came in.

For this disproportional representation the reasons are fairly clear.

The simplest and most paradoxical reason is lack of racial prejudice. There are a number of American unions—notably the miners, the longshoremen and the needle trades—in which the tradition against racial or national discrimination is so strong that it never emerges as an electoral issue. In his capacity as a labor leader, no member of the GEB thinks or acts as Jew or Gentile, and everybody in the union knows it. In fact, in large organizations, which consist of many stocks without mutual prejudice, the tendency is apt to be toward mutually preferential treatment among the various groups. For all groups have a strong vein of self-criticism, of which the most likely objects are people of their own background. This helps to explain why Dubinsky is especially popular among the Italian workers and Antonini among the Jews. As one cynic, who is a friend of both men, put it, "Their own people know them better."

Of course, a much stronger reason for the preponderance of Jews in the top leadership of the ILGWU is the weight of oligarchic continuity. They were there first. An oligarchy may be defined as an almost irremovable body which can meet almost any irresistible force. It takes a long time to develop leaders, who flourish on entrenchment, and even a longer time to get rid of them except by revolution. And if an oligarchy is reasonably faithful, competent and honest, rebellion against it is well-nigh impossible. On the other hand, it is also true that in an alert and liberal organization—in which tradition does not impede but motivates progress—the established leaders, even when they hark back to an earlier period, are more valuable and effective than the coming men until the latter have really arrived.

There is another reason. The older leaders of the Italian workers—such men as Ninfo and Antonini, who have been outstanding members of the oligarchy for many years—are a good deal more than labor leaders in the eyes of the Italian-American community. They are among the pioneers and social leaders of this community at large. This kind of leader finds it difficult to share his prestige with rising men from his own group. Almost unconsciously he is apt to encourage the secondary leader or the hired technician rather than the forceful personality.

Though all these factors are understandable, Dubinsky's common sense tells him that the new groups, especially the Italians, should be encouraged in every way to develop top leaders as soon as possible—"if only because it would look better."

"But there are so many difficulties beyond those which are obvious," he told me. "Few people realize, for instance, that the labor movement, for all its great strides in recent years, is now losing more of its competent younger people than ever before to other walks of life. The only exceptions are those few CIO unions whose entire leadership is of recent vintage.

"Practically all of us old-timers had no more than an elementary schooling, if that much. We rose from the sweatshop in an atmosphere of class antagonisms. We began as agitators rather than executives. Our base was the picket line—we belonged to a pioneer movement of militant ideals. We became administrators by actually building the union itself. 'To go over to the boss' seemed like a betrayal.

"Today the picture is very different. Most of the coming men have at least a high-school education. After half a dozen years in the International, which is a large organization and plays the most important single role in the industry, they have had a great deal of executive and industrial experience. They can double or treble their income any time they want to; business is glad to have them. And they need not feel that they are leaving the workers in the lurch. On the contrary, they may feel that they are bringing to management an enlightened labor point of view.

"In the International we are lucky in having a number of what one might call career men and women, able and well trained, who wish to make the union their lifework. But there are not many of them.

"Anyway, time will solve this problem. After all, only four men on our General Executive Board were on it in 1920. . . ."

Almost 75 per cent of the members of the International are women, yet more than 95 per cent of their leaders are men. The selective process of leadership among women workers is almost hopelessly inhibited at every turn.

To begin with, as we have already observed, women leaders meet very much the same kind of prejudice in the labor movement as they meet elsewhere. But masculine prejudice is not the only thing that holds them back.

The vast majority of women in industry, especially young women, hope to escape from it through marriage. And those who are married work not for a career but for a supplementary income. This attitude does not make for leadership. Moreover, unlike her middle-class sister, the professional or business woman, the woman labor leader must have followers, she must lead. And she is not likely to have followers except in virgin territory, where the union is comparatively new and the men are not entrenched. But in general women workers want men leaders out in front. The labor leader has to deal with the employer, the community, the government, wherever the union touches society. And everywhere he has to deal with men, many of whom have risen in the world because they are cunning and unscrupulous.

This combination of reality and prejudice discourages the more ambitious women in the labor movement. They are apt to drop out and go into some social or government agency. Those who stay are usually of the sentimental-idealistic type, whose devotion makes them good organizers of other women; or they make

places for themselves, sometimes important ones, as office managers or in the social and educational activities of the union.
They seldom reach the seats of strategic power.

All these reasons help to explain why the leadership of the International has changed so little while the rank and file has
changed so much. But the fundamental reason, underlying all
others, is the simple fact that the present leadership has made the
International what it is. The NRA was a historic opportunity;
but it took a forceful and experienced directorate to exploit it.
And the rank and file is satisfied with this leadership. Some of the
leaders are, of course, much abler and more dynamic than others.
Some are slowing down. But they have all gone through the same
hard school and can function as members of a team with a great
tradition, which has never tolerated corruption and would not
shield utter incompetence for long.

Today the International is a vast trade union empire spreading across the United States and Canada. Some of the members
of the GEB—such men as Morris Bialis in the Middle West,
Meyer Perlstein in the Southwest, Louis Levy in the Far West—
administer vast autonomous territories. When we cover this empire we shall discuss them and their work. Now let us meet the
leaders in New York, which is still the heart of the industry.

Julius Hochman

One of the most colorful personalities in the International is
Julius Hochman, the general manager of the New York Dress
Joint Board. He represents 70,000 workers but somehow one
doesn't think of him as a labor leader.

The union hierarchy and rank and file, the manufacturers
and jobbers, the stylists and designers, all regard him as the im-
presario of the trade—picturesque, temperamental and creative
Nothing human is alien to Julius because his nature is so rich in
contradictions. Disillusioned yet idealistic, self-centered yet un-
selfish, politically ingenuous but extraordinarily perceptive of
human motives, avid for recognition but without any real desire
or capacity for power, Hochman is full of those inner conflicts

which hamper but enlighten the gifted individual. He is the kind of man who is both "impossible" and lovable, whose friendship is at times more trying than his enmity and whose enemies seem to be as fond of him as are his friends.

And his talk is wonderful—and uninterruptible. To follow his conversation is like walking through caves of treasure. It flashes with wit and illumination and even his absurdities are brilliantly suggestive.

Hochman considers it his thankless task to infuse the manufacture of women's dresses with such efficiency, imagination and élan that the American woman can't escape being the best-dressed woman in the world. This high purpose could be achieved only if the dressmaking industry turned itself into a miniature Good Society, which would pay reasonable profits, the best possible wages, maintain high standards and conditions, and educate the consumer to want useful and lovely things at a fair price. Hochman has a long history of browbeating both the manufacturers and his union colleagues into accepting this exalted notion of their social function. In a way they are flattered, but as practical men they are always worried about what he may think up next. Yet they follow him to a remarkable extent.

Hochman looks like a mellow and world-weary version of John L. Lewis. But he is weary only of the absurdities of mankind which he discusses with unflagging energy and wit. He has a positive genius for twisting an idea into ludicrous self-illumination. "Well," he once greeted me in his booming voice, "I've just signed a contract for still more wages and still fewer hours, and one of these days we'll have such an overwhelming victory that the industry will have to close shop altogether."

Once a manufacturer lost his temper with Hochman on some minor point in a contract. "For God's sake," he yelled in his slightly cockeyed idiom, "why are you holding things up just for a drop in the bucket?" Without a word Hochman poured out a glass of water and shook into it a drop of ink from his fountain pen. "Go ahead," he said, "drink it, it's only a drop."

Hochman has no political machine—he is incapable of building one. He is neither a good nor a bad politician; he is just no politician at all. But though he has no political power in the union, he has great influence in the industry. His imaginative approach to industrial problems has come to be genuinely appreciated. Then, he is a superb negotiator. He knows the industry, he understands the psychology of collective bargaining and above all he knows his dress manufacturer. Having all these skills and no flair for power, he enjoys the continuous support of his colleagues. They can always endorse him without fear of competition.

If you want to know the latest political doings in American labor, don't ask Julius. He is apt to consider politics petty stuff and he absolutely refuses to gossip. Inside dope bores him. But he is full of interesting ideas—at times he can be profound—on the nature and conflicts of institutions, on the psychology of leaders, on the attitude of the workers, on the basic drives in contemporary life, all of which he discusses with the air of an anthropologist making observations on primitive society.

Some years ago he visited England. He called on very few labor leaders and brought back no latest news. But he did get the feel of things. "You know," he told me, "the British are ahead of us —and not because they have a Labor party, which is all right too. The point is that the English workers and the English industrialists, the English people in general, are not afraid of themselves or each other. They do not have to bluster so much on the 'right' or on the 'left,' for they don't have to prove anything to themselves. They love freedom because they are historically mature."

His reading is vast and unorganized, mostly in American history, anthropolgy, economics and psychoanalysis. He considers Freud the most seminal mind of our times. "Too bad Freud couldn't analyze Marx," he once remarked and went on to speculate on what kind of world this might be if Marx had had all his complexes fixed up. Julius refuses to psychoanalyze friends and colleagues; in such matters, he implies, truth and good taste do not go together. But God help your self-esteem if he is in a mood to help you understand yourself!

Hochman was born in a small town in Bessarabia in 1892. His father was a ladies' tailor. He had no early schooling whatever and at eleven he went to work as a tailor's apprentice. At thirteen he took part in a strike which was lost. "That decided me to become a socialist and join the revolutionary movement—against my father," says Julius, with a characteristic psychoanalytic twist.

In 1907 his father came to America and brought Julius with him. The boy went to work as a skirtmaker, but during the next ten years he spent every spare moment reading, attending evening classes and taking courses at the Rand School. In 1916 he passed his high-school Regents'. "Originally I wanted to be a doctor or a lawyer," he says, "but I got so involved in the labor movement that I just never could get out of it."

In 1910 he joined Local 23 of the skirtmakers and in 1913 he transferred to Local 25 of the waistmakers. During the strike of 1916 he became assistant organizer of Local 25, and has been a union official ever since. In 1919 President Schlesinger sent him to Chicago to organize the dress market. A few years later President Sigman sent him to organize the garment workers in Boston, Toronto and Montreal. Hochman is a good organizer of a certain type. Though a great admirer of efficiency, he is not particularly efficient. But he can get people excited about ideas. He is an effective speaker, curiously combining after-dinner wit with agitational passion. And he has a sure instinct for publicity and public relations. Like Schlesinger, he knows how to involve all sorts of people on the side of the union.

In 1921 he became a department manager in the dressmakers' union and a year later the general manager of the New York Dress Joint Board. But when in 1923 Sigman amalgamated the Joint Boards of the dressmakers and cloakmakers, Hochman resigned because he was opposed to the fusion, and spent a year studying at Brookwood Labor College. In 1925 he was elected a vice-president of the International and during the civil war he was tireless in his efforts to save the union from Communist disruption. After the disastrous strike of 1926, when the Communists were purged, Hochman was the manager of the reorganized Joint Board, which still included both dress- and cloak-makers. But he continued agitating for a separate Dress Joint Board. And when it was finally re-established in 1929 he became its general manager, which he has been ever since.

Soon after the NRA was inaugurated, Hochman got an industrial engineer to work out the "unit system," based on a time study of piecework operations, as a substitute for the hit-or-miss method of fixing piece rates. He campaigned for almost three years to get it accepted by the union and the employers. In 1939, when conditions in the New York dress market began to deteriorate ominously because of the inroads made by the new and more efficient factories in the Middle and Southwest, Hochman wrote a pamphlet, *Industry Planning through Collective Bargaining*, and started a ceaseless campaign for greater efficiency in the New York dress industry and for the national promotion of its output.

His "industry planning" became the basis of the agreement of 1941 and in that year his pet idea of a New York Dress Institute was realized. The Institute was to study styles and costs and to promote New York as the fashion center of the world. For the duration it is marking time. "But after the war," Hochman says, "we're going places."

Of late Hochman has been obsessed with the necessity of "planned, systematic public relations work by the labor movement." He has talked about it before colleges, universities, clubs and labor organizations all over the country and has written on the subject for magazines and newspapers. In 1942, at the AFL convention in Toronto, he introduced a resolution calling for a large-scale public relations program. "It is not a question," he says, "of concocting some slick sales talk about labor but of bringing the facts and the spirit of the labor movement before the American people."

"Would you bring the 'facts' about the racketeers in the AFL and the 'spirit' of the Communists in the CIO before the American people?" I asked.

This got Julius awfully mad. Like all labor leaders he believes that racketeering and disruption "cannot be eliminated overnight." "They are deep-seated sociological phenomena which labor shares with other movements and institutions in American life," he lectured me. "American labor did not invent graft or totalitarianism. The problem is to get rid of these infections without killing the patient. And education is probably the best way of doing it.

"Labor's job of public relations should be just that, education in a twofold sense. It must try to convince the public that trade unionism is here to stay and that without it there can be no industrial democracy. And it must educate itself to live up to its own publicity."

Isidore Nagler

Through the long years of the depression and the New Deal— from 1928–39—the general manager of the New York Cloak Joint Board was Isidore Nagler.

Nagler represents the modern type of AFL leader who has risen from a highly skilled craft. A cutter by trade, he is up to date and a good mixer, with all the earmarks of the amiable politician, though he is a bit too ingenuous to be the politician he fancies himself. As is the case with most cutters, his background and his outlook are thoroughly middle-class. It would be difficult to imagine him as a leader of dressmakers, for he lacks completely the romantic-proletarian touch which always lurks in the temper of men like Antonini, Zimmerman or Hochman, who began in the sweatshop and who move in an atmosphere sprayed with idealism as a barbershop is with bay rum. Nagler never was a socialist, Communist or radical of any kind. He has always been first and last a trade unionist, to whom all collectivist ideals are slightly ridiculous.

Nagler was born in 1895 in Austria and came here as a boy of fourteen. His father was a merchant and Isidore was not brought up in a "class struggle" environment. After finishing elementary school he decided to become a cutter. Young rebels like Dubinsky or Hochman went into the shop with the vaguely contradictory ambition of leading the workers toward "emancipation" while saving enough money to study medicine or law. Nagler became a cutter because he thought that cutting was a nice, clean trade at which one could make a good living. And he worked at his trade for almost ten years, earning as high as seventy-five dollars a week.

During his years at the bench he was an active member of Local 10. In 1920 he became a business agent and from then on his rise was steady. At various times he served as a member of the local's executive board, as its recording secretary and as a delegate to the Central Trades and Labor Council of New York. By 1928 he was the general manager of the Cloak Joint Board and a year later a vice-president of the International.

Whatever job Nagler fills he handles like the sound businessman he looks. He knows the cloak industry through and through and is a good negotiator from sheer expertness. Unlike Hochman he is less interested in the psychology of the employer than in the number of stitches which goes into a garment.

For eleven years Nagler ran the Cloak Joint Board. He loved his job, which was important and impressive. Good-natured, sensible and well-adjusted, Nagler rose in the esteem of others and himself. He made close connections with the AFL hierarchy, especially with its leaders in New York City and State, and was a perennial delegate to AFL conventions, national and local. In 1934 the ILGWU sent him abroad as its representative to the International Clothing Workers Congress, which in turn appointed him a delegate to the International Federation of Trade Unions.

But in 1939 an emergency arose in his own union, Local 10. The powers that be decided that it was essential for the good of the International to defeat Samuel Perlmutter, who was running for re-election as manager of the local. The best man to lick him was Nagler. And like the good organization man he is, he reluctantly resigned as general manager of the Cloak Joint Board and ran for his old post as manager of Local 10. He was elected and has been the head of the New York cutters ever since.

Nagler likes public life. He is a natural born committeeman and he has the energy to cope with the many honors he enjoys having thrust upon him. Since the founding of the American

Labor party in 1936 he has been on its State Executive Committee. In 1937 he came near being elected borough president of the Bronx on the ALP ticket. The next year he ran for Congress; his expected defeat did not in the least mar his pleasure in his candidacy. In 1942 he was elected to the Executive Committee of the New York Federation of Labor. All these distinctions he takes very earnestly and is as busy at his various social activities as a boy spearing snakes. He is also prominent in all sorts of Jewish causes, from philanthropy to Zionism.

There is something very attractive about his roly-poly energy, his chronic optimism and the artless zest with which he pursues his public life. To Nagler the labor movement is a sort of Workers' Rotary for the advancement of their interests and the service of society. Not a bad idea.

In 1943 Nagler was one of two fraternal delegates of the AFL to the British Trades Union Congress. This annual junket is one of the prize honors in the gift of American labor. But in the fall of 1943 it was much more than a junket—great issues of international relations were to be debated. The main issue was the relation of Anglo-American labor toward the Soviet trade unions. In a speech of remarkable lucidity Nagler gave the reasons why the AFL must refuse to become part of any proposed joint council with the Russian unions. The AFL, he pointed out, has the deepest fraternal feelings for Russia's workingmen and -women in their heroic fight against the common enemy, but it could not recognize something which did not exist. There were no trade unions in Russia, he said. There was only a state-controlled labor front in the grip of the dictatorship.

Whereupon the *Daily Worker*—both in London and New York—went into simultaneous conniptions. Nagler, the Communists screamed, "echoes Goebbels"; he is part and parcel of the "defeatist clique" which "stabbed in the back our heroic brothers of the United Nations" and is "prolonging the war regardless of cost in human lives." For a day or two Nagler beamed at every visitor, called for the clippings and quoted the most slanderous epithets against himself in the presence of his delighted office staff. He was proud of drawing such a hysterical smear campaign by the totalitarians. Surely no greater accolade can come to an American, a democrat and a labor man!

Louis Stulberg and Moe Falikman

Local 10 is really an amalgamated union, consisting of cloak cutters, dress cutters and cutters in the miscellaneous trades. Nagler himself is in charge of the cloak department. The manager of the dress department is Louis Stulberg; and the miscellaneous department is headed by Moe Falikman.

Stulberg represents the best type of the younger leaders in the International. Clean-cut and alert, he is a good executive who knows the trade and the people he deals with. And he is one of the most popular union officials among the workers.

Louis joined the union in 1915 as a boy of fourteen, and while working in the shop he managed to get through high school and to attend the University of Chicago for a year. In 1924 he was appointed an organizer in Toledo, and five years later he became an officer of Local 10 in New York. In 1933 he was made the manager of its dress department.

Moe Falikman joined Local 10 in 1916 at the age of twenty-three. He worked at his trade until 1929, when he became an organizer for his union. In 1933 he was promoted to his present post. Falikman is the quiet and studious kind whose effectiveness is taken for granted and whose wide popularity is as unobtrusive as the man himself.

Israel Feinberg

Isidore Nagler's successor as general manager of the New York Cloak Joint Board is Israel Feinberg.

Feinberg has an unusually rich background in the social and labor movements of the last forty years. In his early teens he got a strong whiff of the Russian Revolution. Then, at the turn of the century, he went to England, where he spent eight fruitful years as an active trade unionist at a time when British labor was beginning to shape its future as we have come to know it. He made

friends with many of the leading personalities among the trade
unionists, co-operators, anarchists, Fabians and left-wing socialists. Feinberg still has a great admiration for the British, for their
capacity to combine progress with tradition, imagination with
discretion.

He founded the Jewish tailors' union in Manchester, which
was then a center of Russian Jewish immigration. His English
experience more or less fixed the patterns of his social thinking.
In his political views he is a right-wing socialist—in his own
words, "a conservative progressive." But there is a lot of the
philosophical anarchist in his make-up, of the unreconstructed
libertarian who cannot conceive of any movement for social betterment which is not deeply rooted in personal freedom and common decency. Feinberg's personal culture lacks the amateurish
touch of the self-taught workingman. Mellow, philosophical and
widely read, he is really an old-time intellectual who grew up in
the labor movement.

Feinberg was born in 1885 in Berdichev, the heart of the Russian Jewish pale, in the province of Kiev. His father was a high-
class tailor and as a child Israel did not have to work and went to
school until he was sixteen. Then he learned the tailoring trade.
In 1912, after his Manchester days, he came to this country and
went to work as a cloak operator, joining Local 1. His reputation
had preceded him and he soon became one of the rank-and-file
leaders in his union. He was friendly with John Dyche, who was
then the power in the International, and who had lived with
Feinberg in Manchester. In course of time he was elected to the
executive board of Local 1, then he became its chairman and one
of the delegates to the Cloak Joint Board. Later he became
chairman of the Joint Board itself. In 1922 he was elected a vice-
president of the International and, with the exception of a three-
year period at the height of the civil war, has served on the GEB
ever since.

In 1922 Sigman left the managership of the Cloak Joint Board
and Feinberg took his place. But when, three years later, the
Communists captured the New York cloakmakers, they insisted
on his resignation. Sigman, who at the moment thought it best

to appease them, got Feinberg to resign, and he went back to work in a shop—a rather unusual procedure for a vice-president of a union.

When Schlesinger became president in 1928 he appointed Feinberg to take charge of the Boston area. Two years later he went to Toronto and Montreal and for several years was the leader of the International in Canada. In 1933 President Dubinsky sent him to the West Coast, where he organized the garment workers in Los Angeles, San Francisco, Portland and Vancouver. He remained as the head of the International in the Far West until 1939, then returned to his old post as general manager of the New York Cloak Joint Board.

Though not yet sixty, Feinberg today is one of the elder statesmen of the union. His experience, his knowledge of the industry, his forty years in the trade union movement, have rooted him in the inner circles of the hierarchy and won him the confidence of the rank and file. To the cloakmakers he represents the best in their tradition, the easygoing philosopher and shrewd negotiator who doesn't annoy them with high-pressure efficiency. But though as an executive he may seem more relaxed than streamlined, there is no doubt that as a pinochle player he is more streamlined than relaxed.

Benjamin Kaplan and Eduardo Molisani

The two big unions of cloakmakers in New York are Locals 117 and 48. Local 117, which has gone through a number of mutations and has 9000 members, is headed by Benjamin Kaplan. Local 48, made up of 8500 Italian cloakmakers, is in charge of Eduardo Molisani.

Both men are old-timers who have been in the International for almost thirty-five years and officers in their respective unions for over two decades. Molisani became manager of Local 48 in 1938, and Kaplan of Local 117 in 1939. Together they have jurisdiction over half the workers affiliated with the New York Cloak Joint Board. And each of them is as familiar with every inch of his bailiwick as an Indian guide is with his neck of the woods.

Joseph Breslaw

Joseph Breslaw is the perennial leader of the New York cloak pressers and has been one of the powers in the International for a generation. He is full of character and mother wit, shrewd and practical. By nature a machine politician, he resembles a Bill Hutcheson of the carpenters or a Dan Tobin of the teamsters a good deal more than he does a Schlesinger or a Sigman. He has the rough-and-ready manner of the presser.

Hearty and likable, he is so apparently aboveboard as to make one suspect that he might very well be. To the progressives in the union he has always been the symbol of reaction. Sigman and his numerous followers detested the "Breslaw crowd" and in 1925 they forced Breslaw out of the union. But his machine remained intact and after four years he came back to the old stand. The Sigman attitude toward Breslaw still lingers among the professional reformers in the union—the ex-Communists, the anarchists and others—who view a political machine not of their own making as something to deplore. To his own pressers Breslaw is the peerless leader of the common man. They swear by him—and well they may, for their wages range anywhere from $80 to $150 a week.

Breslaw was born in 1887 in Odessa and came here at the age of twenty. After a brief spell as a dress operator he became a cloak presser and in 1909 joined Local 35, where he was immediately elected to the executive board. Later he was secretary, then chairman of the local, then a business agent and in 1916 manager. In 1922 he was elected a vice-president of the International.

Breslaw's power in the union is far greater than the size of his local, which has only 3800 members, would indicate. No man can build a Tammany on such a small constituency. "On what, then," I asked a friend in the International, "does his power feed?" "There is no mystery about it," was the answer. "Breslaw's power rests mainly on his tactical ability and on his really superb common sense. For years I have watched him cut through to the heart of some complicated problem and settle it in a way that was acceptable all around." To this one might add that he has the homely virtues of the machine politician: he is loyal to his friends and, once he gives his word, he keeps it.

But Breslaw undoubtedly has also the ultraexpedient touch of his kind. Though frank and loyal, he is also crafty—qualities which are by no means incompatible. Of late years he has been playing quite cynically with the Communists. In his own union he gives short shrift to any left-winger who dares to raise his head. But he will join all sorts of popular front organizations to keep in the good graces of the comrades and their fellow travelers.

While the *Daily Worker* and the *Freiheit* bitterly attack Dubinsky, Antonini, Nagler and other leaders of the International as "enemies of labor," they go out of their way to point to Brother Breslaw as a sterling progressive. Such tactics give him prestige in the fellow-traveling "liberal" world and authority among the left-wingers in the labor movement, including the International. And he laughs off any suggestion that he plays footsie with the Commies under the table by pointing to his own "reactionary" record. All Brother Breslaw does is to give his name to good causes.

Max Cohen

For many years Joseph Breslaw's sidekick in Local 35 was Max Cohen, who is now the manager of Local 60 of the dress pressers.

In spite of his high position in the union hierarchy Cohen is very much the congenital business agent—at once canny and simple-minded, just one notch above the rank and file, who think of him as their champion and crony. And indeed Max is constantly "out in the market," visiting shops to see to it that his pressers get "a square deal"—to the tune of anywhere from $80 to $120 a week. He also runs an unemployment department which distributes the available work in slack times.

Cohen was born in 1891 in Bessarabia. He came to this country in 1909 and went to Toledo, where he got a job as a cloakmaker. "I was soon blacklisted," says Brother Cohen with a touch of nostalgia for the heroic days. "Conditions in those days were terrible and of course I fearlessly stood up for my fellow workers."

In 1910 he moved to New York and joined Local 35, which then included all the pressers in both the cloak and the dress trades. He immediately moved way to the left in union politics in opposition to Breslaw, and his dissidence was finally recognized when Breslaw invited him to join the official family. "It was like this," Cohen explains. "One day Breslaw called me in and told me that an able fellow like me should use his talents constructively. Naturally, I agreed with him." In 1915 he became a member of the executive board of the local and three years later its chairman.

Cohen worked at his trade for twenty-two years, which explains his real closeness to his membership. That type of leader resembles an army officer who has spent half his life in the ranks. It was not until 1931 that Cohen became a paid union official. But his big chance came in 1933 when the dress pressers were separated from the cloak pressers and given their own local, of which Cohen became the manager. In 1937 he was elected a vice-president of the International.

Conscious that pressers have the reputation of being plain and uncultured folk, more at home on the picket line than at symphony concerts, Cohen makes quite a fuss about the cultural and educational work which he promotes. For a number of years he had a part-time educational director. And the pressers would listen dutifully to Columbia professors discoursing on the history of trade unionism or the gyrations of the business cycle. But they did much better in sports events in which they could knock hell out of most challengers.

Jacob Heller

The stormy petrel of the New York cloakmakers for over a generation has been Jacob Heller. For years he was the leader of the reefer makers—the children's cloakmakers—until they were finally amalgamated with the other cloakmakers in 1936. Heller fought amalgamation bitterly and his jurisdictional forensics have become part of the tradition of the International.

He is one of the few old-time leaders in the AFL who has a higher education. He was born in 1889 in Russia and there he studied at a *Yeshiva* for the rabbinate. He is still quite a Hebrew scholar, a sort of emancipated theologian whose scholastic turn of mind flavors his utter skepticism. In this country, while he worked in the shop or as a union official, he continued his studies and graduated from the School of Commerce in New York University. In his social views he is very conservative.

"Were you always a conservative in your social and political views?" I asked.

"Of course I was," he said. "At twenty-five I was a right-wing socialist and conservative trade unionist, just as I am today. It's one of the silliest notions that a young man must begin way on the left and spend a lifetime winding up on the right track. To me there is nothing noble in that kind of wasteful evolution. My observation has been that this kind of 'growth' usually runs a man's character ragged: the journey from left to right is generally nothing but a progressive school for opportunists." Heller has a flair for bringing out the disturbing side of a half-truth.

He came to this country in 1906 and he worked as a children's cloakmaker for eight years during which he was very active in his beloved Local 17, whose manager he became in 1916. In 1920 he was elected a vice-president of the International. In 1925, when Sigman purged the "Breslaw-Heller machine," Heller opened an office as an accountant. And for four years he did very well as business adviser to various unions. With the fall of Sigman he went back to his old post as head of Local 17. But the jurisdictional fight between the reefer makers and the cloakmakers went on until it was finally settled through amalgamation in 1936, and Heller was made the manager of the reefer makers' department of the New York Cloak Joint Board. But the unreconstructed individualist in him found it difficult to function without a union of his own, and in 1942 he was put in charge of the newly created Local 105 of about 3000 snow-suit workers.

Heller is a man of great force, which time has mellowed but not subdued, and his Gridiron Club satire is so felicitous that even his victims quote his barbs after they have lost their sting.

He is the perennial editor of, and sole contributor to, the *Kibitzer,* a humorous journal issued at the conventions of the International, whose mordant wit appeals to everybody's best friends and severest critics. After the immense expansion of the International since the NRA and the liquidation of his jurisdictional fight, Heller has lost some of his strategic power in the oligarchy but none of the prestige which his colorful personality commands. And he still enjoys the unswerving loyalty of the New York children's cloakmakers no matter in what local they may find themselves.

Harry Greenberg

In 1933 the unions in the so-called minor trades became an important part of the International. With the emergence of these trades during the NRA, two of their leaders rose high in the councils of the union—Harry Greenberg of the children's dressmakers and Sam Shore of the undergarment workers.

Harry Greenberg is the traditional right man in the right place. The membership of Local 91 is almost entirely composed of NRA babies; in 1932 the local had fewer than 500 members, within a year it had grown to 6000. Virtually all of these new members were young girls who had no trade union experience. And Greenberg was, and still is, just the man to lead them.

He is the efficient bureaucrat—self-assured, tenacious, fussily conscientious and benevolently high-handed. He knows exactly what is good for his members and proceeds to do it for them. With the cloakmakers such streamlined management just wouldn't work. To the average cloakmaker, efficiency connotes autocracy and has to be hidden behind the smoke screen of leisurely kibitzing. In the vast dressmakers' unions the machinery of administration has to be garlanded with the ivy of idealism. But the girls of Local 91 want a manager that is a manager— as long as they are sure that he is competent and honest. Harry Greenberg more than fills the bill.

Greenberg was born in 1891 in Rumania but came here as a little boy, and at the age of ten he went to work in an underwear shop. He joined Local 25 of the waistmakers just before the great strike in 1909, and in 1913 he was appointed business agent for the local. Two years later he became the manager of Local 50 of the children's dressmakers, which at the time had twenty members. In 1921 this local was merged with Local 41 of the housedress and bathrobe makers and became the present Local 91, which today has over 12,000 members.

By 1925 Greenberg was a vice-president of the International. But as an ardent follower of Sigman he was purged from the GEB in 1928 when Schlesinger came to power and he remained out until 1934, when the Dubinsky regime was in full bloom. Though ambitious, Greenberg just wouldn't play with Schlesinger, whom he cordially disliked. But all through this period he retained his leadership of Local 91.

For all his hard-boiled qualities Harry is a sentimentalist at heart, like a real-estate promoter who falls in love with the development he is boosting. I doubt if anything means more to him than the "progress" of Local 91. In 1943 he prevailed upon his executive board to buy Tammany Hall as headquarters for his beloved union. This new home symbolizes to him a combination success story and moral victory: the saga of the working girl routing the Tammany tiger from his lair.

Greenberg prides himself on his pioneering in trade union welfare work. Local 91 was the first union in the country to inaugurate vacations with pay. The employer pays for one week's vacation for every worker in his shop and the union administers the funds. Greenberg also takes a strenuously paternal interest in the health of his members. He sees to it that the workers actually use the facilities of the Union Health Center maintained by the International. On two occasions he got the Health Center to move its X-ray equipment to his local headquarters and then practically browbeat the members into submitting to an examination. "We found 150 cases of tuberculosis and set aside $25,000 to cure them all," Harry boasts. "No member of our local has any business being sick with such a splendid Health Center at her disposal."

In his dealings with the employers Greenberg has the attitude of a banker being approached for a loan. His first reaction to anything is no. He has to do business with the employers but he lets them know that they are under suspicion. This attitude sometimes gets him into unnecessary difficulties—not only with the manufacturers but with his union colleagues as well. But his single-mindedness and boundless energy, his busy devotion to his union, his paternal solicitude for his members really make him the success he thinks he is. Local 91 has the atmosphere of a highly successful Chamber of Commerce which tells the world that Zenith is the greatest little town on earth.

What makes Greenberg's bullheadedness rather attractive is his utter humorlessness where his loyalties are concerned. You can always get a rise out of him by suggesting that the International is not the greatest union in the world, that Local 91 is not the greatest union in the International, or that the heart of Harry Greenberg ever misses a beat for his children's dress, bathrobe and house-dress makers.

Samuel Shore

Samuel Shore is the only member of the General Executive Board who never was a garment worker, though he worked at almost everything else under the sun. He has been a dishwasher, streetcar conductor, pharmacist, millinery worker, free-lance writer and theatrical producer.

Shore came to this country from his native Bessarabia in 1903 at the age of fifteen. The family settled in Philadelphia, where Sam joined the anarchist movement. His hero was Prince Kropotkin and in his teens he made street-corner speeches refuting Darwin's theory of the struggle for existence and strongly advocating the doctrine of mutual aid. Very soon he began writing for the anarchist papers, contributing short stories, essays and literary comment. Later he published a volume of short stories.

To be in the anarchist movement a generation ago meant that one had to be active in the trade union movement, and in 1909 Shore became the secretary of the bakers' union in Philadelphia. But Philadelphia was too tame for him and in 1911 he came to New York, where he made friends with John Dyche, then secretary of the International, and Rose Schneiderman, one of the founders of the Women's Trade Union League. Both of them were interested in organizing the underwear and "white goods" workers and Shore was chosen to head Local 62, which had just been founded. In 1913 he persuaded Dyche to let him call a general strike. "The response was terrific," he says. The strike lasted six weeks and ended in a great victory—the agreement provided for a 50-hour week and a 20-cent hourly minimum wage.

Shore stayed with the International until 1920. Then he went into business and later worked for the International Union Bank. He remained in business for ten years and in 1930 he came back to the International as manager of his old Local 62. During the NRA drive the local grew from 2000 to 10,000. Today it has over 15,000 members and is one of the most prosperous unions in the International. In 1940 he was elected a vice-president of the International.

The young anarchist of a generation ago has become one of the most respectable labor leaders in New York. As a labor leader he has a way of looking at industrial problems from the point of view of an enlightened businessman. In 1943 Shore called together the manufacturers and made a little speech. "Gentlemen," he said, "for the purposes of this meeting I am the president of Samuel Shore and Company, manufacturers of ladies' underwear. I'm in trouble. Many of my girls are leaving to go into war production where they get more money. I'll just have to raise wages. But I'm afraid that the War Labor Board won't let me raise them the usual 10 per cent, though in these prosperous times I can very well afford it. And so I'm going to see my namesake, Sam Shore of Local 62, who is a most reasonable fellow, and get him to agree with me to petition the Labor Board for a 5 per cent increase."

His little speech described the actual situation to perfection and then and there Mr. Samuel Shore, the manufacturer, and Sam Shore, the labor leader, got a rousing vote of confidence and approval for this little scheme, to which Washington was only too glad to agree.

The members of Local 62 are, if anything, even more satisfied with Mr. Shore than the manufacturers. For Shore is essentially the politician who considers his membership his constituency which he has to please. He is ever the diplomat. When a member of Harry Greenberg's local gets fired, Harry's first instinct is to fight. Shore's technique is very different. On one such occasion he called up the employer, who was a Syrian, and told him that the local had intended for a long time to send a little check to his wife for the Syrian hospital in which she was so deeply interested. After the employer had expressed his effusive appreciation for this unexpected union generosity, Sam suggested that perhaps the little misunderstanding about the firing of Bessie could be amicably adjusted. It was—right then and there.

Shore loves to be active in public affairs. He is an excellent after-dinner speaker—shrewd, tactful and vastly amusing. He is a member of the Selective Service Draft Appeals Board of New York City, a member of the American Jewish Congress, a director of Freedom House and chairman of the National Labor Division of the Citizens for Victory Committee. He has been one of the moving spirits in the American Labor party and it was he who trotted out his friend Dean Alfange for the gubernatorial nomination on the ALP ticket in 1942.

Politically Shore is far less astute than in his trade union leadership. He is apt to be impressed with the politically great and a "call from Washington" is treated more or less like a command. Glamour, political or social, he finds irresistible.

But above all, Sam is a great mixer. His zest for life is Falstaffian. He is, I think, the best storyteller I have ever heard and his repertoire ranges from the subtlest to the broadest. I remember when, at a party for William Green, he gave some of his celebrated imitations. We were all in convulsions. But through the tears of laughter we had the sense that we were watching a great comic artist at work. A superb comedian was lost to the American stage when Sam Shore became a labor leader.

Luigi Antonini

The top-flight Italian leaders of the International are almost as much leaders in the Italian community as they are in the labor movement. This is especially true of Luigi Antonini, the first vice-president of the International.

Antonini is far more than the general secretary of Local 89 of the Italian dressmakers. He is America's number 1 anti-fascist, the president of the Italian American Labor Council, which has over 300,000 members, a leading spirit in the Mazzini Society, one of the most important Italian democratic organizations in the country, and for years he was chairman of the American Labor party. He is as well known among Italian-Americans as Count Sforza or Professor Salvemini, but his influence is greater, for he has spent thirty-five out of his sixty years in this country.

To be sure, Antonini is a professional labor leader. But unlike Dubinsky, who is a public figure because he is a labor leader, Antonini is a public figure who is also a labor leader. The other leaders of the International today are not pioneers in the organization of the garment workers as were Dyche or Rosenberg or Schlesinger; they are the second or even the third generation of leaders. But Luigi Antonini and Salvatore Ninfo are themselves pioneers of Italian organized labor in this country. Moreover, Antonini is not only a pioneer trade unionist among his people but one of the early intellectual leaders of the Italian-American working-class community, in this respect comparable to Abraham Cahan and Morris Hillquit when they first began to organize the Jewish workers in New York.

Antonini is an impressive personality. Expansive, colorful and warm, he has the Latin gift of combining the patriarch with the good fellow, genuine dignity with infectious joviality. In Italian he is a superb orator. To his discourses in English I could listen by the hour. His absurdly delightful accent serves as a sort of running emphasis on his satirical wisdom. Antonini is a very shrewd customer. But he impresses one as much bigger than that. His shrewdness seems lost in his general sagacity.

During the two decades of Mussolini's dictatorship Antonini was the leading Italian-American anti-fascist. It was a courageous part to play, for during most of that period the Little Italies of this country were largely pro-Mussolini, not because they were fascist but because they felt that Mussolini had "put Italy on the map." Antonini never faltered. He was never vague or general in his attacks on fascism, especially on its activities in this country. He named names, gave details of fascist skulduggeries, and for years was in real danger from Mussolini's gangsters, who were murdering far less telling opponents in Europe and in this country. After each radio speech (and he made hundreds of them) he would receive scores of threatening letters—and not all of them from cranks.

Antonini was born at Vallata Irpina in central Italy on September 11, 1883. His father was a teacher and the home environment was intellectual and socialist. The boy received a sound elementary and high-school education. He came to this country in 1908.

The first few years in the United States he spent in Boston and New York, always close to the Italian labor and socialist movements. He had a hard time finding himself. Few Italian intellectuals in those days went to work in a shop. They went into business or the professions or they became agitators and journalists, like the late Carlo Tresca, one of the noblest figures in the history of American radicalism. But Antonini had to go into a shop. He worked at various garment trades, first as a cloakmaker, then as a dress operator, then as a cutter and finally as a dress presser. This shows that he was never a craftsman at heart because your true cutter doesn't become a presser. Antonini was an intellectual working in a shop—a type cut out for leadership.

In 1913 he helped to form a committee to get the Italian dressmakers to join Local 25, of whose executive board he became a member. In 1916 he started his career as a paid union official. His first job was as an organizer for Local 25, then he became the assistant editor of L'Operaia, the Italian paper of the New York garment workers. Finally, in 1919, the International decided to charter a separate Italian-speaking union of dressmakers in New York, Local 89, of which Antonini was really the founder and has ever since been the general secretary. Local 89 is one of the half-dozen largest local unions in the country. It has a membership of about 37,000.

During the civil war in the union Antonini was a tower of strength to the Sigman administration. In the early twenties he had been for a brief period a Communist but he broke with the party as soon as he realized that trade unionism can do no business with totalitarianism. Ever since then he has been fighting the Communists as hard as the fascists, not only in the labor movement but in the Italian-American community at large. He is both tireless and astute in exposing the Popular Front technique of the Communist party—the fifth column technique of "uniting" with liberal and labor groups of all kinds in order to exploit them as a "front" for Communist purposes.

Thus he forced the Communists and their stooges out of the Italian American Labor Council, although their maneuvers were directed by a powerful clique headed by August Bellanca of the Amalgamated Clothing Workers. In the Mazzini Society, too, Antonini drove them into bolting the organization.

But his most trying fight was his effort to purge the Communists from the Italian section of the OWI. It was a rather short-lived fight. Antonini soon gave in to pressure from Washington and soft-pedaled his criticisms. It seems impossible for any labor leader who has been tied up with the New Deal to resist the specious argument that criticism of the Administration is tantamount to sabotage of the war effort.

Antonini's job as manager of Local 89 is both less and more than a trade union executive post. He tends to his job very much as Dr. Nicholas Murray Butler tends to Columbia University: he keeps his eye on it and watches policy rather than detail. He knows how to pick his aides and is able to keep track of things in the local while working up a committee for some Italian-American cause or rushing off to Washington to see Attorney General Biddle. It was Antonini more than anyone else who persuaded the government to lift the stigma of "enemy alien" from Italian residents in this country while we were still at war with Italy. The Administration listens to him not because he is a labor leader but because of his long record as an indomitable democrat in the Italian community in America.

Salvatore Ninfo

Salvatore Ninfo is also an Italian community leader, but he is far more the traditional trade unionist than Antonini. For years before the New Deal Ninfo was the head of Local 48, the Italian cloakmakers' union in New York, who—unlike the girls of Local 89 over which Antonini presides—have been part and parcel of the organized labor movement for decades.

Ninfo is the typical AFL hierarch with progressive leanings. His whole life has been spent in the labor movement. He came here from his native Sicily as a boy of sixteen in 1899 and three years later joined Local 9, when the International was only two years old. In 1903 Samuel Gompers borrowed him from the ILGWU and appointed him a general organizer for the AFL to unionize Italian workers in various crafts—cabinetmakers, roofers, tunnel workers, painters, carpenters, bakers and longshoremen. Ninfo's territory included New York, Philadelphia and Boston. During the Gompers era he was undoubtedly the leading trade unionist of Italian origin in this country.

Ninfo continued working for Sam Gompers until 1906, when he returned to Local 9 of the cloakmakers and became a member of its executive board. In 1908 he was elected a delegate to the Cloak Joint Board and was appointed by John Dyche a general organizer for the International. During the great strikes of 1909 and 1910 Ninfo was the acknowledged leader of the Italian garment workers. After these strikes he was elected a business agent of the New York Cloak Joint Board, then a strategic organizing post.

In 1916 Ninfo became vice-president of the International, when Dubinsky and most of the other present-day leaders were still young fellows working in the shop. During the next two decades he was one of the best-known leaders in the International and from 1922–34 its first vice-president. During the interregnum between the resignation of Schlesinger and the election of Sigman in 1923 he served as acting president of the union for four months. In the civil war he contributed as much as anyone to the final victory of the right wing. His Italian cloak-makers voted as a bloc with the Sigman administration and there was never a moment's doubt where Ninfo stood—he was Gompers' man.

Sensible, by no means brilliant, none too forceful, a man of obvious integrity, Ninfo is more the respected coleader than the power politician. His career was steady and distinguished. But the victory of fascism in Italy, with its reverberations in Italian-American life, and later the rise of the New Deal, which changed the whole trade union picture in this country, combined to push Antonini ahead of Ninfo, and in 1934 Antonini displaced him as first vice-president. For one thing Local 89 is nearly six times as large as Local 48, and for another thing Antonini, precisely because his roots are not so deep in the older labor movement, is more in the current of events.

Today Ninfo is in charge of the Passaic area for the International. In 1937 he was elected to the New York City Council on the ALP ticket and he served through 1943.

Anthony Cottone

A completely different type of leader of the Italian workers is Vice-President Anthony Cottone. Born in 1880, he came to this country at the turn of the century and worked at almost every trade in the garment industry. He was a cloakmaker, a presser, a dress operator and a cutter. In 1910 he was elected to the executive board of Local 35 of the cloak pressers. Then he became an organizer and later the manager of the Harlem cloakmakers, and since 1927 he has been in charge of the cloakmakers in Brooklyn. In 1939 he became a member of the General Executive Board of the International.

This is the career of the trade union leader who remains a Jimmy Higgins at heart. Such men never attain power by themselves because they are interested only in the parish work of their own locals.

THE PASSING OF THE NRA

In 1933 the International had nothing but praise for the New Deal and the NRA. An industrial union under energetic leadership, it had been able to take full advantage of the government's green light to go ahead and organize the workers in its industry. But in 1934 and 1935 the question of organizing the basic industries came to the fore. In these industries the AFL had been able to make very little headway. And so General Johnson and Donald Richberg, who ran the NRA, began recognizing company unions, almost nullifying the original intent of the act. The company unions, on the other hand, could not hold down labor's end of the industrial seesaw. They were unable to keep minimum wages from freezing into maximum wages or to improve conditions; in short, they were unfit to help in the policing of the codes because they were controlled by the industrialists who had created them.

The whole labor movement became restless. It felt that the NRA had failed to live up to its early promise, that wage increases were being canceled out by the rising cost of living and that Section 7A was being repudiated by all sorts of phony interpretations and exceptions. The International shared this critical attitude. But the progressives in the union, headed by Zimmerman, felt that mere criticism was not enough. They wished to put themselves on record as "class-conscious" radicals who recognized only too well the "capitalist" nature of the NRA and weren't going to be fooled by the liberal chatter of the New Deal.

The NRA became the subject of a full-dress debate at the 1934 convention of the International in Chicago between President Dubinsky and Charles Zimmerman, who arrived with a long treatise on "The NRA and the Labor Movement," replete with the hackneyed phrases of the class struggle, which he introduced bodily as a resolution. The only specific recommendation Zimmerman made was that union leaders should refuse representation on code authorities since all such representation was but a form of "class collaboration." They should, he insisted,

merely present their demands before the NRA and then "be prepared to back them with their organized power."

Dubinsky knew that Zimmerman's position was but a grand-
stand play to the traditional left-wingers, with whom he had been
identified for so long. There really was no difference of opinion
between the two men. In his reply Dubinsky pointed out that
the NRA, for all its imperfections, was a great boon to organized
labor and he objected to the fantastic idea that the trade unions
should refuse representation on the code authorities. The whole
debate, conducted in an atmosphere of friendly unreality, was
the last effort of the progressives to play the opposition to
Dubinsky, and as time went on they identified themselves completely with his administration. When the NRA was declared
unconstitutional in May 1935, the so-called controversy of the
year before was hardly a memory. Zimmerman was as deeply
dismayed as any conservative in the AFL.

The liquidation of the NRA posed for the International, as
it did for the whole labor movement, an alarming problem.
Would the union be able to hold its new membership and maintain its gains without the NRA? Or would the abolition of the
NRA lead to the breakdown of the whole industrial setup erected
under its authority? Under Dubinsky's leadership the union acted
promptly and energetically. When the Supreme Court decision
was announced the GEB happened to be in session in Philadelphia. It immediately issued a ringing declaration to the membership:

We are facing today an emergency situation growing out of this
frightful setback. . . . The Supreme Court could nullify the NRA,
but it cannot take away the economic power of the workers to
organize, to strike, and to protect through their organizations work
standards gained at the cost of untold sacrifice. . . . Meet with
strikes every attempt by either individuals or groups of employers to
weaken our organization or to reduce our standards of life and labor.

Then, instead of waiting to see what happened, the union
intensified its organization work, especially in the weaker centers
of the industry. It was remarkably successful in maintaining its

gains and even in extending them. The membership actually increased, though only slightly, during the next few months and industrial standards were kept up. Moreover, the International did everything to communicate its high morale to the rest of labor. It lobbied effectively for the National Labor Relations Act which, for all its miserable draftsmanship, was essential as a substitute for Section 7A of the defunct NIRA. It contributed heavily to the campaign for organizing the textile workers. It came out squarely for the industrial form of organization in the basic industries. And it almost doubled its budget for educational and propaganda activities.

To replace the NRA code in the coat industry the union got together with the manufacturers and established a voluntary National Coat and Suit Recovery Board; and it proceeded to expand and tighten the regulative machinery in the dress industry and in the minor trades.

For the ILGWU the NRA had done precisely what it should have done. It had successfully primed the pump of union organization and after it was abolished the union was able to continue on its own.

THE PASSING OF FACTIONALISM

The curse of factionalism, inherited from the civil war, continued to plague the union up to the very eve of the great revival of 1933. The coming of the NRA completely changed the picture. What neither Dyche nor Rosenberg nor Schlesinger nor Sigman could accomplish—a unified International—Dubinsky did accomplish by exploiting the New Deal as an absorbent for intraunion discord. The NRA cemented the union into a united front, the united front of howling success.

Three political groupings emerged from the Philadelphia convention of 1932. First, there was the old right wing, the Breslaw-Heller "crowd," which dominated the New York Cloak Joint Board and therefore was a power in the International. The second group, which fancied itself as an official opposition, consisted of the so-called progressives; it was a loose conglomeration of old-time Sigmanites, the followers of Zimmerman, Nelson and other ex-Communists, a number of left-wing socialists, and a large but vague group of "non-partisans." These progressives were dominant in Locals 1 and 9 of the cloakmakers, in Local 22 of the dressmakers and in the new Local 155 of the knit-goods workers. They also had a considerable influence in other local unions throughout the country, partly because they represented the spirit of traditional opposition to whoever was in power. The third group were the Communists and their fellow travelers. Most of these had quit the International and were now in the dual Needle Trades Workers Industrial Union but they had left behind their nuclei within the ILGWU.

During the NRA the Breslaw "elements," being practical politicians, tended to their business of building up their local unions. The progressives worked closely with the Dubinsky administration and forgot all about their official dissidence. Zimmerman, who became a vice-president in the convention of 1934, joined Breslaw in making Dubinsky's re-election to the presidency unanimous. The Communists were in the doghouse, for they insisted that the New Deal was a "fascist" setup, which seemed like a huge joke to the garment workers.

All that was left of the old fratricidal bitterness were the routine sneers of the progressives at the "reactionaries" of the Breslaw camp, who reciprocated with the amused contempt of the machine politician for the fiery revolutionists tamed into respectable members of the oligarchy. Dubinsky, the congenital centrist, sided in his general outlook with the progressives without giving offense to the right wing, an attitude of conciliation which was not difficult to maintain in a union that had quadrupled its membership in less than a year and where there was very little to fight about.

But towards the end of 1934 some factional tensions reappeared. The Comintern decided to dissolve all dual trade unions and ordered the comrades back into the "reactionary" unions to renew the old game of "boring from within." A year later the Communist party officially abolished the Trade Union Unity League and the Needle Trades Workers Industrial Union, and

told their members to return to the International in any way
they could. Most of them drifted back into their old bailiwicks
—Locals 1, 9 and 22.

In 1936 their fifth column activities were reinforced when the
Comintern launched its famous Popular Front policy which invited everybody but open fascists, and even some of them, to
"collaborate" for "peace and democracy." In the International,
as everywhere else, they abandoned every vestige of principled
opposition and offered a united front to all and sundry who
would unite with them.

Breslaw reacted with characteristic expediency. Though he
kept the Communists down in his own union, he lent his name
to their innumerable Popular Front organizations and supported
their trumped-up public causes, which is what they wanted from
him and for which they praised him as a constructive statesman.

The progressives, under the leadership of Zimmerman, could
not deal with the Communists that way. For one thing the progressive locals had thousands of liberal and radical members who
fell for the Popular Front. Besides, romantics like Zimmerman
always feel impelled to raise every political problem to a high
ideological level. Accordingly he and his group, though refusing
to join the Popular Front, entered into formal discussions with
the Communists and agreed to collaborate with them on various
specific union questions. In Local 22 of the dressmakers the
groups issued a joint declaration and in 1937 elected a joint
slate. In Local 117 of the cloakmakers (Locals 1 and 17 had just
merged into Local 117) the progressives and the Communists
actually fused and some Communists were given positions of
importance. Manager Louis Nelson of Local 155 of the knit-
goods workers was the only progressive who refused all dealings
with the reds. Nevertheless, they gained some influence even in
his local by supporting him enthusiastically against his will on
every issue which came up.

Local 9 of the cloak finishers was actually captured by the
Communists. The manager of this local was Isidore Sorkin, a
right-winger in the Breslaw camp. But when the Popular Front
began to make inroads in his union he made common cause

with the Communists and became their man. The Sorkin-Communist machine dominated the local until the spring of 1942 when our old friend Louis Hyman, the reconstructed fellow traveler of civil war days and now a Dubinsky fan, defeated Sorkin in a close election.

But in spite of all these more or less successful infiltrations, the Communists did not make significant headway in the International. When in 1935 they dissolved their dual union, Dubinsky laid down a clear policy for their readmission: all garment workers are entitled to belong to the union but they cannot enter as a group. "If the Communists want to support our administration," he said, "well and good. But we shall hold them strictly accountable for their acts. And we shall make no horse trades with them, for the union has nothing to trade about with outside-dominated groups." In other words, Dubinsky was glad to "collaborate" with them on his own terms, and being an expert in detecting Communist skulduggery, he was pretty well able to frustrate their disruptive tactics.

In 1938 the Communist party once more changed its line, foreshadowing the scuttling of the Popular Front and their return to "revolutionary" sabotage. The New Deal once more became a "fascist" racket, F.D.R. a "warmonger" and the AFL a "reactionary" outfit. By 1939 Dubinsky was again, as of old, one of their pet hates in the labor movement. But the Stalin-Hitler pact of 1939 rendered them completely harmless, for the vast majority of the garment workers did not agree with Comrade Molotov that "fascism is a matter of taste."

To be sure, when Hitler attacked Russia in June 1941 the position of the Communists improved considerably and for a while they were able to carry on the most vehement agitation with impunity. But curiously enough this agitation did not perceptibly strengthen their factional influence in the union. The International was now a rich and powerful organization, whose members felt secure, wages were comparatively high and conditions good, and even the left-wing rank-and-filers were not anxious to precipitate a second civil war. It is an interesting fact that precisely when the general influence of the Communists was getting stronger by the minute, when they were able to infiltrate into so many institutions of American life and government on the strength of the magnificent fight the Russians were putting up against the Nazis—that just at that moment the women's garment workers defeated them in every local. The Communists lost the elections in Locals 9, 22, 117 and wherever else they put up a slate. The Dubinsky administration won all along the line.

Today the Communists amount to very little in the International. There is no correlation between their noise and their power. In Local 22 they can draw about 3500 out of 26,000 votes in an election, but neither in that local nor in any other New York organization of the International do they have a single officer, paid or unpaid. Out of nine hundred elected delegates to the forthcoming Boston convention only six are Communists. There is one Communist business agent in Los Angeles and one in Toronto. Otherwise not a single Communist can be found in the entire ILGWU in an official post.

The Dubinsky administration no longer has to take the Communists into serious account. Dubinsky is the first president of the International who can function without having to fight a continuous and disruptive opposition. One reason is that the civil war has taught the membership the danger of the totalitarian virus; another reason is the expansion and strengthening of the International during these last ten years; and the third reason is Dubinsky's resourcefulness as a tactician.

His resourcefulness was evident in the way he used the New Deal to bring about the "depoliticalization" of the top leadership in the union. In the old days almost every prominent figure in the International was a member of some political movement. Schlesinger, Dubinsky and Hochman were members of the Socialist party; Sigman and Louis Levy were anarchists; the left-wingers were Communists. Leaders without a strong political or ideological affiliation, such as John Dyche in the early days or later Meyer Perlstein or Isidore Nagler, were the rare exception.

In 1936 Dubinsky gave up his lifelong membership in the
Socialist party. He was a Roosevelt man and wanted to work
for his re-election. The Socialist party split—and opened a way
for him to leave it. He realized that the best way to liquidate
the remnants of factionalism was to set the example of dis-
affiliation from the old-line radical movements. He became a
presidential elector in the Democratic party of New York, which
is a very different thing from belonging to a political faction
within the labor movement. Most of the other leaders of the
International followed suit. The old Sigmanites remained anarchists in sentiment, which is nowadays nothing but a sort of
libertarian nostalgia. A few philosophical socialists on the GEB
—Israel Feinberg, Jacob Heller and Harry Wander—retained
their membership in the Social Democratic Federation, the right-
wing socialist group in New York, which amounts to very little
and is indeed nothing but an adjunct of the American Labor
party. Zimmerman, Nelson and other ex-Communists in time
were instrumental in dissolving the Independent Labor League,
the so-called Lovestone movement, of which they were prominent members. All the leaders of the International became politically New Dealers, and in New York virtually all of them joined
the American Labor party, which was not a party but a tactical
device of the New Deal to promote its own political fortunes in
New York.

THE END OF LOCAL 17

At the height of the NRA boom Dubinsky felt that now was
the time to do something about the generation-old jurisdictional row between the cloakmakers of Local 1 and reefer makers
of Local 17. The GEB recommended the establishment of a
reefer makers' department in the New York Cloak Joint Board
to co-ordinate the jurisdictions of the two unions and to eliminate overlapping.

But this halfhearted proposal merely exacerbated the conflict.
The convention of 1934 took up the matter and referred it back
to the GEB with the recommendation that the two locals be

merged, if possible, on a voluntary basis. The Board tried its best to bring about the merger but for a long time it could make no headway against the stubborn recalcitrance of Jacob Heller and his reefer makers, who simply refused to give up Local 17. Finally the GEB, thoroughly disgusted, set January 1936 as a deadline for the fusion. And this time the leaders of the two local unions worked out an agreement.

It was decided to amalgamate Locals 1 and 17 into a new union, Local 117. The Cloak Joint Board and the new Local 117 were each to establish a children's cloak department to be administered by former officers of Local 17. No officer of either local was to be squeezed out in the merger, and the reefer makers were assured that in future elections they would be entitled to one fourth of the officers of the amalgamated union.

The merger took place on February 18, 1936. Everybody heaved a long sigh of relief but the new arrangements failed to work out smoothly. The leaders of the cloakmakers, especially Louis Levy, who had been the manager of Local 1 and was now the head of Local 117, felt that they could not accomplish very much as long as Heller remained in charge of the children's cloak department in the Joint Board. Heller was hell-bent on "protecting the interests" of his reefer makers and the old quarrels were revived. Finally a happy solution was worked out. Heller was made the manager of the newly created Local 105 consisting of some 3000 workers who make children's leggings and snow suits. For a while Local 105 was affiliated with the Cloak Joint Board but in 1941 it became completely independent. Heller is now again the head of a union of his own, whose members swear by him. But Heller has not forgotten his reefer makers and the reefer makers have not forgotten him.

THE RISE AND DECLINE OF THE INDUSTRIAL GANGSTER

The most ominous development in the needle industries during the thirties was the dominant position achieved by the industrial gangster. These gangsters were no longer the mere hirelings of industrial warfare but robber barons who terrorized and dominated whole industries in metropolitan New York.

The professional gorilla entered the industrial picture way back in the eighties when the employer would hire him to break up strikes. In time he developed into a mob leader and in the great ILGWU strikes of 1909 and 1910 a plug-ugly named Dopey Benny (Fine) was already running a strike-breaking service. Industrial thuggery became one of the main sources of income of the old East Side gangs who operated under the protection of Tammany and produced such specimens as Dopey Benny, Big Jack Zelig, Kid Dropper, Little Augie (Orgen) and Curley (Holtz). These criminals were spawned by the poverty and degradation of the slums whose industrial symbol was the sweatshop.

In the beginning the labor movement fought back on the picket lines with young and brawny militants who were willing to stand up against the thugs and cops. But in time the gangsters became too powerful for amateur strong-arm men and the unions had to hire gangsters of their own.

Then came the New Deal for the American underworld—prohibition. During the prohibition nightmare the small-time gangster gave way to the big-time bootlegger who organized crime as Big Business. The leading crime entrepreneur in the twenties was Arnold Rothstein, whose role in the civil war in the International I have recorded. Rothstein tried to consolidate crime in much the same way as the elder Rockefeller or Morgan tried to consolidate the oil or the railroad and steel industries.

His main lieutenants were such gentlemen as Little Augie, Jack (Legs) Diamond and his brother Eddie, Lepke (Louis Buchalter) and Gurrah (Jacob Schapiro). Rothstein was killed in 1929 before his monopolistic labors were completed. His main successors in the industrial field were Lepke and Gurrah, whose strong-arm department became celebrated as Murder, Inc. Lepke and Gurrah, especially Lepke, were moral idiots of great business ability who built up an industrial empire in New York City which by the mid-thirties yielded them an annual income of some $2,000,000.

Lepke and Gurrah invaded a number of industries—the flower, trucking, bread and apparel industries. These trades were especially vulnerable because they all employed drivers and truckmen, "outside workers" whom the gangster could easily intimidate—and organize. Once the gangster has muscled into an industry he can always find employers and labor leaders who will deal with him.

In the garment industry unfinished goods as well as finished products are being constantly shuttled between the manufacturers or jobbers and the contractors, who in turn farm out a good deal of their work to subcontractors. Trucks crisscross the streets of the metropolitan area and the highways to and from the "out-of-town" markets. This transportation system is the arterial network of the industry. Lepke and Gurrah first muscled into the garment trades by getting hold of the truckmen and organizing them into a Truckmen's Association. This Association included bosses who operated a number of vans, men who ran their own trucks, and ordinary teamsters who were union members.

The pay-off was very simple. The Truckmen's Association—that is, Messrs. Lepke and Gurrah, whose organizational department was Murder, Inc.—would raise the price of the delivery of garments by a few cents per garment. This increase, which was, of course, handed on to the consumer, was divided between the racketeers, many truck owners and some drivers. The lion's share naturally went to the racketeers. And Murder, Inc., saw to it that the honest bosses and drivers, of whom there were quite a few, fell in with the racket and kept their mouths shut.

After they had wormed themselves into the trucking end of the industry, it was not very difficult for Lepke and Gurrah to muscle into the industrial relations between labor and management. They offered "protection" to the employers against "labor trouble" and some firms paid as much as $10,000 a year not to have Lepke and Gurrah's stink-bomb squads ruin their goods or wreck their premises. Then the racketeers would offer their services to local union officials for the settlement of any difficulties with the employers, whom they claimed, with some justice, to control. Business agents and other union officers who couldn't see the light were beaten within an inch of their lives. "Control" of the union could then in turn be sold to the employer.

By the mid-thirties the gangster was one of the dominant factors in the garment trades. The ILGWU fought back as hard as it could. But it could do very little until the state interfered. It is folly to expect either labor or management, or both, to get rid of the industrial gangster as long as he is protected by corrupt politics. Lepke and Gurrah, who were at their height throughout the earlier part of the La Guardia administration, were broken only when District Attorney Thomas Dewey in Manhattan and District Attorney William O'Dwyer in Brooklyn went after them.

And even then Dewey and O'Dwyer, for all their earnestness and ability, could not have accomplished this job until the end of the thirties—until industrial developments had sufficiently undermined the position of the gangster in the economic setup. For, fantastic as it may sound, the gangster of the twenties and early thirties was able to enter and then to entrench himself in certain industries because he offered a stabilizing force in the chaos which resulted from the murderous competition among the manufacturers and the impotence of the labor unions. The NRA, which forced some degree of organization upon both management and labor, cut the ground from under the feet of the industrial gangster. Dewey and O'Dwyer were then able to deliver the knockout blow, which, to be sure, only the police power of the state can deliver.

The ILGWU fought desperately against the industrial racketeer. In many cases the racketeers are the union leaders themselves. In the women's garment industry the gangsters were an outside Maffia, not an inner clique. As Dubinsky put it, "In our union the gangster was never a partner. He was misfortune."

INDUSTRIAL RELATIONS, 1935–40

The International has never known a dull moment. Its story is like a pageant staged by a great director. The major strikes in the industry remind one of historic campaigns followed by memorable treaties. The civil war in the union was a veritable Greek drama, and when it was over the exhaustion seemed less an ordinary collapse than a catastrophe.

Then came the revival of 1933, as amazing as a resurrection. And yet the resurrection was not a miracle. It was conditioned by the readiness of the union to exploit a great opportunity. No other large American union, except the miners, grew after the NRA with such inner stability, taking in its stride the industrial recession in the mid-thirties and then the rebellion of the CIO. When the International held its 1937 convention in Atlantic City, the women's garment industry was better organized than ever before in its history.

Cloaks and Suits

Still it was not all smooth sailing. As soon as the excitement over the revival of the union died down in 1934, the cloak jobbers in New York launched an attack on the system of limitation of contractors, the provision in the code they resented most. The New York Cloak Joint Board mobilized to meet the attack. It voted and quickly collected a ten-dollar "preparedness tax." In April 1935 negotiations began for the renewal of the 1933 agreement, which was to expire in two months, but they got nowhere and broke down.

The whole social atmosphere was against the jobbers, who personified to the public the "chiselers" whom General Johnson was just then excoriating. To be sure, the NRA was on its way out. But the New Deal was still at its height, and in New York Governor Lehman was distinctly favorable to labor. He called the employers and the union together and an agreement was finally worked out. The limitation of contractors was retained and even strengthened. The demand of the union for a 20 per cent wage increase was referred to the impartial chairman of the cloak industry, who recommended a 10 per cent increase.

The cloakmakers were jubilant. Their victory was clear-cut and held every promise of stability. The new agreement lasted until June 1937, when it was peacefully renewed, this time for three years, with an additional increase of five dollars a week for week workers and 10 per cent for piece workers. On the whole the period from 1935–40 was one of steady advance for the coat and suit unions throughout the country.

The Dress Trade

The jobbers in the New York dress industry, just like those in the cloak industry, were restless under the agreement they had signed after the strike of 1933. The union was even more restless and complained of the widespread chiseling among the jobbers. In January 1934 it called a stoppage of 20,000 dressmakers in the lower-price shops and for a while the jobbers behaved themselves. But everybody knew that the real trouble in the dress industry was the hit-or-miss method of determining piece rates. These difficulties in wage determination were further aggravated by the constant drift of shops from metropolitan New York to near-by communities where the employers hoped to escape union control.

Julius Hochman had a group of efficiency engineers work out a scientific "unit system" of fixing piece rates, based on a time study of operations. The union was determined to sign no more agreements which failed to rationalize piecework pay. As the day of the expiration of the agreement approached, the Dress Joint Board called a series of meetings and rallies to prepare for a possible strike. And for a while a strike did seem unavoidable.

But on February 10, 1936, a new agreement was signed. It provided for the limitation of contractors and for the "unit system" of piece rates. Moreover the wages of the workers in the contracting shops were to be determined by negotiations between the union and the jobbers and not by individual bargaining with each contractor. Finally, no manufacturer was to be

permitted to move his plant beyond the "five-cent fare" limit.
Harry Uviller became the new impartial chairman. He had been
for many years the manager of the American Association of
Coat and Suit Manufacturers and has played a leading role in
stabilizing the dress industry in New York.

During the next few years the Dress Joint Board, under the
leadership of Julius Hochman, did a great deal to rationalize
the industry. Rigid union control was gradually bringing a sem-
blance of order out of the old chaos. The notorious "auction
block" system, under which contractors underbid each other
mercilessly to get work from the jobbers, disappeared. Between
1936 and 1940 contracting shops declined 26 per cent and the
big inside shop was slowly making headway. The size of the
average plant increased from thirty-one workers in 1934 to
forty-one workers in 1938.

In December 1938 the agreement was renewed. But for all
the reforms introduced, the dress business in New York was
merely limping along. In 1937 its sales volume was $400,000,000
—by 1939 it had shrunk to $350,000,000. And employment
shrank in almost the same proportion—12 per cent. The seasons
were short and fitful, unemployment was rife and the annual
income of the worker was less than $1000.

The main reason for this decline in the New York market
was competition from other centers. The efficient mass production plants which had sprung up in the Middle West and the
South were cutting in on the older dress markets, especially on
New York. These brand-new modern plants were not hampered
by the traditional ways of production and doing business. They
were highly rationalized and, operating in non-union territories,
they could underpay their help. This competition had to be met
by organizing the new fields and by trying to jack up the twenty-
five-cent hourly minimum wage under the Wages and Hours
Act.

The International had some succeess in organizing the garment workers in the South and West, and it managed to raise the
hourly minimum to forty cents. But in the long run these efforts
could not in themselves solve the problem of the New York dress

market. Its weakness sprang from technological conservatism, managerial inefficiency and poor merchandising. It was not until 1940, when Julius Hochman brought forward his Industry Planning program—an industrial efficiency and sales promotion plan —that a basic approach toward the problem of the New York dress market was even envisioned. The Hochman plan was embodied in the agreement signed in February 1941.

In the other organized dress centers—Philadelphia, Chicago, Cleveland, Boston, Canada and the Pacific Coast—the union was also able to maintain its NRA gains and even to improve upon them.

The Minor Trades

In the two outstanding "minor trades"—the children's dress and the underwear industries—the agreements were peacefully renewed with higher wages and improved conditions. These industries had the advantage of being largely confined to New York City. Moreover, as we have seen, Local 62 of the underwear workers and Local 91 of the children's dressmakers proved of such great value in stabilizing the industries in which they functioned that the employers soon learned to rely upon their collaboration.

A newcomer in the International family was Local 155 of the knit-goods workers. This union was born during the NRA and its jurisdiction covered everything from cheap sweaters to expensive knitted suits and dresses. After two successful strikes in 1934 and 1936, Local 155 became solidly established and its place in its own industry became very much like that of Locals 62 and 91 in theirs.

Louis Nelson

The manager of Local 155 is Louis Nelson, who began his career in the Amalgamated Clothing Workers, from which he was ousted for his intransigent opposition to the Hillman administration. He moved over to the International, where he aligned himself with the Zimmerman group. In 1934 Dubinsky selected Nelson, whom he liked for his integrity and his efficiency, to head Local 155. Nelson has helped to improve and stabilize conditions in the knitwear industry to a remarkable degree.

In the union Nelson is regarded as a bit of a fanatic on trade union ethics and proletarian proprieties. He refuses to accept more than fifty dollars a week—with an air of implied disgust at labor leaders who do better by themselves. His expense account reads like the budget of a Salvation Army worker and in his office every postage stamp has to be accounted for—"It's the workers' money." Once Louis invited me for dinner. "I'll be damned," I said, "if I'll eat a six-course dinner for fifty cents." "All right," Louis said with contempt at my sybaritic tastes. "I'll treat you to a dollar dinner."

X

In and Out of the CIO

T HROUGHOUT its entire history the International has been closely tied up with the general labor movement. It has partipated intimately in every major struggle—ideological, economic and political—which has animated American labor. Though its status in the AFL is, of course, autonomous, it has never hesitated to invite such AFL dignitaries as Gompers, Green or Woll to act as arbiters in its internal troubles. The International is one of a dozen of the oldest affiliates of the AFL and to the women's garment workers the AFL has always meant home.

To be sure, the garment workers do not enjoy—nor do they have to endure—the crucial position which the miners, for instance, occupy in organized labor. The least economic stress or strain affects the United Mine Workers because they have to operate at the very heart of industrial society. The women's garment workers are engaged in a consumers' industry and therefore do not reflect the social weather quite as sensitively. But for that very reason they always could afford to view life and labor in a more theoretical light. Dyche was a "pure and simple" trade unionist, Sigman an anarchist, Schlesinger a socialist, and they fought for their ideas as philosophers as well as politicians. Their rows created no national emergencies which might force a Theodore or a Franklin Roosevelt to take over their industry in the public interest. And being ideologues, the tailors—whose archetype is the cloakmaker—have always been far more emotionally involved with the rest of labor than the necessarily ultrapractical union politicians in key industries. The garment workers were

missionaries within the trade union movement—which makes for
profounder and more intimate relations, whether friendly or
hostile. Industrial unionism, for instance, meant very little one
way or another to the building trades until the issue was on top
of them—and then they were against it. But to the garment
workers it was a great cause long before it was a burning question, and its acceptance or rejection by the House of Labor was
to them a momentous issue.

Naturally the participation of the International in the general
labor movement has varied in intensity according to its own
strength and the energy it had left for "outside" activities. These
activities were very meager when the union was down and out
in 1932. At the AFL convention of that year President Dubinsky,
the only delegate whom the union could afford to send, was denied a seat because it was in arrears with its per capita tax.
With the dawning of the new day in 1933, its "outside" activities
expanded enormously. It began to contribute lavishly to various
causes, its educational work spilled over into the general labor
movement; it took the initiative within the AFL in the fight
against fascism; it got the 1933 convention of the Federation to
endorse the anti-Nazi boycott and to declare its solidarity with
the underground trade union groups in Germany and Italy.

When the AFL, because of its craft limitations, failed to exploit under the NRA its opportunities for organizing the basic
industries, the International became a leading advocate of industrial unionism, which had always been part of its own tradition. At the San Francisco convention of the AFL in 1934 it
stood foursquare behind the industrial union faction which was
emerging within the Federation. And the next year, at the Atlantic City convention, Dubinsky joined with John L. Lewis in the
epoch-making fight which gave birth to the Committee for Industrial Organization.

The rise of the CIO precipitated a psychological conflict
within the International. On the one hand, the ILGWU had
always been intensely loyal to the AFL, a loyalty based on its
identification with the dominant labor movement and its tradi-

tional horror of dual unionism. On the other hand, the International was just as intensely committed to industrial unionism in the basic industries.

Throughout the civil war between the AFL and the CIO, Dubinsky's policy was guided by an effort to resolve this conflict. His entire strategy and all his shifts in tactics between 1935 and 1938—while the ILGWU was in the CIO—can be explained by the fact that he insisted on riding these two horses through all the burning hoops. It explains why the International went into the CIO, why it refused to remain when the CIO became a rival federation, why it became an independent union for a while and why it finally returned to the AFL. All these tergiversations, far from breaking its back, strengthened its position in the labor movement. Dubinsky's gifts as a tactician were never more strikingly brought out than in those critical years.

Until 1933 industrial unionism was a somewhat academic issue in the AFL. Progressive labor was for it as a matter of course, and after the fatal steel strike in 1919 even the conservatives in the AFL came to feel that the basic industries eventually would have to be organized along industrial rather than craft lines. In 1927 and again in 1930 the conventions of the AFL passed pious resolutions to refer this problem to the studious researches of the Executive Council. But that is as far as things went. The craft union oligarchy in control of the AFL showed no particular enthusiasm for reorganizing itself out of power. They were wedded to the ancient craft system and instinctively viewed industrial unionism as a utopian dream for the workers —and as a nightmare for themselves.

But the NRA made further procrastination impossible. Some form of industrial unionism in organizing the mass industries became unavoidable. The workers in the basic industries, in a fever of self-organization, were demanding charters from the AFL. The question now was whether the AFL would pitch in and really organize them into affiliated unions or would turn its back on them because they could not fit into the craft union scheme. The AFL had to choose and the necessity of a choice threw it into a panic of confusion. The old craft unions could not organize the basic industries: the vast majority of the automobile workers are not skilled mechanics but animated screwdrivers. Nevertheless, these craft outfits claimed jurisdictional squatters' rights in the mass production fields and thwarted every effort to unionize them.

In January 1934 William Green called a conference of presidents of AFL unions "for the purpose of giving consideration to the question of organizing the unorganized, particularly those employed in mass production industries." Dubinsky was appointed to a committee, of which Matthew Woll was the chairman, to probe the possibility of unionizing the basic industries by means of "federal locals." (A federal local is a single union of all workers in one plant or company directly affiliated with the AFL.) The purpose of this "federal local" policy was to avoid jurisdictional disputes in a plant in the hope that in time the workers could be peacefully distributed to their respective crafts. In short, it was an industrial union strategy to accomplish craft union ends. And of course it was bound to defeat itself.

At the 1934 convention of the AFL in San Francisco the issue of industrial unionism could no longer be ignored. The workers in the mass production industries were clamoring for organization and every attempt the AFL had made to unionize them during the preceding year had proven a miserable fiasco. John L. Lewis, the strongest personality in the AFL, demanded action—he was deeply interested in the organization of the steel workers because steel and coal are so closely interconnected. He was willing to compromise. He accepted a resolution which recognized the advantage of craft unionism "where the nature of the industry is such that the lines of demarcation between crafts are distinguishable." But he insisted that the AFL grant industrial charters in such mass production fields as automobiles, cement, rubber, aluminum and oil. Above all he wanted steel organized.

The ILGWU delegation at this convention remained in the background. Dubinsky was anxious for Lewis to lead the fight, partly because the miners were by all odds the most powerful group in the Federation and partly because the International's advocacy of industrial unionism was an old story. The compromise resolution was adopted. Like all such compromises it was really a jumble—which enabled the craft unions to sabotage the convention's mandate to launch the drive for industrial unionism. The resolution really added up to very little, for it left to the Executive Council the privilege of doing nothing about it, which the Council promptly proceeded to do. But evasion only exacerbated the issue and at the Atlantic City convention of the AFL in October 1935 the explosion came.

John P. Frey, one of the most conservative of the AFL leaders, was chairman of the resolutions committee. He spoke for the majority of the committee who wanted to stand pat on the San Francisco declaration. But the minority, again headed by John L. Lewis, would not stand for further procrastination. "I refuse to be seduced again," Lewis roared. The minority report came out for unqualified industrial unionism. It called upon the convention to order the Executive Council to launch an all-out campaign to organize the mass production industries and to issue industrial charters unqualified by craft union reservations.

Dubinsky, who was on the resolutions committee, backed up Lewis to the hilt. The fight was on and the debate was extraordinarily bitter. The minority report was, of course, defeated. But the traditional taboo against industrial unionism in the AFL was broken just the same, for over a third of the votes of the convention upheld the minority report. And the leaders of the industrial union faction felt justified in going ahead and forming a permanent agency within the AFL to propagate their cause.

Shortly after the convention, in November 1935, Lewis called a conference for this purpose. This conference was attended by John L. Lewis, David Dubinsky, Sidney Hillman of the men's clothing workers, Charles P. Howard of the typographers, Thomas F. McMahon of the textile workers, Harvey C. Fremming of the oil refinery workers, Max Zaritsky of the millinery workers, and Thomas H. Brown of the mill and smelter workers. Together they represented about a million workers, almost a third of the membership of the Federation at the time. They decided to form a Committee for Industrial Organization. They were careful to state that the CIO was to function *within* the AFL, and that its sole purpose was to promote the organization of the unorganized workers in the mass production industries on an industrial basis.

Dubinsky especially was determined that every suspicion of rival unionism be carefully avoided in the program and activities of the CIO. The CIO was not to be a dual movement.

But there can be little doubt that the germs of dual unionism were already present. The mere formation of such a committee, with significant objectives but no official standing, was bound to lead to a widening of the breach. Then, John L. Lewis was by no means hell-bent on staying within the AFL; less than two weeks after the formation of the CIO he contemptuously resigned from the Executive Council of the AFL. And the Communists were already speculating on the advantage they might derive from a split in American labor.

THE INTERNATIONAL TAKES ITS STAND

In December the GEB of the International met in Cleveland to thresh out the entire question. Dubinsky, who had just been elected to the Executive Council of the AFL, reaffirmed his conviction that AFL unions had every right to form the CIO, provided they sincerely meant to function within the framework of the Federation. He did deplore "the tone and approach by some of the leaders of the CIO"; he was resentful of Lewis's unceremonious resignation from the Executive Council without consulting even him, although he was the only other CIO leader on the Council. Nevertheless he urged the GEB to endorse his commitment of the International to the CIO. "Nothing," he said, "can overshadow the fact that the CIO represents a movement with which the ILGWU has profound sympathy, whose policies we have traditionally advocated for years past and whose objectives are close to the hearts of our members."

The Board was sharply divided. The leaders of the cloakmakers—Nagler, Breslaw, Heller, Feinberg, Ninfo—were opposed to joining the CIO. They stressed the traditional loyalty of the ILGWU to the AFL and warned that the CIO would develop into a secession movement. The leaders of the dressmakers—Antonini, Hochman and Zimmerman—strongly supported Dubinsky. They felt that the union was historically committed to industrial unionism and should not alienate the workers in the mass production industries.

The Board decided to continue membership in the CIO by a vote of 12–10—in other words, the margin was so narrow that Dubinsky's own vote was decisive. The closeness of the vote justified his double strategy of encouraging the CIO without disrupting the AFL. And even though his theory of a peaceful resolution of the conflict was implausible, his strategy was sound just the same—and very cagey. His centrist instinct stood him in good stead. His policy bridged the wide divergence of opinion within the International; and later, when the International left the CIO, enabled it to work effectively for peace.

AMERICAN LABOR SPLITS

During the next five years organized labor was torn by the gigantic struggle between the AFL and the CIO. The International, which remained in the CIO until 1938, hewed to its centrist line. It threw its weight skillfully one way or the other, whichever held out the greater promise of a negotiated peace that would recognize industrial unionism in the basic industries. During the first two years—through 1936–37—the initiative for peace could hardly come from the CIO for the simple reason that it was then engaged in its epic campaigns to organize the steel, automobile, rubber, oil and textile industries, while the Executive Council of the AFL kept on insisting that it dissolve itself and cease its activities. Dubinsky considered this attitude on the part of the Executive Council absurd, and the International lent its organizers and poured hundreds of thousands of dollars into the various CIO drives.

But after the CIO had laid the foundations of unionism in the mass production fields, the picture changed. Green, Woll and other AFL leaders who were not bitter-enders were now ready to accept industrial unionism in the basic industries as an accomplished fact and willing to make peace on a reasonable basis. But by this time John L. Lewis had become too successful to listen to any reasonable overtures from the AFL. Whereupon the International shifted its line of attack, welcomed the conciliatory attitude of the Federation and sharply criticized the intransigent position of the CIO.

The real fight opened in 1936. The Executive Council of the AFL, with only Dubinsky dissenting, branded the CIO as a dual movement and ordered all Federation affiliates to have nothing to do with it.

It appointed a committee headed by George M. Harrison of the railway clerks to deal with the rebels. The committee issued an ultimatum to all CIO unions to dissolve their "illegal body" or else to forfeit their charters. The International rejected the ultimatum and even refused to appear before the Executive Council to justify its stand. For Dubinsky held all along that only a convention of the AFL could discipline autonomous unions, let alone revoke their charters.

The CIO, of course, denied any dualist intentions. But it did a lot more than engage in verbal battles with the AFL hierarchy. In June 1936 it set up the Steel Workers' Organizing Committee, put up $500,000 as a starter and began organizing steel. Dubinsky stuck to his double policy: though a member of the Executive Council of the AFL he appointed Julius Hochman to represent the International on the SWOC.

The Executive Council met in the summer of 1936 and considered the question of expelling the recalcitrant unions. Dubinsky pleaded with his colleagues on the Council to postpone the whole CIO issue until the fall, when the regular convention of the AFL would meet in Tampa. He was confident that at this convention the balance of forces in favor of industrial unionism would be even greater than it had been the previous year in Atlantic City; Dubinsky always believed that the CIO, if only it could avoid dual unionism, would in the course of time win the battle within the Federation. He warned the Council of the disastrous consequences of hasty and arbitrary action. But he failed. His plea was rejected by a vote of 13–1—all against himself. The Council voted to suspend the unions affiliated with the CIO, giving them a period of grace until Labor Day, September 5.

The General Executive Board of the International again refused to recognize the right of the Executive Council to suspend AFL affiliates and simultaneously decided to levy a dollar tax for the CIO's steel campaign. This time the GEB was unanimously behind Dubinsky's leadership. The more conservative members of the Board were still dubious about the CIO but they refused to put up with the arbitrary methods of the Executive Council of the AFL.

On September 1 Dubinsky resigned from the Executive Council. Five days later, on Labor Day, the International found itself outside the Federation to which it had belonged from its birth thirty-six years before.

FRICTION WITH JOHN L.

Meanwhile the CIO was developing internal problems which had nothing to do with its efforts to organize the basic industries. The main problem was how to tell the CIO from Mr. Lewis. As usual his attitude and methods were flamboyantly highhanded and picturesquely arbitrary. He consulted no one—even his perennial stooges in the miners' union were seldom given a chance to rehearse their parts. He made all sorts of pronunciamentos about the nature and aims of the CIO, to which Dubinsky for one could not subscribe. From the very beginning Lewis proceeded on the assumption that the CIO was, and intended to remain, a rival federation.

Needless to say, John L. used his new eminence as a platform for displaying his genius for vituperation. His style has a touch of biblical grandeur with a gift for transmuting prophetic denunciation into modern abuse. And he has great wit. Every suggestion

of possible unity with the AFL he dismissed with devastating
felicity. Dubinsky was for peace and did not enjoy, at least not
officially, Lewis's celebrated cracks at the AFL dignitaries who,
after all, were the men with whom peace would have to be made.

Dubinsky was also disturbed by the rapid infiltration of Communists and fellow travelers into the CIO. Lewis put a great many
of them into key positions; he considered them excellent agitators
and organizers whom he could always control. Dubinsky, who
had had his experiences with them, knew better. But no one can
ever tell Mr. Lewis anything. "Who gets the bird—the hunter or
the dog?" he once roared at me. My answer was, "The dog—if
he is a totalitarian dog trained in Moscow to get the bird away
from the hunter." (Within the next two years the Communists
dominated the inner councils of the CIO and by 1941 Lewis was
out—and the comrades who were within were abusing him as
America's leading "fascist.")

Almost as soon as the CIO was formed Dubinsky turned himself into a promoter of peace and unity in American labor. He
addressed trade union conventions, issued statements and engaged in voluminous correspondence. His activities put the International in the forefront of the peace movement, but otherwise they were in vain. In November 1936 Lewis called a meeting of the CIO in Pittsburgh and made it pretty clear that he did
not care to discuss even the possibility of peace and that he considered Dubinsky an "unreliable" customer in the CIO who continued flirting with the AFL. The AFL convention, which took
place in Tampa a few days later, was equally intransigent and
confirmed the suspension of all CIO unions by the Executive
Council. The labor movement was split wide open and the war
was on.

THE INTERNATIONAL CONVENTION OF 1937

The great issue at the 1937 convention of the ILGWU at Atlantic City was the CIO. There was no open conflict between
those who had originally differed about joining it. Though an

undercurrent of tension could be felt, there was no attitude of "I told you so" on either side. By this time the achievements of the CIO in organizing hundreds of thousands of workers in the automobile, steel, rubber and other basic industries were so colossal that even the right wing could no longer advocate a break with it. Moreover, everybody felt that the AFL and the CIO were equally to blame for the continuation of the civil war. Accordingly the convention unanimously endorsed Dubinsky's double policy of staying within the CIO while trying to reunite the labor movement.

John L. Lewis was invited to address the convention. The CIO enthusiasts among the delegates, mainly from the dressmakers' unions, staged an uproarious demonstration to greet him. Lewis's speech was a masterpiece in his particular genre—aggressive, histrionic, displaying his peculiar gift for combining bombast with impact and demagogy with clarity. He touched upon the question of unity in the labor movement only to dismiss it with contempt. The speech made an impression.

The resolution on the CIO, which the convention adopted unanimously, endorsed the action of the GEB in affiliating with the CIO and comended "all the activities of President Dubinsky and the GEB within the CIO since its formation, including their resistance to the grossly illegal conduct of the Executive Council of the AFL in suspending the CIO unions." The resolution also blamed the AFL for continuing "the present division in the forces of labor." It insisted that industrial unionism "is the only basis for a lasting peace in the American labor movement" and voted $100,000 to the Steel Workers' Organizing Committee. At the same time the convention went on record that the International should continue "to work in the direction of an honorable and realistic reconciliation in the ranks of labor for the ultimate attainment of a united labor movement." This was a muffled slap at John L. Lewis and his Communist allies in the CIO. The Communists were even more opposed to peace than Lewis, since in a reunited movement they could not hope to play a leading part.

THE GROWING RIFT

The Atlantic City convention marked the high point of pro-CIO sentiment in the International. Soon after this convention, which took place in May, events began moving rapidly towards a break. Within a year the International was out of the CIO—and in three years it was back in the AFL.

The irreconcilable issue between Lewis and Dubinsky was unity. Dubinsky was consistently against anything that might widen beyond repair the rift between the CIO and the AFL. He even objected to the admission into the CIO of the United Radio, Electrical and Machine Workers on the ground that the AFL already had semi-industrial unions in these fields. He was irritated by the vituperative bitterness displayed by CIO leaders against the leaders of the AFL, which made reconciliation psychologically almost impossible. And he was forever urging that the two sides get together to discuss seriously the bases of a negotiated peace.

In this desire for peace Dubinsky undoubtedly expressed a growing undercurrent for unity among the masses in both the CIO and the AFL. Even Lewis had to take account of this swelling sentiment. And in October 1937 he proposed to the AFL convention in Denver that a committee of one hundred from the CIO meet with an equally large committee of the AFL to consider "methods and means whereby a united labor movement can be brought about in America."

This was Lewis's disdainful way of taking the wind out of the sails of those who were preaching unity in his own camp, for obviously a committee of two hundred could never settle anything. William Green replied that the AFL was ready to enlarge its standing committee of three empowered to deal with the CIO, but that surely nothing could be achieved by Lewis's frivolous suggestion of mob arbitration.

Finally it was agreed that two comparatively small committees should meet in Washington on October 25. The AFL committee consisted of George M. Harrison of the railway clerks, G. M.

Bugniazet of the electrical workers and Matthew Woll. The CIO
appointed a ten-man committee headed by Philip Murray of the
miners and the SWOC. The others were David Dubinsky, Harvey C. Fremming of the oil workers, James B. Carey of the radio
and electrical workers, Homer Martin of the automobile workers,
S. H. Dalrymple of the rubber workers, Michael J. Quill of the
transport workers, Abraham Flaxer of the municipal and county
workers, Joseph Curran of the maritime workers and Sidney
Hillman of the men's clothing workers, who was too ill to serve.
The composition of this committee was significant since six of its
members were either Communists or fellow travelers who were
covertly against unity.

The CIO committee proposed that the AFL unconditionally
accept industrial unionism as the only form of organization in all
basic industries; that it create a CIO department to have "complete and sole jurisdiction" over all CIO unions; and that a special convention of the AFL be held as soon as possible to ratify
these provisions. The AFL, on the other hand, proposed that all
CIO unions which had originally been in the AFL be readmitted
immediately; that all unions founded by the CIO adjust their
jurisdictional conflicts with the AFL before readmission; that the
CIO thereupon dissolve itself; and that all other problems on
which no agreement could be reached by the negotiators be left
to the next regular convention of the AFL.

The program of neither group was acceptable to the other,
though the AFL had gone a long way towards a negotiable peace.
Discussions continued and in the course of these discussions the
AFL made even more significant compromises. It now agreed
that the twelve AFL unions which had gone over to the CIO need
not apply for readmission until all CIO unions could enter in a
body. The AFL was also ready to amend its constitution to the
effect that only a convention, and not the Executive Council,
could suspend or expel affiliated unions. Finally it agreed "to
specify certain industries where the industrial form of organization would apply." In effect the AFL was ready to grant the
fundamental demands which had led to the split. It merely sought
to prevent the domination of a reunited labor movement by

Lewis and Company through their control of a CIO department, which would include the unions in the basic industries.

For Lewis there was real danger that the peace discussions might succeed. Philip Murray was ready to go ahead negotiating on the basis of the AFL terms, when Lewis called the CIO peace committee together and stormed and raged against all compromise. Thereupon Murray, who in those days was Lewis's man Friday, issued a statement in which he made no mention of the AFL proposals but declared that the peace conference had adjourned sine die.

Dubinsky was outraged. As a member of the CIO peace committee he knew all the intrigues which had taken place and he became convinced that Lewis and his Communist allies were determined to block any peace effort, no matter how reasonable. Since he was equally determined to promote unity, the issue between him and Lewis was now definitely joined, and the International openly became the opposition in the CIO.

To clarify his position and to place the issue in all its seriousness before the members of the International, he called all the officials of the International in New York to a joint meeting at Manhattan Center on January 11, 1938. His address was a model in democratic leadership. It was a detailed report of what had taken place and a clear program of action for the International. It expressed Dubinsky's philosophy of trade unionism—simply, lucidly and without demagogy.

Essentially his program was what it had been all along: industrial unionism must be upheld, dual unionism must be resisted, labor unity must be re-established. Peace on these terms, he insisted, could now be achieved if it were not for obstructionary forces in the CIO. "Industrial unionism in the mass production industries has been vindicated and historically justified," he said —and the AFL had admitted as much. Moreover, the Executive Council of the Federation had agreed to abandon any claim to the right of suspending or expelling affiliated unions. In short, he contended, there was no longer any reason for prolonging this fratricidal conflict.

The speech made a sensation. It received nationwide publicity and brought the issue squarely before the workers of the country. It charted the road for the International to follow and prepared it for the inevitable break with the CIO.

BREAK WITH THE CIO

Three months after Dubinsky's Manhattan Center address Lewis announced that in the fall the CIO would hold a constitutional convention in order to transform itself from a temporary organizing committee into a permanent labor federation. Dubinsky promptly issued a statement indicating that the International could not possibly join in such a dualist development. But before taking final action the ILGWU decided to make a last gesture at conciliation. Antonini, Hochman and Nagler were instructed to approach both sides with an appeal to reopen peace negotiations. They interviewed both Green and Lewis. Green was willing. But Lewis informed them that the resumption of union discussions would be futile unless the AFL was ready to accept his terms. And if the AFL found his terms unacceptable it might, he suggested cynically, apply for admission into the CIO—on the same terms.

The International refused to attend the constitutional convention of the CIO which was held in Pittsburgh in October 1938 and at which the CIO officially transformed itself into a rival federation by adopting a permanent constitution and by changing its name from the Committee for Industrial Organization to the Congress of Industrial Organizations. This refusal was tantamount to a withdrawal from the CIO.

The GEB presented its reasons for the break in a special resolution. It gave the CIO all due credit for its successes in organizing the mass production industries. But it refused to join in "the formation of a permanent national union. We do not believe now, and we have never believed," the GEB declared, "that two separate labor movements are required to achieve the common objectives of labor. . . . We therefore decide that we remain an independent union until peace is established in the labor movement or until it is otherwise decided by a regular or special convention of our union."

Dubinsky's policy was vindicated. The International had done its share in helping to organize the basic industries—but it would have nothing to do with legitimating a permanent schism in American labor. Professor Selig Perlman, of Wisconsin, our leading historian of labor, has pointed out that the organized labor movement of this country is a "job empire" consisting of affiliated "principalities"—with here and there independent kingdoms such as the railway brotherhoods—permitting no encroachment upon their sovereign jurisdictions. Hence the deep taboo against dualism in the history of American labor. The miners and the women's garment workers were the only two important and seasoned AFL unions in the CIO. The garment workers returned to the AFL in 1938 and the miners have been negotiating since 1943 to do the same.

The CIO, of course, had every right to challenge the sovereignty of the AFL, but it was the right of revolution. And the International did not believe that a revolutionary breakup of the American labor movement was called for or desirable. When the CIO proclaimed its revolutionary independence from the AFL, the International withdrew. It had been in the CIO for exactly three years, from November 1935–November 1938.

"TWO SIDES OF THE MEDAL"

For the first time in its history the International was an independent union and it remained unaffiliated for almost two years. It was in no danger of attack, for its position in its own industry was so secure that neither the AFL nor the CIO could possibly encroach upon its jurisdiction. Still, as Dubinsky put it, independence was "but one side of the medal." There were decided disadvantages in standing alone. "We derived our moral and spiritual sustenance from being an integral part of the entire labor movement," Dubinsky pointed out. "It cannot be denied that our influence in framing general labor policies, in aiding to shape labor and social legislation, is bound to be less pronounced and effective without the support which affiliation with the central body affords."

Dubinsky expressed the nostalgic longing of the women's tailors. They wanted to go home—to the AFL. And when in his opening address at the New York convention of the International in May 1940 Dubinsky admitted, "We are frank in stating that the position of isolation is not a permanent solution for our union," his sentiments were applauded to the rafters.

The AFL was eager to welcome the errant daughter, for the return of a quarter of a million workers would be a major victory over the CIO. Knowing this, Dubinsky felt that he could couple his application for readmission with certain conditions. He asked that the AFL drop its one-cent monthly per capita assessment for the purpose of fighting the CIO, for he did not believe in levying taxes for intensifying the conflict. He called upon the Executive Council to abandon its claim to the right of suspending or expelling affiliated unions. And his third condition was that the AFL clean up the racketeers in its own house. Like all presidents of international unions he believes in the complete autonomy of each affiliate in the AFL but he doesn't think that such autonomy should serve as a protection for hoodlums, racketeers or gangsters.

The 1940 convention of the ILGWU had before it forty-two resolutions calling for reaffiliation with the AFL. Only Local 97 of Los Angeles, which was then under Communist control, wanted the International to rejoin the CIO.

While the convention was in session President Green of the AFL, by prearrangement with Dubinsky, sent him a letter in which he dealt with two of Dubinsky's three conditions. He promised that the Executive Council would recommend to the next convention that the Federation give up the penny anti-CIO tax—and substitute for it an increase in the per capita tax of one cent a month, a measure "long overdue." In short, Mr. Green removed Dubinsky's objection by a bookkeeping device. He also stated that the Executive Council would recommend a constitutional amendment prohibiting the suspension or expulsion of any union by the Council. On the question of racketeering Mr. Green was silent.

The convention of the ILGWU decided to return to the AFL on the basis of Green's letter. The fact is that if the International wanted to rejoin the AFL at all, it couldn't seriously insist that the racketeers be driven out of the AFL then and there. Green, Woll and other Federation leaders could not eliminate racketeering from the building trades and elsewhere simply by issuing an order any more than a man can get rid of cancer by autosuggestion. The International had made its gesture and for the time being that was about all it could do.

On June 6 William Green appeared before the convention of the International and brought with him the old charter, the very same certificate of affiliation the International had received from its parent body exactly forty years before.

THE INTERNATIONAL AT NEW ORLEANS

The AFL convention met in New Orleans the following November. The reappearance of the International, with its widely publicized anti-racketeering resolution, created a good deal of tension in the bars and hotel rooms of the city. By this time Westbrook Pegler had gotten considerably under the skin of the AFL bureaucrats—both clean and dirty. Decent leaders, such as Green, Woll and Harrison, knew that they could do very little about racketeering and therefore resented Pegler's perpetual gibes about "consorting with white slavers and grafters." The grafters, of course, resented Pegler for more obvious reasons. And here was the International, full of moral superiority, "harping on the same string."

The ILGWU introduced a resolution which would give the Executive Council summary power to remove any officer of an affiliated union who was convicted of crimes involving "moral turpitude." ("Moral turpitude" was a rather unfortunate phrase, for it might refer to the recreational activities of labor leaders without relevance to their professional rectitude.) The resolution was rejected by the convention as an invasion of the traditional autonomy of AFL unions. Instead the convention adopted an innocuous substitute admonishing the Executive Council to use its "full influence" against notorious crooks in AFL unions. And there was nothing the International could do about it, unless it was willing to leave the AFL once more—which it wasn't.

But the International delegation did have a change to stage a demonstration against racketeering on the floor of the convention when George E. Browne's re-election to the Executive Council came up. Browne was then president of the stagehands and was notorious for his connection with Willie Bioff, a former pimp, who had been the boss of Browne's outfit in the motion picture industry. Browne's re-election to the Executive Council was a foregone conclusion, though he himself was soon to follow Bioff to prison for shaking down movie magnates for hundreds of thousands of dollars. The International made a formal protest against Browne's re-election, giving its reasons without pulling punches.

The other two "conditions"—by this time the word had best be put in quotation marks—were more easily disposed of. The penny "war" tax against the CIO was abolished—and the regular monthly assessment was raised to compensate for the loss. Then there was the issue of the right of the Executive Council to suspend affiliated unions. The one promise in Green's letter which Dubinsky felt would be kept was the pledge that the Executive Council would recommend that only the convention could suspend affiliated unions. But what the Executive Council actually recommended was something very different. It proposed that it be deprived of the power to suspend individual unions but that it retain the power—Dubinsky claimed that it never had either right—to suspend a combination of unions if they were "conspiring together to set up a dual movement." In other words, by making a distinction without a difference, the Executive Council justified its arrogation of power in suspending the original CIO unions. Dubinsky rose to protest that Green's pledge to the ILGWU had been repudiated.

From all this, however, it must not be inferred that the International received a trouncing in New Orleans. The only unpleasant incident was the assault on Dubinsky in the bar of the Roosevelt Hotel by Joe Fay, a notorious hoodlum and vice-president of the stationary engineers. In his cups, Mr. Fay had the courage of his convictions and objected in his favorite manner to Dubinsky's aspersions on racketeering. Otherwise the atmosphere was very friendly. Between politicians—God bless their innocent souls!—it is understood what can and cannot be done. The International had not expected too much. In politics compromise often takes the place of principle—and when even compromise fails the beau geste has to suffice. President Green showed his exuberant good will to the International by facilitating its return to the Federation through promises he could not deliver; and the International showed its appreciation of this gesture by remaining in the AFL without holding Mr. Green to his promises.

What mattered—both to the AFL and the ILGWU—was that the garment workers were back where they belonged.

XI

Pins and Needles

EDUCATION is one of those catchall words beloved by mediocrity. Dr. Johnson's celebrated crack that "patriotism is the last refuge of a scoundrel" might be paraphrased that education is the first refuge of a fool.

The reason is that "education" is a term which may be stretched to cover the whole of life. It is not in itself a discipline like history or mathematics, but an attitude on the relation between the individual and the world. It can be made to embrace everything from the sublime to the ridiculous, from the study of Greek drama and modern physics to courses in table manners or "household engineering" in the Babbit warrens of our teachers' colleges. In short, like all fundamental human needs—love, religion, art—the desire to know can be endlessly organized and exploited by frauds, nitwits and careerists.

But never before has education lent itself to a highfalutin racket as it does today. For not until modern "techniques" of education were contrived could these techniques be used to create a vested interest in trained and diversified ignorance at the expense of the pursuit of knowledge. While authentic learning has progressed amazingly in the last generation, pseudo-learning has progressed a great deal faster. The opportunities for intricate and professionalized stupidity have never been as rich as they are today.

Gresham's law, according to which bad money tends to drive good money out of circulation, is just as valid for the diffusion of culture in a society. In the chaos of our times the pseudo learning of the professional educator has come to be considered a liberal-izing and "progressive" force in American life. It was this type of educational reformer in the early twenties who became the apostle of adult education, of which workers' education is an important part.

For years the spirit and jargon of this vulgarized enlighten-ment, appealing to the innocent remanticism of proletarian yearn-ing for culture, dominated the field of workers' education. What saved workers' education was the fact that it derived its real inspiration and sustenance from the needs of an authentic social movement with a long tradition of its own.

VARIETIES OF EDUCATION

Education has four main objectives: cultural and scientific education for its own sake; professional education; vocational education; and propaganda. All four are legitimate provided they are not confused with one another.

The first type of education—the pursuit of learning for its own sake—has always been and always will be an individual enter-prise. It requires a formal and systematic training which is gen-erally acquired academically but may be acquired by oneself.

Professional education, such as medicine, law, engineering or theology, offers formal disciplines directed towards vocational purposes, in the realm of higher education. Today chiropractors, undertakers, even beauticians, consider themselves professional people, which is so much nonsense, for a profession implies the mastery of an established body of knowledge based on a wide traditional culture.

Vocational training is just what its name implies. It is the acquisition of knowledge and skill in a field not rooted in intel-lectual discipline and culture.

Propaganda is concerned with the dissemination of ideas, usu-ally a system of ideas. They may vary from the highest to the lowest, from religious faith or libertarian doctrine to race hatred or statolatry. Propaganda can be used by great leader like Samuel Gompers or by demagogues like Huey Long. There is nothing wicked about propaganda as such—it all depends on who does the propagating and what he propagates.

Obviously every great social movement, including labor, has been interested in education. Organized labor could not exist without it. The question is, Which of the four varieties of education or combination of them can a trade union use significantly for the advancement of its aims?

The women's garment workers have been in the forefront of labor education ever since Reconstruction days. They are the recognized pioneers in this field and have had an enormous influence on the educational activities of American labor, indeed on adult education as a whole. The influence of organized labor, and particularly of the ILGWU, on adult education—university extension, evening classes in the public schools, courses offered by private institutions such as the YMCA—is comparable only to the influence of pre-Civil War labor in bringing about free compulsory education in this country.

There are many reasons why the garment workers led in the movement for workers' education. The immigrants who came to this country in droves in the eighties, the nineties and the first decade of this century had an unusually large proportion—say 5 per cent instead of the usual 1 per cent—of individuals with a driving urge for self-improvement. The Russian Jews among them, moreover, had a traditional veneration for the man of learning.

Then there was the fact that the earliest trade unions among the garment workers, unlike those in the building trades, for instance, were organized by intellectuals or semi-intellectuals who were exponents of some ideology or social faith. We have only to remember such names as De Leon, Hillquit or Cahan. The unionization of the garment workers was not only an economic but also a romantic movement. And romantic movements are based on panaceas—that is, on rounded theories of social progress. The propaganda of an intelligible utopia is in itself a task in education.

Many of the early cloakmakers' unions actually grew out of

socialist or anarchist educational societies. In 1890 the New York cloakmakers founded the Cloakmakers' Educational Club, which not only propagated socialism but also taught its members how to read and write English and prepared them for citizenship. It also launched a general educational program consisting of lectures and debates. Philadelphia, Boston and Chicago had similar educational societies among the garment workers. The Knights of Labor assemblies in the garment trades encouraged discussion of contemporary "reform questions" at their meetings.

All these radical groups insisted upon "class-conscious" education. They believed as a matter of course that the universities and schools taught history, economics and the other social sciences from the capitalist point of view and that therefore it was incumbent upon workers' education to present social problems from the standpoint of the common man. Hence the radicals, and their fellow travelers in the middle-class world, set up a number of educational ventures and institutions which looked at society from a left or proletarian "angle." The best-known of these institutions are the Labor Temple, Cooper Union and the Rand School of Social Science. All these institutions gave lectures on trade unionism, economics and history, and also ran forums, debates and mass meetings.

At the 1902 convention of the International in New York, Benjamin Schlesinger introduced a resolution urging local unions to arrange "bimonthly or at least monthly [sic] lectures and discussions on all educational subjects. . . . Labor's intellectual power," he explained, "is the only effectual weapon in the struggle for emancipation." Similar resolutions were adopted by subsequent conventions and were carried out in sporadic fashion by a few local unions in New York. The International and the New York Joint Board also got out a number of educational leaflets and pamphlets in various languages. But during the first decade of this century, from the founding of the International until the cloakmakers' strike of 1910, the union did very little sustained educational work. It was felt that the various left-wing schools filled the need. Besides, it was at just about this time that the abstract utopian factionalisms of the various radical groups within the union were being translated into painfully concrete rows, which were hardly conducive to the pursuit of learning.

EDUCATION IN A BIG WAY

By 1912 the picture had changed considerably. The Uprising of the Twenty Thousand dressmakers in 1909 and the Great Revolt of the cloakmakers in 1910 had brought tens of thousands of new members into the union. Like the "NRA babies" of a later day, they had to be assimilated and given some idea of the most elementary notions of trade unionism—which is one of the really indispensable objectives of workers' education. For workers' education, all romantic talk to the contrary notwithstanding, is essentially propaganda education—education in a faith and in the public relations of this faith. Hence whenever the International experienced a great upsurge in morale and membership its educational activities automatically intensified.

The rapid growth of the union, moreover, necessitated a considerable increase in the number of trained officials in the middle and lower ranks; and the new and complicated problems which arose from the Protocol of Peace required a good deal of clarifying not only for the officers but for the membership as well. Above all there was the constant pressure from the dressmakers, the "girls" of Local 25, for educational and cultural activities which would put a "soul" into the union.

In June 1913 the English-speaking branch of Local 25 held a "coming-out party" to mark its spiritual debut, at which the speakers were Zona Gale, Hamilton Holt and Arthur Bullard, well-known liberals of the period. The local also gave musical entertainments and popular lectures in Jewish and Italian as well as English. The "girls" of Local 25—later of Local 22—have always been the ferment behind most of the educational enterprises of the International, especially of a cultural nature.

At the 1914 convention of the International in Cleveland a resolution was adopted which declared that "the time has come to dwell particularly on the more solid and preparatory work of education and not to devote so much time to the more superficial forms of agitation and propaganda which have been the main features of our educational work in the past." The resolution was verbose and confused but a committee was appointed to shape a new program.

During the next few years the union tried to introduce some elementary training for officers. It arranged with the Rand School for special courses on trade unionism and some of the New York locals conducted classes in "union service." But interest in these courses soon flagged and vocational courses in trade union management were given up until their revival in the thirties. The trouble with the early courses was that they emphasized training in "leadership" and leadership as distinct from technical knowledge cannot be taught. One can train leaders of Boy Scouts or baseball teams, but one cannot train leaders of social movements. Political, religious, industrial or trade union leaders are leaders by nature and not by vocational guidance. Lewis, Tobin and Dubinsky never took a course in "leadership" and if they were the kind of people who would register in a school for leaders they of course wouldn't be where they are. Courses in leadership are given by people who have no understanding of leadership or they would not attempt to teach it; and they are attended by people who have no instinct for it or they would play the game of power instead of studying it.

But in general educational work the union was more successful. Sigmund Haiman, then the chairman of the educational committee of the dressmakers, obtained the use of a public school for weekly lectures and concerts. That caught on and in the spring of 1915 Juliet Stuart Poyntz, a former teacher of history at Barnard, was engaged by Local 25 as educational director.

Miss Poyntz was a gifted and striking personality, a woman with a rare combination of charm and force. She was by nature a zealot and later became a revolutionary extremist, winding up as a GPU agent, and one fine day she mysteriously vanished. Her work as the educational director of the dressmakers soon established her as a leader in the field of workers' education. She was really the creator of the educational department of the International. She persuaded the public school authorities to place increased facilities at the disposal of the International and introduced an extensive schedule of classes and activities. In the summer of 1915 Local 25 founded a vacation center, called Unity House, with accommodations for fifty people, at Pine Hill, New York. In 1919 Unity House was moved to Forest Park, Pennsylvania; in 1924 the International took it over. Today it is one of the most magnificent summer camps in the United States.

The 1916 convention of the International in Philadelphia felt justified in adopting a rather ambitious educational program. The program was still vague but it was considerably enlarged. And what was more important, the convention directed the GEB to set up a General Education Committee and instructed the local unions to appoint educational committees of their own. The General Education Committee was to canvass other labor organizations with the idea of "creating a workingmen's college"—a suggestion directly inspired by Professor Charles A. Beard of Columbia who was one of the founders of Ruskin (Labor) College at Oxford. This idea ultimately led to the foundation of Brookwood Labor College and to the various summer schools for workers in our leading institutions of higher learning. The chairman of the new Education Committee was Elias Lieberman, then the chief clerk of Local 25 and now the general counsel for the International. Miss Poyntz was made educational director and Fannia M. Cohn was appointed organizing secretary.

After this reorganization the ILGWU went into educational work in a big way. In New York the use of eight public schools was obtained for evening classes open to any trade unionist. In January 1918 the International opened the Workers' University at Washington Irving High School, where courses were offered in labor problems, industrial economics, American history and government, literature and psychology. On a much smaller scale Philadelphia and Boston followed New York's example. All this educational exuberance reflected itself at the next convention of the International in Boston in 1918. The work of the educational department was enthusiastically approved and its budget was increased to $10,000 for the next two years.

In December 1918 Miss Poyntz resigned. The Socialist party had been split by the Russian Revolution, and Juliet Poyntz became a Communist sectarian and was lost to the trade union movement. Fannia M. Cohn, the secretary of the department, was put in charge of it.

Fannia M. Cohn

Fannia Cohn has been secretary of the educational department of the International ever since it was established in 1917. She was born in 1885 in Russia, where she received a good private-school education. In 1904 she came to this country and became a waistmaker. Just before the dressmakers' strike of 1909 she joined the International and for a few years was very active as an organizer and strike leader among the women garment workers in New York, Chicago and other centers. From 1916–28 she was on the General Executive Board, the first woman vice-president of the International. For over a quarter of a century her passion in life has been workers' education.

Miss Cohn's temperament and outlook have deeply colored her views on the subject and have had considerable influence on the whole field of labor education in this country. From the first she has stressed that the primary function of workers' education is to strengthen character, "to develop discrimination and to create ability to form sound judgments." Fundamentally, however, she views workers' education as a school in inspiration, for she believes that it is labor's function to change and to enlighten the world at large. "The workers' education movement," she wrote in an article in *Justice* on June 1, 1923, "is a movement for special education in the subjects which will enable the workers to accomplish their special job, which is to change economic and social conditions so that those who produce shall own the product of their labor."

Since then Miss Cohn has somewhat modified this utopian

conception of labor's mission. But deep down she still retains the romantic concept of the Worker as the Redeemer of Society. Such a lofty and amorphous notion does not tend to clarify the educational function of a trade union, which is to make its members good trade unionists and to create the best possible public relations for the union.

But in spite—or rather, because—of her sentimental approach, Miss Cohn was extremely valuable in the formative days of workers' education, for all pioneering must have a romantic drive behind it. She is a dedicated personality who has stuck to her job with devotion and tenacity. Were it not for her, it is almost certain that the International would not have maintained even a skeleton Educational Department during the dark days of the civil war and the depression. Her dynamic exaltation intrigued and involved a great number of people in universities and colleges and in public life, and the Educational Department, under her solicitous care, did a great deal for the public relations of the International. She has made hundreds of distinguished friends for the union through her endless correspondence, which is really propaganda for an idealistic labor movement—quite an achievement during a period that has produced a Bioff, a Scalise and other such hoodlums. College professors, liberal bigwigs, reformers of all sorts have lectured, written, served on committees in behalf of labor and adult education. Miss Cohn is a missionary who must be judged by her good works among the heathen, not by the quality of her theology.

And she has done a lot to keep alive, especially among the women workers, the emotional folklore of the union—the Triangle fire, the Uprising of the Twenty Thousand, all the "struggles" the girls have gone through to build the ILGWU. She is essentially an old-fashioned feminist in the labor movement. And she represents the long tradition of the women in the garment unions who combined radical agitation on the picket line with a yearning for sweetness and light, a joint appeal which proved almost irresistible to the middle-class apostles of good will. It resulted in a rapprochement between working and middle-class women which proved a beneficent force in American life.

THE HIGHER LEARNING

At the 1920 convention in Chicago the International appropriated $15,000 for education, and at the Cleveland convention two years later this amount was increased to $17,500. This, of course, did not include the money spent by individual Joint Boards and local unions, many of which now began to take educational work seriously. In New York City the various Unity Centers, housed in public schools, and especially the Workers' University, took on new life. In 1920 Dr. Alexander Fichandler, a Brooklyn public-school principal, was appointed educational director in special charge of the Workers' University. An extension division was added which provided programs and furnished speakers for clubs and colleges, for union meetings, conferences and forums. Recreational and sports activities were initiated and encouraged.

On the whole, classroom work in higher education was not a great success, and after many years of experimentation the International has practically given it up. The difficulty is that higher education permits of no gaps in the formal training of the student. A grade-school graduate gets very little out of a seminar in economics. He must have a secondary-school grounding, whether acquired by himself or in a high school. If he lacks it, the higher learning floats over his head. Those few workers who do have a secondary education or its equivalent generally do not attend workers' colleges but use whatever further education they acquire to work themselves out of the shop and behind a desk, often as union officials.

It was soon discovered that the motives which made the average working girl enroll in the Workers' University had rather little to do with a thirst for knowledge. More often than not these students were moved by some different urge—a desire to make new friends, especially young men; interest in a sentimentally rather than academically fascinating instructor; or the plain wish to escape loneliness or a narrow and dreary family circle.

I remember the time way back in 1923 when Professor Paul Brissenden of Columbia and I gave a series of lectures on trade unionism at the Workers' University. We naturally assumed that the workers would flock to our classes, for we took it for granted that union members would be interested in trade unionism. Across the hall from where we held forth, a Columbia instructor offered a course in English poetry—Shelley, Keats, Byron and Tennyson. The gentleman looked like the late William Faversham, the celebrated matinee idol. His stage presence was romantic and his wares were inspiring, though later I learned from an expert that they were more glittering than genuine.

Well, our Faversham packed them in by the hundreds while Brissenden and I would talk to a dozen earnest souls, more willing than comprehending. For economic problems cannot be oversimplified without falsification. All democratic theories to the contrary notwithstanding, most dressmakers cannot very well follow a discussion of the wage structure of the United States or of the economics of the mining industry as it affected the history of the United Mine Workers. Serious class work in the Workers' University, even in the social sciences, quickly petered out. In a sense the early twenties were the goofy period in workers' education as they were in almost every other phase of American life.

THE ILGWU AS EDUCATIONAL MISSIONARY

From the very beginning the International considered itself the apostle of workers' education in the trade union movement. At the St. Paul convention of the AFL in 1918 the ILGWU delegates pointed with pride to the educational work of their union and urged organized labor as a whole to follow its example. The AFL appointed a committee "to investigate the educational system of the ILGWU and other similar schools and to report to the next convention." And in 1919, at Atlantic City, the Federation endorsed the educational work of the International and called upon the rest of labor to follow suit. The 1920 and 1921 conventions adopted workers' education as part of the AFL program. In the latter year the Federation set up the Workers' Education Bureau. At the same time Brookwood Labor College, a residential school, was founded in Katonah, New York, under the direction of the Rev. A. J. Muste, who had been the leader of the Lawrence and Paterson textile strikes in 1919. Many trade unions, particularly the International, established scholarships at Brookwood for their members.

During the twenties and thirties a number of AFL unions launched educational programs more or less modeled after the International, though none of them ever reached the same proportions. The seminal influence of the women's garment workers in promoting workers' education cannot be exaggerated. Soon after Brookwood Labor College was founded, Bryn Mawr initiated its Summer School for Women Workers. The idea of affiliating workers' education with institutions of higher learning spread rapidly. Summer schools, special seminars or fellowships for trade unionists were established at Barnard, Wisconsin, Penn State, Yale and Harvard. Independent summer schools and residential labor colleges sprang up here and there, though most of them disappeared very soon. The Harvard fellowships are maintained partly by the International and partly by the Harvard Alumni Association. At Wisconsin the scholarships are paid for by the union and the state. Most other institutions merely offer free tuition.

Years later the WPA spent literally millions in workers' education. The basic patterns of its activities were taken directly from the International, which for a while was intimately involved in these government ventures. But, as so many other New Deal adventures in culture, WPA Workers' Education soon became a madhouse of high-minded confusion and a happy hunting ground for the Communists and their fellow travelers, who in time took it over bodily and finally wrecked it.

RETRENCHMENT AND DECLINE: 1926–33

In 1923 and 1924 the educational program of the International reached its high point before the New Deal, but soon after

the decline began. The more hard-boiled members of the GEB
—always accused by the yearners of lacking "vision"—had
never been quite sold on such fancy enterprises as the Workers'
University. They went along with the expansion of the educational activities of the union because they found it difficult to
oppose anything offered in the name of Education. But when
the increasingly fierce internal struggles of the civil war forced
the union to pare down all expenses, the GEB naturally cut the
budget of the educational department to the bone. To be sure,
the GEB report to the Boston convention in 1928 still devoted a
good many high-flown phrases to "educational work," but the
work itself had almost ceased. Four years later at the Philadelphia
convention the GEB admitted the sad truth. That the educational department survived at all must be credited to the invin-
cible perseverance of Fannia Cohn, who during the civil war
days constituted its total personnel.

REVIVAL: 1933-37

The astonishing revival of the union in 1933 gave new life to
its educational activities. Now the International had the money
to resuscitate the educational department. But Dubinsky, the new
president, was determined to make education serve the real needs
of the union and not some vague conception of proletarian
culture. He felt that the union should inaugurate a propaganda
drive to assimilate the "NRA babies" and make them into good
union citizens.

Dubinsky wanted the educational program to create inner
cohesiveness, not to dispense general culture—which may lead
to catholicity of taste but does not serve as a binding force in a
local union. He did not believe that it was the function of a
union "to educate people out of the labor movement." Neither
did he believe that leaders—as distinct from functionaries—
could be trained in the classroom. He knew damn well that gentlemen like Breslaw or Zimmerman, whose political prowess he
had experienced, had not been developed in a seminar on "leadership" at Ruskin College. But the union did have to hire hun-

dreds of new functionaries and organizers, young men and women to carry on as administrators and business agents, all the way from New York to Vancouver. And though these tyro bureaucrats needed no courses in either English poetry or the psychology of leadership, they did need some knowledge of the headaches of a business agent. They had to know how to cope with their own jobs and how to deal with green workers in the shop. Accordingly, the educational program which Dubinsky advocated at the 1934 convention in Chicago was short and simple. "The task of the union," he said, "is to weld and keep together the masses who until now were strangers to our organization," and to train people for service in the local unions and the International.

The actual revival of the educational work was initiated by Local 22 of the dressmakers. Within a few months a large-scale and many-sided program was inaugurated, devised to serve the needs of the union. To be sure, the dressmakers, with their long tradition of cultural self-improvement, insisted on some academic classroom work, and of course they got it. But on the whole the program was directed toward union citizenship and practice. Other locals more or less followed this lead.

In January 1935 the educational department was completely reorganized. Fannia Cohn remained as secretary. Mark Starr was appointed director, Louis Schaffer was put in charge of a cultural and recreational division, and Julius Hochman became the chairman of the Educational Committee of the GEB. Hochman has the perfect temperament for this job: he has a talent for constructive interference, believes profoundly in education and yet is highly skeptical of its romantic illusions.

Mark Starr

Mark Starr was born near Bath in England in 1894 and went to work as a hod carrier's helper at the age of thirteen. The next year he got a job in the mines in Somersetshire. His father too was a miner.

He soon became active in his union and a devoted follower of Keir Hardie, the Christian Socialist and founder of the British

Independent Labor party. Starr is still a Christian Socialist in spirit—that is, an ethical rather than a political socialist. But above all, he is practical.

Starr became one of the leaders of the workers' education movement in Great Britain, writing a number of textbooks widely used in labor colleges. In the early twenties Brookwood Labor College invited him to this country to teach British labor history. Since then he has traveled widely, lecturing, teaching, serving on innumerable committees of an educational nature. In 1943 he was the only candidate qualified for the directorship of adult education in the city of New York but the Board of Education turned him down on the absurd grounds that he was a "protagonist of labor." This gave him wide publicity. The same year the OWI sent him as a labor consultant to Britain for an extended tour through factories and army camps.

The first thing Starr did as educational director was to make a survey of the educational work of the International, to find out just what was going on and just what needed to be done. Then he proceeded to carry out the plans of the 1934 convention. In New York City the International, as distinct from its affiliated unions, instituted classes in officers' training. These training courses were brief and to the point and were given by specialists, mostly experienced union officials. The department also issued pamphlets and study outlines dealing with practical union problems.

In 1937 the lectures in officers' training became obligatory. The convention of that year at Atlantic City ruled that "an applicant for a paid office in the ILGWU, who has not previously served, shall not be qualified to run as a candidate unless he or she shall first have completed a satisfactory course in training conducted or approved by the educational department of the ILGWU in localities where such courses are available."

Starr devotes a great deal of his time to cultivating public good will. He visits periodically the various centers of the International and tries to integrate the social activities of the union with community life. And, with a shrewd eye to public relations, he encourages the dramatic and recreational activities of the union which have now become a really significant part of the work.

DRAMA—AND LOUIS SCHAFFER

In 1935 the union also employed Louis Schaffer as the general supervisor of its cultural and recreational activities. Schaffer is a veteran newspaperman and labor editor with a long background in the socialist movement and in business. He is the typical New Yorker—breezy, sophisticated and extremely likable. His sense of publicity is keen and his conception of the theater is far more Broadway than "proletarian." He is a sort of link between the theatrical world and the New York labor movement. In 1936 he got the union to take over the old Princess Theater in the Times Square district and named it Labor Stage. The original idea was to have Labor Stage supported by the entire labor movement of New York, an inspiration which grew out of a casual discussion at the home of Eugene Lyons, editor of the *American Mercury*. The International put in about $25,000 but the other unions did not respond, and so Labor Stage became part of the ILGWU.

The upper floors of the theater were converted into studios for dramatics and dance group recitals. But the main interest centered around the production of plays. The actors were recruited among union members who had been putting on one-act "proletarian" plays for their own local unions in and around New York City. The girls were mostly dressmakers and the men were cutters, cloakmakers and truck drivers. The young actors were eager to do some good old-fashioned working-class plays, chockfull of Social Significance. And so Labor Stage began with one of the most popular one-act plays at the time, *Steel*, by John Wexley, a "proletarian document." At the height of the CIO steel drive Labor Stage presented the play fifty times in New York and in the Pittsburgh areas, and took in $10,000. Even so, according to Louis Schaffer, the results were pretty disappointing. What people really wanted, he insisted, was amusement and not class consciousness. And he was right.

One day Harold Rome, a law student who at the time was working in the WPA Theater Project, dropped in on Schaffer and read him some lyrics he had written. "I'd like to hear the music," Schaffer said, and Rome played some of the tunes which later became famous in *Pins and Needles*. Schaffer knew a good thing when he heard it, got some of his actors together and began rehearsing after working hours. They kept it up for a year while the whole program of skits was being perfected.

In midsummer of 1936 two performances of *Pins and Needles* were given but nobody paid any attention to it. And so Schaffer went to see Dubinsky and got him to send out tickets to a long list of public dignitaries—Mayor La Guardia, judges, politicians and labor leaders. They came not for the play but to please Dubinsky. The play, however, was so tuneful and funny that no more invitations were needed to pack the house. The actors had to be taken on at full time at their shop wages. The rank and file of the union stormed the theater, and Schaffer organized a second company which played late matinees for members at an admission of twenty-five cents.

And now the general public began to flock to the revue. The critics raved. Big manufacturers would call in their shop chairmen and force on them hundreds of dollars for tickets: the buyers, it seems, insisted on being taken to *Pins and Needles*. The cast trooped down to Washington for a command performance at the White House. A gala performance was given in Hollywood. Two companies went on the road for four years. New editions of the revue were presented in New York in the course of a phenomenal run of almost 1200 performances. The total box office receipts were nearly $1,500,000.

Pins and Needles had a profound effect on the educational policy of the International. The experience confirmed Dubinsky's feeling that the educational work of a labor union should emphasize the cultivation of sound public relations. *Pins and Needles* created an enormous reservoir of good will for the ILGWU.

And this lesson was not forgotten after *Pins and Needles* closed its doors.

But *Pins and Needles* also taught the union that professional success is death on amateur standing. After *Pins and Needles* ordinary amateur dramatics were bound to seem flat and stale; everything was judged by the standards of a Broadway smash hit. The effect was unwholesome. In 1943 Labor Stage folded up; the cultural and recreational division took modest quarters in the home of the International and is now trying to reorganize its program along less ambitious lines.

All through the furore created by *Pins and Needles* the ILGWU continued developing choral and instrumental groups, staging pageants and dance recitals, promoting what might be called the folk aspects of recreation. And it is upon this type of cultural recreation that the union lays its main stress today.

ATHLETICS

The International centralized the athletic activities of the New York locals in an athletic division under Phil Fox, an experienced director of amateur sports. In the beginning competitive sports among local unions—baseball, basketball, soccer— were emphasized. The "girls" of Local 22 played nice clean basketball and tennis, and everything was fine.

But after a while things took a somewhat unexpected turn. The cutters, the pressers and finally the teamsters became enthusiastic about ball games and organized a number of teams. They played against schools, YMCAs and Sing Sing, and usually knocked the hell out of all comers. And to make sure of victory some of the locals would take in ringers. The poker-playing contingent in the union would bet on games, and for a while "athletics" became quite a problem. "Now I appreciate," Dubinsky said, "why Dr. Nicholas Murray Butler isn't crazy about football." In 1940 the General Executive Board diplomatically but firmly suggested that the union lay greater stress on such activities as tennis, bowling, swimming and gym work rather than on competitive games which lend themselves to professional abuses.

UNITY HOUSE

The vacation center of the International is Unity House, a vast estate in the Pocono Mountains in Pennsylvania. Unity House is in fact the largest vacation center in the United States. It has magnificent grounds, a private lake, facilities for every conceivable sport, and offers rich musical programs as well as stage and screen entertainments. In 1943, over 12,000 people, the vast majority of them members of the International, spent their vacations there. Unity House is the largest single enterprise of the ILGWU and takes in over $300,000 a year. Its director is Alfred Taxin, who had been an auditor for the International.

HEALTH AND BENEFITS

In the old sweatshop days the garment worker lived in an environment, industrial and social, which was a major outrage to every rule of public health. His occupational ailments were legion—tuberculosis, rheumatism, arthritis, skin diseases, anemia, postural defects and premature old age. Even the earliest unions in the garment trades, before the founding of the ILGWU, were aware of the problem and tried to help their members by including sickness provisions in their benefit systems.

In 1905 the International's constitution was amended to include disability and death benefits, and in 1910 it initiated a sickness insurance scheme. But the scheme soon collapsed and ever since all such mutual aid has been decentralized and carried on, if at all, by the local unions.

The International found that it could not maintain an effective benefit system for the simple reason that no private institution can offer social security to its membership. Only an over-all national scheme, in which the state, the employer and the worker pool fiduciary risks, can do that sort of thing. But the International could furnish an outpatient health department and clinic to provide medical services to its members. And way back in 1913 Dr. George M. Price, one of our great pioneers in public and industrial health, prevailed upon a number of local unions of the ILGWU in New York to collaborate in establishing the Union Health Center. The institution was popular from the start, and in 1930 the International took it over.

Today the Union Health Center occupies two floors of a large office building in the heart of New York's garment center. It has a staff of almost two hundred physicians, pharmacists, laboratory technicians and nurses. The Center furnishes ambulatory medical care and its clinic is one of the best equipped in the city. In 1942 over 50,000 people made use of it, 90 per cent of them members of the International and the rest members of other unions. The Health Center also does a splendid job in preventive medicine. It has a visiting nurse service and does extensive work in health education, with special reference to the problems of the garment workers.

Dr. Price died in 1942 and was succeeded by his son and collaborator, Dr. Leo Price. Pauline Newman, a former garment worker and general organizer for the International, has been the educational director, really the liaison officer between the medical staff and the local unions, since 1923. A woman of great efficiency and tact, she has devoted her life to the medical care of the women's tailors.

RESEARCH

The research department, one of the most effective enterprises of the International, is also the most unobtrusive. No ideological storms cross its threshold and no visionary notions disturb its economic studies.

Quickie research in connection with its industrial problems was done by the International sporadically as far back as 1910. Whenever the union needed such services it would hire outside experts. In the early twenties it set up an economics bureau of its own but the depression and the civil war killed the undertaking. In 1935, however, a permanent research department was established with Dr. Lazare Teper, recently out of Johns Hopkins, at its head. When Dr. Teper went into the Army in 1943 he was succeeded by Professor Broadus Mitchell, formerly of Johns Hopkins and now of New York University.

When Dr. Teper set up his department his greatest difficulty was the appalling lack of information on almost every aspect of the economics of the industry. Union officials knew their specific trade problems but in a purely practical fashion. Accurate data on current production, technological changes, earnings, industrial standards, retail sales, consumer trends and other similar problems were almost unobtainable. The department had to develop its own techniques for gathering and analyzing material and preparing it for use by the union administrators. In time the bureau found it necessary to make more fundamental studies, going into those phases of the national economy that affect the women's clothing industry. Such studies, particularly those on the relation between wage rates and the cost of living, proved invaluable in the negotiation of collective agreements.

The department has a staff of a dozen members and keeps in close touch with every branch and center of the industry and every section of the International. It has become a sort of national clearinghouse on the economics of the women's garment trades, especially for various government agencies.

OFFICIAL JOURNALS

The International publishes four official journals in as many languages. We have already touched upon the history of *Justice,* the semimonthly mouthpiece of the union, edited by Max Danish, who is also general supervisor of the foreign-language press of the ILGWU.

The Italian organ, *Giustizia,* is edited by Raffaelo Rendi, Serafino Romualdi and Vanni Montana. The Jewish paper, *Gerechtigkeit,* is run by Dr. B. Hoffman and Simon Farber. And Antonio Reina gets out the Spanish *Justicia.* They are all monthlies.

All of these editors are veterans in the socialist and labor movements and all of them, except Simon Farber, are intellectuals by origin. But being journalists, they are a very different type of intellectual from a Ph.D. in the research department, who thinks of himself as a hired expert. Most of them took a leading part either in the factional struggles of the International or in the controversies in the socialist movement in years past. In the days of the Hourwich affair thirty years ago, Dr. Hoffman would think nothing of writing a scorching editorial denouncing President Rosenberg and Secretary Dyche as "misleaders" of labor. Those days, of course, are gone. Nowadays even Dr. Hoffman wouldn't dream of attacking Dubinsky in the official journal of the union. The editors of the International are no longer involved in union politics. But they are still political personalities and play quite a public role in the Italian, Jewish and Spanish communities. Montana, for instance, is active in almost every Italian anti-fascist and democratic organization and has been extremely valuable to the OWI in its Italian broadcasts and propaganda. And Romualdi has been borrowed for the duration by the government as a labor liaison officer for Latin America; it would be hard to find a better man.

THE WAR

By 1938 the educational activities of the International were no longer concentrated in New York. There were now fifty educational departments in various parts of the country and twenty-four of them had full-time directors. The Joint Boards and local unions pitched in financially and did their own work. And yet there was a noticeable decline in the interest and participation of the membership. Education was beginning to lost its glamour and was becoming more or less a routine activity.

Even the war could not revive the original crusading spirit about workers' education as the hope of the labor movement. But it did bring about drastic changes in the educational program. First aid, civilian defense, home nursing and nutrition classes sprang up in almost every local union in the country. In New York City the International formed its own uniformed Women's Brigade, which co-operates closely with the American

Red Cross and the OCD and participates in all sorts of civilian war activities. The Brigade girls, all dressed up in their blue and red capes with matching overseas caps, made such a hit in New York that the idea spread to other garment centers and brigades were formed in Chicago, St. Louis, Los Angeles and elsewhere.

Miss Cohn, characteristically, has tried to interest the union in a postwar outlook. Even before Pearl Harbor she arranged a panel discussion—whatever that may mean—on "Where Is America Going from Here?" Since then she has organized three more such round-table talkfests on similarly grandiose topics. But this kind of thing could not catch on, for most union members are too busy and sensible to attend vague discussions on the role of labor in the coming world. Panel discussions by liberals and college professors about what American labor should do after the war are quite meaningless. Labor's place in the postwar world no doubt requires considerable thought but it is not a job for round-table devotees or even for workers' education. It is a job for the official labor movement, and both the AFL and the CIO have formed committees for that purpose.

WHAT USE WORKERS' EDUCATION?

In 1943 the educational department of the ILGWU celebrated its twenty-fifth anniversary. The purely educational work of the union—and I am excluding research, journalism, the Health Center and Unity House—has cost the International and its affiliates over $1,000,000. Of late the leaders have begun to ask themselves just what the union has gotten out of all this expenditure of cash and effort. And the more hard-boiled among them point out that at no time were there more than 10 per cent of the members of the union directly involved in its educational activities.

The answer is that the International got a good deal out of what it put in. The experience has enabled it to clarify and define the purpose of trade union education. It has learned that the union is not the institution to provide its members either with a formal education or with "a way of life." Classroom work in advanced subjects has on the whole failed, for the worker has neither the interest nor training to absorb it. And the union cannot constitute a way of life, educationally or otherwise, because the only way of life for an American is America itself.

The union is also not concerned with trade education, which can be had at a number of public institutions. Moreover, the ILGWU, like all other unions, has a defined jurisdiction; in other words it is a labor monopoly in its field. And like all monopolies it does not encourage newcomers. But it is definitely interested in the vocational training of its officers of all ranks. Hence the emphasis on officers' training courses. There again experience has shown that one cannot train "leaders," but one can help union administrators to increase their effectiveness.

Finally, the International has learned that education undertaken by a social movement is primarily a twofold propaganda: making the union member a better union citizen and cultivating the best possible contacts with the public. As Dubinsky put it: "Our educational activities in the widest sense should be looked upon from the point of view of the union's public relations— and sound public relations presuppose a sound union."

XII

The State of the Union

WHEN WE ENTERED the war, the union and the manufacturers alike anticipated that the women's clothing industry would be sidetracked as virtually non-essential. They also feared that the already noticeable decline of the established markets in favor of the new territories would be accentuated. But their anxieties proved groundless. The war brought unprecedented prosperity to the industry and all centers began producing at their optimum capacity.

For over a quarter of a century New York, though always the hub of the industry, had been losing to the other big markets, such as Chicago and St. Louis, while these markets were in turn losing to the newer plants in the smaller towns in the West and Southwest. The war reversed this process of gradual decentralization, at least for the duration. Higher wages and a tighter labor market reduced enormously the competitive advantage of the newer centers, which had thrived on a cheap and plentiful labor supply.

Another reversal brought about by the war was in the price structure of the industry. Between 1927 and 1937 the average price of dresses, for instance, was almost halved. This was due to many reasons—the prudent buying habits contracted during the depression, the increasing use of rayon and other cheap synthetic fabrics and the simplification in style. But war production put money into the pocketbooks of the consumers and consump-

305

tion increased by almost 50 per cent. The manufacturers could meet this swelling demand partly because they had large stocks on hand and partly by greater resourcefulness in the use of synthetic materials.

Ever since the last war there has been a consistent tendency towards simplicity in women's styles. The increasing participation of women in sports, the use of the automobile for all sorts of purposes, the modern passion for streamlining made for functionalism in dress. The present war accelerated this trend by necessitating the conservation of materials and by throwing millions of women into production and other war activities in which utility was the prime consideration.

SLACKS

The sudden eruption of slacks in 1940 was the symbol of this tendency towards simplicity in style. By 1942 the epidemic of pants for women had become a big headache for the International. A feeling of anxiety pervaded the entire industry. Were slacks going to cut in seriously on skirts and dresses? Jurisdictional worries and rivalries quickly developed among the various crafts. Julius Hochman deplored "the rage for slacks" on aesthetic and industrial grounds, but accepted the unsightly reality and demanded jurisdiction for his dressmakers because slacks were mainly replacing dresses. Sam Shore put in his claim on the ground that an increasing number of his negligee workers were also making slacks. Israel Feinberg demanded jurisdiction over slacks for the skirtmakers and Charles Kreindler for the waistmakers. And Jacob Heller, our doughty old jurisdictional feudist, demanded slacks for his union of snow-suit workers on general principles.

A committee of the GEB, appointed to iron out these conflicting claims, recommended a complicated plan which merely stabilized the existing confusion and which naturally satisfied nobody. The jurisdictional antagonists wanted a clear-cut settlement. But Dubinsky urged delay because it was impossible to foretell whether slacks were here to stay, or what, in fact, the rapid trend towards style simplification might mean to the industry as a whole. The provisional arrangement was accepted. All the trades were booming and everyone agreed to let things slide until after the war.

WAR WORK

Soon after Pearl Harbor, when a prolonged crisis in civilian production seemed imminent, the ILGWU tried its best to get recognition in war contracts. The women's garment trades could easily produce such items as cartridge belts or parachutes, not to mention uniforms for nurses, Red Cross workers and women in the armed services. The cloak industry wanted to get some contracts for men's uniforms since it was well equipped to contribute in this way to the war effort.

The government procurement agencies were giving a lot of work to non-union plants and even subsidizing the erection of new plants in the low-wage areas. And whatever work did go to union shops went almost entirely to the men's clothing industry. Sidney Hillman was at the time the rear end of the Knudsonhillman combination and he saw to it that the International got as little as possible. Dubinsky protested vigorously that the Amalgamated Clothing Workers were "monopolizing" government orders. The International made it a public issue, a storm was raised in Congress, the press and radio took it up, and finally the WPB promised to award 20 per cent of its contracts for uniforms to the women's clothing industry.

But very little came of this promise. And the whole issue soon lost its urgency when it became obvious that the women's garment trades were in for a boom without benefit of heavy war work. Whatever war work the International managed to get— and it got a good deal in the way of parachutes and women's uniforms—was so much to the good. When there's enough for everybody there's no urge to fight for crumbs.

COLLECTIVE BARGAINING SINCE THE WAR

The collective bargaining relations of the industry were not markedly affected by the war. The International renewed its various agreements peacefully and with considerable gains. Some of these gains were of unusual significance. In the New York dress industry the agreement of 1941 included the promotion and efficiency schemes of Julius Hochman's Industry Planning program. In the New York cloak and suit market the agreement of 1943 established an old-age pension system, paid for by the employers and administered by a board of trustees representing the employers, the union and the public; the board is headed by Arthur J. Altmeyer, chairman of the Federal Social Security Board. Paid vacations covered about 85 per cent of the membership of the International throughout the country. In all the markets and in every trade of the industry wages were increased, standards were raised and in general the steady progress since the NRA was maintained.

Like the rest of American labor the International has had to curb its organizing drives for the duration. The no-strike pledge and the Little Steel formula put a damper on militant campaigning. Moreover, the draft cut in heavily on the organizing staff, especially in the outlying districts where most of the organizers are younger men. By and large, the ILGWU had to be satisfied to extend unionism through the elective machinery of the National Labor Relations Act. Nevertheless the International kept on growing right through the war. Early in 1940 it had a membership of 240,000; by January 1944 the membership had risen to 310,000.

MRS. DONNELLY AND SENATOR REED

A noticeable fly in the ointment was, and still is, the troublesome and expensive fight between the International and the Donnelly Garment Company of Kansas City, Missouri. The Donnelly Company operates one of the largest dressmaking plants in the Middle West, employing 1200 people, and its owner is Nell Donnelly, a high-spirited personality in her own right, triply reinforced by the militancy of her husband, that stout octogenarian warrior, ex-Senator Jim Reed.

The International tried to organize the Donnelly workers in the days of the NRA, but Senator Reed insisted that they were already represented by an organization of their own choosing, confined to the Donnelly plant. The NLRB ruled that this plant union was company-dominated, and the fight was on.

In 1937 the Atlantic City convention of the International voted $100,000 to buck the old Roman and to organize his wife's plant. To make a long story short, the Donnelly case has gone before every relevant government agency and shuttled back and forth through the federal courts, including the United States Supreme Court—with both the company and the union suing each other. This has been going on for seven years. The International is determined to organize the Donnelly plant. The Senator is equally determined that it shall not be unionized.

NEW DEPARTURES

Every labor union is, of course, vitally involved in the technology of the industry in which its members make a living. The real education of a trade union—education in the sense of self-clarification—is twofold: (1) a growing awareness of the engineering factors which condition the process of collective bargaining; and (2) a deepening appreciation of the economic impact of technological change on the lives of the workers, so that it may protect them adequately against exploitation.

Many unions—and I am here not referring to plain rackets—have been unable to educate themselves so as to meet industrial and social change. Obsessed by jurisdictional jealousies or intent on exploiting their job monopolies, these unions ignore the economic forces within whose logic they have to function.

The International has always been keenly alive to technological pressures (within the limits of bureaucratic expediency). The Protocol of Peace way back in 1910 showed a clear appreciation of the importance of technological problems. In 1913 the New York waistmakers, Local 25, pioneered in industrial efficiency studies at a time when the manufacturers showed not the slightest interest in scientific management.

In 1919 the Cleveland Joint Board, headed by Meyer Perlstein, and the local manufacturers hired a leading firm of industrial engineers to make an exhaustive study of production methods in relation to wage structure. On the basis of this study a Joint Board of Standards, with a large staff of time-study experts, was established to formulate production norms as a guide to the perplexities of wage determination. The Cleveland Experiment was one of the earliest attempts to turn scientific management to the advantage of labor as well as to that of the employer and the consumer. The civil war in the International short-circuited this type of union-management co-operation just as it did all other expansive projects of the union.

INDUSTRIAL PLANNING IN NEW YORK

Two decades later, in 1940, the idea behind the Cleveland Experiment was revived and developed by Julius Hochman in an effort to halt the decline of the New York dress market. Hochman got Dr. N. I Stone, the distinguished industrial engineer and statistician who had headed the short-lived Wage Scale Board of the dress industry in 1913, to make a survey of conditions in the trade. Dr. Stone's report showed an alarming obsolescence in equipment and management in most of the New York dress factories. Even more astonishing were the chaotic and haphazard sales and promotion methods prevailing in the market. Handicapped by such self-sabotage, the New York market was losing ground to the newer centers with their modern plants and efficient management.

Something had to be done, and Hochman worked out a well-conceived program of rehabilitation. He put forth two minimum demands—greater industrial efficiency and sounder sales promotion. And he insisted that these demands be implemented through the collective bargaining machinery.

The agreement signed in February 1941 provided for obligatory standards of efficiency in plant management and empowered the union to hale before the impartial chairman any manufacturer who failed to live up to these standards. Unlike the Reuther and Murray plans, which would have labor partake in management under government supervision, the Hochman plan leaves the right of management to management, but imposes upon it the obligation of efficiency. It avoids the Reuther-Murray totalitarian corporatism and accepts the premises of free enterprise.

The agreement also provided for the creation of a New York Dress Institute to promote New York as the fashion center of the country, indeed as the successor of Paris as the fashion center of the world. The first thing the Institute did was to adopt the "New York Creation" label, to be sewed on every garment manufactured in the market. It engaged the J. Walter Thompson agency for a large-scale advertising and promotion campaign.

The Institute's budget was $1,000,000 a year and its program correspondingly ambitious. It was going to be a sort of combined Academy of Arts and Sciences and Chamber of Commerce for the New York dress industry. But the war came along and the Institute had to curb both its ambitions and its expenditures for the duration.

The "Industry Planning" program was not accepted by the employers without a fight. They signed up only because the union had public opinion on its side. The press all over the country hailed the Hochman plan as a "new departure" in industrial relations. But even after the agreement was concluded many of the employers remained unreconciled. One manufacturer challenged the efficiency and promotion clauses in the courts. Finally, in June 1942, Justice Philip McCook sustained the legality of these provisions in a memorable decision which ruled that a trade union had the right to insist on efficient management and merchandising by the employer.

INDUSTRIAL PLANNING IN ST. LOUIS

A very similar venture was successfully carried through by Meyer Perlstein in the Middle West.

When Perlstein came to St. Louis in 1934 as regional director of the International he found the market in the women's clothing industry in serious difficulties. The industry depended entirely on New York for style and design. Fashion piracy was the accepted order of things, which killed initiative, embittered competition and aggravated the prevailing inefficiency in production methods. Although labor costs were high, both profits and wages were low.

Perlstein had been interested in industrial planning for many years. It was he who had guided the Cleveland Experiment in the early twenties. And now he went to work in St. Louis in the same spirit and with his usual energy. The manufacturers were willing and even eager to co-operate—anything was better than the mess they were in.

Together they decided that the first thing to do was to break away from style dependency on New York, even though Brother Hochman was busy as a beaver promoting New York as "the style center of the world."

It was difficult to compete in fashion with New York for the simple reason that the woman in Peoria was not likely to imitate St. Louis when she could imitate Park Avenue. And so the St. Louis industry set out to create a brand-new demand, the "junior size" garment. Young girls had been wearing women's dresses scaled down to their size. Now St. Louis went ahead on the theory that "juniors," especially high-school and college girls, wanted clothes specifically designed for them. They wanted, or could be made to want, bright colors, tricky and clever styling and youthful lines—clothes which would suit their fancy and fit their figures without the awkward alterations unavoidable in models designed for mature women.

St. Louis began to study the American girl—her contours and measurements, her tastes and fancies, her habits and proclivities, even her caprices. From this study of a delightful subject was born the Junior Size Creation, the profitable pride and joy of the St. Louis industry. In the five years preceding 1943 business jumped from $3,500,000 to $20,000,000. Today the St. Louis market is flourishing and independent.

This expansion would hardly have been possible without improvement in production methods. Through Meyer Perlstein's initiative the industry made time and motion studies, inquired into costs and wages, and set up labor-management committees to promote efficiency.

The women's garment workers in St. Louis probably know more about industrial efficiency than any other group in the International. Perlstein has instituted classes in this field which are attended by foremen as well as by union members. And every summer selected workers are sent to the University of Wisconsin for further training.

Meyer Perlstein

Meyer Perlstein is a New York cloakmaker who has made good in the wide-open spaces of the West. His territory, which has a membership of about 11,000, includes southwestern Indiana, southern Illinois, Minnesota, Kansas, Missouri, Arkansas and Texas. The success with which he has mastered his new environment is an index to his personality.

In spite of his conventional appearance Perlstein is tough-minded, full of drive and originality. When he goes out to organize new territory he goes not in the spirit of a trade union missionary but of an empire builder in the service of organized labor. And like all who are empire builders at heart, he is socially conservative and intellectually radical. He is not afraid of new ideas but there is nothing utopian in his nature. He has no desire to change the folkways of a community, except whatever prejudice he may find against trade unionism. He has no doctrines to promote, except the doctrine that labor must organize for collective bargaining. A conservative trade unionist, he accepts capitalism. But he insists that its rights in a free economy imply the duty of industrial efficiency in order to enable the workers to earn a decent living.

Perlstein was born in Russia in 1886. His father was a tailor, and at the age of thirteen Meyer went to work as an errand boy. In 1905 his father took him to London, where he was an operator in a garment shop. Next year he came to New York and became a skirtmaker.

In 1909 he joined Local 23 of the skirtmakers and the following year was very active in the great cloakmakers' strike. After the strike he was elected recording secretary of the Cloak Joint Board and naturally became involved in the Hourwich affair which was tearing the union to pieces. With his practical bent he could not stomach the dogmatic doctor, whom he considered a wild-eyed extremist, and took the lead in fighting him. The rank and file of the cloakmakers, who worshiped Dr. Hourwich, forced Perlstein's resignation. In 1914 President Schlesinger sent him to Philadelphia as a general organizer. Two years later he was elected a vice-president of the International.

In 1918 Schlesinger transferred him to Cleveland, where he headed the union until 1923. His experience, particularly in the Hourwich fight, had taught him that blind opposition to the employers can only weaken the industry in which the workers make their living. In Cleveland, he felt, he could experiment with the idea of labor-management co-operation which he had been mulling over for some time.

But the Cleveland Experiment died in infancy. The civil war in the International, which was just breaking out, smothered the experiment before it could really get under way. Perlstein's stand in the civil war was exactly the same as in the Hourwich affair: he was an intransigent opponent of the left-wingers, this time the Communists. An outstanding supporter of the Sigman administration, he was put in charge of the ILGWU in Chicago, where he fought William Z. Foster and his Trade Union Educational League.

In 1925 he returned to New York and joined the general staff of the right-wingers in the Cloak Joint Board. But within a few months the Communists had gained control of the cloakmakers and, together with Israel Feinberg, he was forced to resign. For eight years Perlstein was out in the business world.

When the fight with the Communists was over and the International was growing by leaps and bounds, Dubinsky brought Perlstein back into the union and in July 1934 appointed him director of the Southwestern region of the ILGWU.

In 1940 Perlstein startled his union colleagues by coming out for Willkie and against the third term. "Well," commented one vice-president, a pious Rooseveltian, "Perlstein was always a conservative." (Two years later Dubinsky suggested to Willkie that he run for governor of New York.)

Rebecca Taylor

In San Antonio and the surrounding territory a good many garment workers are Mexicans or of Mexican descent. Since 1938 the manager of the San Antonio Joint Board has been Rebecca Taylor, a member of a distinguished Tennessee family who was born on a ranch in the state of Tamaulipas, Mexico. After graduating from Sullins College in Virginia, Miss Taylor taught school in Texas for some years and then joined the International as the educational director of San Antonio, where she helped to organize the Mexican garment workers of the city.

Wave Tobin

Another woman leader in Perlstein's district is Wave Tobin, manager of the Kansas City, Missouri, Joint Board. Like Rebecca Taylor in San Antonio, Miss Tobin comes of old American middle-class stock. Her forebears left England in the early seventeenth century for Catholic Maryland, and later migrated to southern Illinois, where she was born in the town of Vandalia in 1895. They were farmers, lawyers, country doctors and small-town businessmen—not a labor agitator in the lot.

Wave Tobin joined Local 104 of the ILGWU in St. Louis when it was formed in 1933. As soon as she was admitted to membership she became an organizer among the St. Louis dressmakers and the financial secretary of the Joint Board. When Vice-President Perlstein took charge of the Southwestern region, he selected her as a general organizer and she conducted cam-

paigns and strikes in Minneapolis, Kansas City, and in Collins-
ville and Alton, Illinois.

In 1936 she was appointed to her present job as manager of
the women's garment workers in Kansas City. And ever since
then she has been heavily on the mind of Senator Reed, whose
wife's plant is Wave Tobin's biggest problem.

Friendly, attractive and clearheaded, Miss Tobin is just the
kind of indigenous regional leader the International needs in the
newer centers, such as the South and Southwest, where the industry and the workers are so very different from what they are
in the old established markets.

THE GARMENT WORKERS GO IN FOR
ENGINEERING

In time the various ventures of the ILGWU in promoting
productive efficiency emerged into a clear-cut industrial philosophy: organized labor has a vital stake in the health and welfare
of industry, of capitalism, if you please; it has the right to demand efficient production, management and merchandising;
and hence it has the duty to help the employer achieve these ends
—not by participating in actual management but by showing the
way to optimum performance.

To be sure, in the women's garment trades there is a special
situation. General Motors or Westinghouse have great industrial
research departments staffed by distinguished scientists and engineers. The unions in these fields can contribute little to the
technical problems of efficient production. In the clothing trades
it is the other way round. The International is by all odds the
most powerful, the most intelligent and, for that matter, the
richest organization in an industry in which the plants which
employ 1000 workers or more can be counted on the fingers of
one hand, and in which the majority of plants are small-scale
enterprises managed by rule of thumb. The garment manufacturer who thinks he knows "his own business" as well as Ford
or the RCA is just wrong. More often than not, he has neither
the background nor the facilities for that. The industry is still a

jumble of jobbers, manufacturers, submanufacturers, contractors and subcontractors. Seventh Avenue is no River Rouge.

The International, on the other hand, can take an industry-wide view and has the interests of the entire industry at heart. The employers, in fact, are accustomed to look to the union for technical and even business information about their own trade. Dubinsky decided that the union must have an engineering staff, and in 1941 the management engineering department was established under William Gomberg, a trained industrial engineer, who had been a business agent for the children's dressmakers' union.

The department has proven an invaluable asset to the International. Its motion and time study laboratory conducts research in every phase of the technology of the industry. It serves as an information center for manufacturers, union officials, government agencies and industrial engineers. Its main job, however, is to give practical assistance in technological and managerial problems as they arise in all branches of the industry. It also makes long-range studies to develop standard formulas for "ideal" performance—and fair compensation—of every manual operation in the women's garment trades.

The manager of a Midwestern local union complained that the workers in a big shop were unable to earn decent wages, though they were skilled and their piece rates were fair. He couldn't figure out what was wrong. After a brief survey the department discovered that the work in the plant was so poorly routed that 20 per cent of the time was wasted. The employer was no less grateful for the discovery than were his employees.

A New York manufacturer working on government contracts was puzzled by the slowness of his production. He came to the International for help. The department found that the lighting in his plant was grossly inadequate for the kind of work being done.

The workers in a large out-of-town factory protested that the efficiency engineer called in by the employer was "unfair" in the production standards he had devised. An ILGWU engineer made a thorough checkup and showed the management that the workers were right.

A Western manufacturer asked the International to help him plan the layout of a proposed new plant and to advise him on a training program for inexperienced help.

The department handles scores of such problems every year.

THE INTERNATIONAL IN POLITICS

The International, with its long socialist and radical tradition, has always favored, as a matter of course, independent political action by organized labor along the lines of the British Labor party. But until 1936 it was never officially affiliated with a political movement, except fleetingly in 1924, when it endorsed the short-lived Conference for Progressive Political Action, founded by the railway brotherhoods, which campaigned for the presidential candidacy of Senator La Follette. With this single exception, the leaders and the rank and file of the ILGWU generally supported the Socialist party ticket—but only as individuals.

In 1936, however, the International officially took part in the founding of a political party—the American Labor party in New York State. This party was an outgrowth of the New York State branch of labor's Non-Partisan League, the political arm of the CIO when Lewis was the CIO and a strong New Dealer. The ALP was just the thing the International had been looking for. Being nothing but a political instrument of the New Deal, it gave the International a chance of combining all-out support of the Roosevelt Administration with its own traditional belief in "independent" political action. Everybody in the union—conservatives, centrists, radicals—hailed the ALP as the promise of an American counterpart of the British Labor party.

But these grandiose expectations had no basis in reality. For one thing, the ALP was launched by the CIO and pro-CIO liberals, which meant that the AFL looked at it with a fishy eye from the very start. Even when the International, whose members formed the largest single group in the ALP, returned to the

AFL in 1940, the hostile attitude of the Federation leaders did not change. Then, the two leading personalities in the new party were Dubinsky and Hillman and they were poles apart in character, outlook and political morals. Finally, the party started out as a Popular Front affair and therefore quickly became a breeding ground for Communist intrigue and disruption. Before long the Communists and their friends had colonized most of the party clubs in Manhattan and a large number of them in the other boroughs.

Men like Dubinsky, Antonini, the first chairman of the ALP, and its state secretary, Alex Rose, a high official of the millinery workers, know how to handle Communist skulduggery in their unions. A union administration has constitutional powers to deal with Trojan horsemanship which the leaders of a political party obviously cannot enjoy. For instance, a union has every right to forbid the formation of caucuses or membership in hostile organizations. A political party, on the other hand, which is open to the whole electorate, can have no such restrictions. Hence the right-wing leaders, who controlled the state committee of the ALP, were powerless against the fifth column tactics of the Communists, even though they understood these tactics to perfection.

Being responsible trade unionists, the right-wingers suffered under another handicap. They could not, and would not, descend to the lies and gutter demagogy of totalitarianism, which never hesitates to exploit social confusion and the hates and fears which spring from it. Dubinsky cannot meet Earl Browder, who wrote of him as one of America's leading "anti-Semites," on Browder's ground—any more than President Roosevelt, for all his political cleverness, could meet and stop the late Huey Long on his. This is a most important reason why the right wing in the ALP has been constantly losing out to the left. The moral is: one cannot defeat totalitarianism in the same party with totalitarians.

With the right-wingers in control of the state committee (though the party never had anything much in upstate New York) and the Communists gradually worming their way into the party's stronghold in New York City, an unusual Popular Front picture developed. The right-wingers, against their will and better judgment, served as the unhappy front behind which the Communists could carry on.

Of course the right-wingers could have stepped out at any moment and exposed the left wing as a ventriloquist's dummy for the Communist party. But stepping out was by no means easy, for the party grew rapidly until it could throw its weight around with 400,000 votes. Though the right-wingers were losing out within the party, they were gaining influence with the politicians in New York, Albany and Washington, because, after all, they were the official leaders of the party. But even if they had been willing to relinquish this enviable influence, they had behind them tens of thousands of genuinely democratic followers who were always hoping to lick the Communists in the next primary and insisted on staying in to fight it out. Finally, the right-wing leaders were under constant pressure from certain New Dealers in Washington to refrain from doing anything drastic, for the ALP represented the New Deal in New York politics.

The Stalin-Hitler pact in 1939 wrecked the surface unity of the Popular Front in the ALP. Now the Communists branded all those who refused to hail the pact as "fascists" and "imperialist warmongers." At last the right-wingers were free to speak their minds and they fought back with the eagerness of released frustration. But by this time it was too late. The Communists had already gotten a grip on the ALP in Manhattan, Queens and Richmond and were making steady headway in Brooklyn. When Hitler attacked Russia in 1941 the Communists, of course, became good democrats once more—and in 1943 they captured Brooklyn, leaving only the Bronx in the right-wing camp.

Is There a Place for a Labor Party in America?

No labor party anywhere can at this moment of history, and for some time to come, avoid disruptive entanglement with the Communist movement. But this is by no means the only difficulty a labor party in the United States has to face. The easy analogy with the Labor party in Great Britain is seriously misleading. We have forty-eight sovereign states and half a dozen regional Americas and to build a national labor party would take years, at a time when history is moving with insane speed.

Moreover, the United States and Britain have developed very differently. The British Labor party, founded half a century ago, has in the course of time taken the place of the dying Liberal party and is today not a minority or class party but one of the two major parties in British political life, embracing broad strata of society. Twice it was in power and at no time was it in danger of being captured by totalitarian forces.

A labor party in the United States has to assume one grave responsibility and to face three unrelenting facts.

It has to assume the responsibility of undermining our two-party system and atomizing our political life. It was the profusion of mutually hostile parties in the succession of short-lived democratic regimes in the Russia of 1917, in Weimar Germany and in prewar France which opened the path to power for the totalitarians. In a great society the scales of political freedom can be balanced only by two great parties. (This is the reason why proportional representation is a menace.) The progressive task is to work within this system and not to break it up.

The three political facts which an American labor party cannot escape are: first, it is doomed to remain a minority party; second, it is bound to eke out its existence as a poor relation of the trade unions; and third, it is at cross-purposes with the real functions of the organized labor movement.

It is bound to remain a minority party because the American common man, including the worker and farmer, thinks of himself as belonging to our vast middle class, which he considers the bulwark of democracy. And, with few exceptions, he will continue to vote for one or the other of the two great middle-class parties. In other words, there is no chance within the foreseeable future for an American labor party to take the place of one of the major parties. All it can be is a spite party, undermining the two-party system.

A labor party in America is also doomed to depend upon trade union leaders for whatever strength it may develop, no matter how loudly and sincerely it may invite all and sundry progressives to join it. Unlike the British Labor party, which two generations ago was built by socialists and liberals in close co-operation *with* trade union leaders, in America today the liberals and progressives in such a party would have to work *under* the trade union leaders. The chairman of the ALP since 1942 has been Professor George S. Counts of Teachers' College, Columbia. But it goes without saying that the real power in the ALP is wielded by the trade union leaders because it is they who sustain the party with funds and manpower.

Finally, a labor party which is dominated by trade unions cannot afford to operate on the presuppositions of a genuine political party. The main function of the trade union movement is the economic protection of its members and therefore it needs the good will of both major parties, of the government in power in city, state and nation, and of public opinion in general. Movements which are primarily interested in social pressure politics must stay out of partisan party politics. Gompers' injunction that labor must vote for men, measures and platforms and not for parties, let alone form a separate labor party, was never more timely than today.

The success of the ALP in mustering hundreds of thousands of votes, in electing a dozen or so of its candidates to the state Assembly and the New York City Council, and in swinging elections in major campaigns, has obscured these inner contradictions inherent in a labor party. But these contradictions emerge with absurd clarity in reactions of men like Dubinsky, who opposed Willkie in 1940 as a tool of the vested interests and two years later wanted him to run for governor of New York.

The same absurdity we find in the political somersaults of the ALP in its attitude toward Thomas E. Dewey. In 1937, when Dewey was running for district attorney, it lauded him to the skies. Three and then five years later, although its encomiums had been justified by Dewey's record, it fought him tooth and nail

when he ran for governor of New York. Nothing had happened
in the meantime except that in 1937 Dewey was in the best
New Deal company while later he ran as a straight Republican.
In this campaign particularly the ALP was made the cat's-paw
of a highly complicated political game between F.D.R. and Jim
Farley, a game which had little to do with the interests of labor
in New York. The 425,000 votes the ALP got for its own candidate, Dean Alfange, hardly justified the role it played.

Twice the ALP helped to re-elect La Guardia as mayor of
New York, in 1937 and in 1941. In the latter campaign the
party opposed the candidacy of William O'Dwyer, whom it was
glad to support when he ran for re-election as district attorney
of Brooklyn the next year. As district attorney, O'Dwyer had
proven himself not only a competent public servant and a friend
of labor but a man of unusually high caliber, and today every
reputable labor leader in New York wishes O'Dwyer were mayor
of the city.

The ILGWU in the ALP

By virtue of its size and power the International has all along
played a determining role in the ALP. The party's first state chairman, from 1936–42, was Luigi Antonini, and Charles S. Zimmerman was head of its Trade Union Council. Officials of the
International ran for state and city offices. Nathaniel Minkoff,
secretary-treasurer of the Dress Joint Board, served as state
assemblyman from 1937–39, and Salvatore Ninfo as a member
of the New York City Council from 1938 through 1943.

It was the International which carried the burden of the fight
struggle against the totalitarians the greatest difficulty the right-
against the Communists in the annual primary contests. In this
wingers had to encounter was the chameleonlike strategy of Sidney Hillman.

Hillman has a long record—going back to the early twenties—
of playing with the Communists. His political tactics have always
been determined by considerations of a purely personal expediency. In the ALP he defended the Communists until 1939.
The Stalin-Hitler pact strained but did not break their relations.

And in 1942 he once more became the white-haired boy, indeed the patron and protector, of the Communists in the ALP. By that time Hillman, who had lost out in Washington as the Administration's number 1 labor man, was desperately determined to come back as a national political figure. In spite of Phil Murray's dislike of him, he managed, by allying himself with the Communists, to get the chairmanship of the CIO Political Action Committee, proposing to raise millions for political purposes, chiefly to promote the fourth-term candidacy of the President.

Of all American labor leaders of foreign birth—Gompers, Woll, Tobin, Murray, Dubinsky—Sidney Hillman is the only one who has never been assimilated by our institutions. He has never really understood the democratic process. In politics he is an opportunist who will make alliances in the most disparate strata of society. Though no Communist himself, he has never scrupled to make use of Communist intrigue for his own purposes. For in his avidity for power he will form connections wherever it will suit his ends, from the highest circles in government or business to the most ominous groups in society. Fortunately, this adventurer is less dangerous than he seems, for he is the typical ham Machiavelli who almost always outsmarts himself.

Between 1941 and 1943 Hillman stayed away from the ALP. In fact, in 1942 he refused to support Dean Alfange for governor and came out against the party, for he had promised Jim Farley to back John Bennett, the Democratic nominee. Bennett's defeat showed Farley, Roosevelt and the public in general that Hillman had no influence whatever on the labor vote. Hence his desperate effort in 1943 to bore his way back into the ALP with the help of the Communists, with whom he is allied in the CIO. He took over the Communist program for the "democratic" reorganization of the party. He proposed to "root" the party in the trade unions by welcoming the Communist unions en bloc and inviting their leaders into its councils. He even accepted their fantastic scheme that the voting strength of the various unions be determined by the size of their contributions.

The right-wing leaders, headed by Dubinsky, vehemently rejected this Trojan horse plan. They rejected it not only because it would turn the party over to the Communists but also because it would tend to narrow the party base exclusively to the trade unions and close the door upon sympathetic middle-class progressives.

Dubinsky made an open fight against the Hillman plan, and to make sure that the public would understand the issue the International reprinted an editorial from *Justice* as a paid advertisement in the metropolitan papers. In this fight the right-wing leaders had the unqualified support of the press and public opinion of the country. A group of several hundred liberals, some of them of national prominence, also ran ads in the New York dailies expressing their conviction that "control of the ALP by the Hillman-Communist coalition would strike a mortal blow at the cause of the liberal movement in this country."

The question facing the International as well as other right-wing unions in the ALP was whether to remain in the party and fight through the primaries in this presidential election year or to get out of the party altogether and declare it to be a Communist front.

Dubinsky and the other leaders decided to go through another primary. The rank and file felt the same way, only more so. They didn't want to quit without one more fight. At this writing (February 1944) it is unsafe to foretell the outcome. If the Communists win in the primaries, the right-wing unions will certainly step out. "We will have nothing to do with a Communist-controlled labor party," Dubinsky says. But whatever the results of the primaries may be, it is safe to prophesy that sooner or later the reds will gain control of the party. Then the ALP will be just another open Communist auxiliary. With the National Maritime Union under Comrade Joe Curran, the transport workers under Comrade Mike Quill, the fur workers under Comrade Ben Gold, and a number of other such Communist-dominated CIO unions in the ALP—it might just as well join the "disbanded" Communist party, which is an active affiliate of the "dissolved" Communist International. And, of course, the clever Mr. Hillman will have outsmarted himself again, for he cannot but emerge as a Communist ally, a figure totally alien to our history and culture. Moreover, the Communists are bound to throw him over in the long run, for he is not one of them. Paradoxically, if the Communists capture the American Labor party, the real beneficiary will not be Hillman but Dubinsky, who will stand out as one of the leading democrats in American labor.

Outside of New York the International has also been active politically. At first it worked with labor's Non-Partisan League. But the League soon became a Communist front organization, for until 1940 Lewis, who dominated the League, was hand in glove with the Communists. The International thereupon lost interest in the League and broke away completely when Lewis went over to Willkie, taking the League with him.

Since then the ILGWU, outside of New York, has played the orthodox AFL game of "rewarding the friends and punishing the enemies of labor" in the various states and communities.

THE ILGWU EMPIRE

The largest single industry in the city of New York—and for that matter in the state—is the women's garment industry. In the city itself 167,000 of the 513,000 workers engaged in manufacture are employed in producing women's apparel. In the metropolitan market, in which hundreds of contractors work for New York jobbers, the International has 200,000 of its 310,000 members.

But as President Dubinsky and the out-of-town vice-presidents always emphasize, "New York is not the whole country." For one thing, over 100,000 organized and approximately 50,000 still unorganized workers in the industry are not New Yorkers, local or "metropolitan." And for another thing, if these 100,000 workers were not organized, the union in New York could hardly exist. The whole history of the ILGWU—like the history of every union—has been the effort to extend its total jurisdiction throughout the country in order to control the labor market of the industry.

The International, outside of New York City, has 251 local unions, 19 Joint Boards and 7 district councils—in 238 cities, 32 states and 4 Canadian provinces. This is the International empire.

This empire is administered by a machinery which has developed not according to a preconceived scheme but in response to organizational needs. The International has two "out-of-town" departments: one is the Cotton Garment and Miscellaneous Trades Department, which supervises these trades over a large section of the Eastern seaboard; and the other is the Eastern Out-of-Town Department, with jurisdiction over the metropolitan area outside of New York City, which includes parts of New Jersey, Connecticut and New York State.*

The rest of the country is organized by large cities or geographical regions.

Morris Bialis

Next to New York the most important center of the industry is Chicago. The head of the ILGWU in Chicago is Morris Bialis.

Bialis is the son of a cloakmaker who is still working at his trade in Chicago. "My father and I are both members of Local 5," he told me with pride. As a psychological type Bialis strikes one as the traditional "honest workingman" of American legend

---

* The two "out-of-town" departments are located in the national headquarters of the ILGWU. In 1943 the International moved to its new building at Fifty-fourth Street and Broadway, which was formerly occupied by the Ford organization in New York. The offices and furnishings are sumptuous and streamlined, and it is very amusing to see Mr. Dubinsky lose his temper and pound the very desk at which Henry Ford probably chuckled over the Dearborn *Independent*.

Visiting cloakmakers at first felt that all this magnificence was not exactly in accord with their proletarian tradition. "What the hell is this," one of them wanted to know, "the Waldorf-Astoria?" But when they learned that the great automobile showrooms downstairs pay for the upkeep of the entire building, they were reconciled.

—upstanding, intelligent yet simple, and thoroughly trustworthy. There is not much of the politician in Bialis, for that type doesn't need much politics. He rises because he is industrious and reliable, and the people he gathers around him on his way up are pretty much the same kind. His relations with the outside world move on the same decent and sensible level, for no one would suspect him of deviousness or skulduggery. And when he meets skulduggery in others, all he does is to put his cards on the table and fight it out.

Bialis was born in Russian Poland in 1897 and came to this country as a boy of thirteen. Practically his whole life has been spent in Chicago. After finishing elementary school he went to work in a cloak shop. In 1912 he joined Local 5 of the Chicago cloakmakers and held the usual succession of local offices. In 1921 he became a business agent and the next year, at the age of twenty-five, he was chosen manager of the Chicago Joint Board. He has been manager ever since, with the exception of a year and a half at the height of the civil war when the Communists controlled the Chicago union.

In 1928 Bialis became a vice-president of the International. And in 1933, when the Chicago district was enlarged to include a good deal of the Middle West, Bialis was named regional director. Today the Chicago-Midwest region has a membership of about 17,000.

Bialis is a staunch Chicagoan with that certain Midwest feeling about New York. He is enthusiastic about everything in Chicago except its politics.

"Is the International interested in municipal politics here?" I asked him. "No," he said rather primly, "we do not play that kind of game. Mr. Kelly spoke at one of our meetings but only in his capacity as chief magistrate of the city." No ALP for Mr. Bialis.

Abraham Katovsky

The Ohio region, with headquarters in Cleveland, is in charge of Abraham Katovsky.

Katovsky is a fighter without the least touch of fanaticism

and an idealist without any utopian frills. His career, from the picket line up, has been one of sturdy militancy, although personally he is as mild and reasonable as they come.

Born in the Ukraine in 1889, he came to the United States at the age of twenty and immediately went to work as a cloak operator. In 1911 he participated actively in the disastrous general strike of the Cleveland garment workers, and as a result was blacklisted by the employers for almost four years.

In 1914 he managed to get back into his trade, and in 1918 he was Meyer Perlstein's right-hand man in the second great strike in Cleveland. This strike was successful; moreover, by this time Katovsky was one of the local leaders and could not be starved by the employers. In 1923 he and Charles Kreindler took charge of the Cleveland Joint Board. In 1932 Kreindler was transferred to Baltimore and Katovsky remained sole manager in Cleveland; two years later he was elected a vice-president of the International. In the same year he was appointed director of the Ohio region, which today has a membership of over 5000.

Katovsky was a fervent CIO man and, when the CIO got going in Ohio, he did all he could to help it organize the steel and rubber industries of the state. The bitterness between the AFL and the CIO was intense—and one night in February 1937 Katovsky was waylaid and so badly beaten up that he hovered between life and death for weeks.

The leaders of the Cleveland Federation of Labor were shocked by this outrage. And now that the International is back in the AFL, Katovsky is one of the most highly regarded AFL men in the city.

Philip Kramer

Bialis, Perlstein and Katovsky run the ILGWU from the Appalachians to the Rocky Mountains. In New England the outstanding figure in the union is Philip Kramer.

Kramer came to this country from his native Russia in 1905 at the age of seven. After two years of high school he went to work in a garment shop and worked in succession as a cloakmaker, a dress operator and a cutter. In 1920 he joined the union, a few weeks after he was mustered out of the Army, where he rose to a top sergeancy in the field artillery.

During the organizational campaign of the ILGWU in Boston in 1925, Julius Hochman picked Kramer as one of his main lieutenants. And when the drive was over Kramer stayed on as a business agent. While still a business agent he was elected a vice-president of the International in 1928, and four years later he became the manager of the Boston district, which today has a membership of 3000.

Kramer is a dapper, handsome fellow whom one would never suspect of pushing fifty. And he has a gift for popularity. Mayor Tobin appointed him to the Boston Committee of Public Safety. He is also on the State Labor Executive Committee of the OPA and represents the needle industries on the local Manpower Commission and War Labor Board.

Samuel Otto

The Philadelphia district, with a membership of about 13,000, is headed by Samuel Otto. Otto's father was a small-town businessman in the old country and the family migrated to Philadelphia in 1908, when Sam was twelve years old. After a good schooling, which included a year in Temple University, he went to work as a cutter. During the Philadelphia cloakmakers' strike of 1913 he joined Local 53 of the cloak cutters, and worked at his trade for twenty years.

In 1933 Dubinsky appointed him a general organizer for Pennsylvania, and two years later he was advanced to the post of manager of the Philadelphia Dress Joint Board. In 1940 he was elected a vice-president of the International.

Once a cutter, always a cutter. Samuel Otto is a Philadelphia version of Isidore Nagler—active and politically minded. He is quite influential in local affairs and is always trying to get the Philadelphia trade unions into the political arena.

Charles Kreindler

Charles Kreindler has two jobs in one. He is the manager of Local 25, the New York blouse- and waistmakers' union, and he is also the director of the Maryland and Virginia district of the ILGWU. This district, with headquarters in Baltimore, has a membership of 3000.

In 1910 Kreindler, at the age of twenty-one, came to this country from Austria, where he had had a high-school education. His first job was in a knee-pants shop and he joined the old United Garment Workers. But he soon switched to the dress-cutting trade in which he worked for a decade, mostly in Cleveland. In 1916 he was elected financial secretary of his local, and in 1923 he became comanager, with Abraham Katovsky, of the Cleveland Joint Board. In 1932 he took charge of the Baltimore Joint Board and held that office until 1933. Then he became manager of Local 25 in New York and regional director of the Maryland-Virginia district.

There is not a trace of the power politician in Charley Kreindler. And he doesn't need it. For if any man was ever liked simply as a human being it is Charley. Understanding, incapable of intrigue, and with courtesy of heart as well as manners, Kreindler is an unusual kind of trade union oligarch. He neither climbs nor pushes. And he has managed to rise without these arts.

John S. Martin

The director of the Southeastern region of the International is John S. Martin, with headquarters in Chattanooga. His district has about 5000 members. He is an old-time socialist and trade unionist as were his father and grandfather before him. They were all house, sign and carriage painters in Lima, Ohio, where John was born in 1890.

Martin was invited to become an organizer for the International in 1934 and three years later was sent to take charge of the Southeastern district. This was most unusual, for Martin was not a garment worker and American unions seldom go outside to pick their officers. But Martin had had a long career in the labor and socialist movements, beginning in 1910 when he and his father were associated with Max Hayes on the Cleveland *Citizen,* the famous Midwestern socialist weekly. Martin

is the typical native American socialist, whose socialism is Deb-
sian Populism rather than Marxian radicalism. This type, no
matter how high he may rise, always remains the Jimmy Higgins
of the movement—loyal, hard-working, articulate, as ready to
sweep out the office as a to sign a wage agreement, and always
ready to make a speech.

Way back in 1912 John Martin was an organizer for the
Carriage and Wagon Workers Union, which in the early twenties
became the first auto workers' union. In 1918 he became its vice-
president. But in 1921 he took over the publicity for the campaign to free Eugene Debs, who was then in Atlanta for his
opposition to the first World War. Then he worked for the
Socialist party, and in 1924 was as busy as a bee in the La
Follette-Wheeler campaign. For the next decade he worked on
a number of labor papers in New Jersey and helped to organize
the unemployed. In 1934 the Amalgamated Clothing Workers
took him on as an organizer, and Sidney Hillman, who was high
in the NRA, made him a compliance officer for the Cotton Garment Code Authority. "When the NRA began to lose its labor
punch," Martin wrote, "I resigned with a public blast and joined
the staff of the ILGWU." Public blasts, more public than blast-
ing, are a specialty of our old-time radicals—as American as
apple pie. The NRA's loss was the ILGWU's gain. In the
ILGWU this rolling stone in American labor began to gather
moss, but never so thickly as to hamper his movements.

David Gingold

For almost a decade the head of the Cotton Garment and
Miscellaneous Trades Department, which has jurisdiction over
almost 24,000 workers in the Middle East, was Vice-President
Elias Reisberg, who died in 1943. His place as head of the
department was taken by David Gingold, who had been Reisberg's assistant for Pennsylvania.

Gingold was born in Poland in 1896 and came to this country in 1912. A year later he joined Local 20 of the raincoat
workers, and from 1924–31 he was the manager of the local.

From 1925–29 he was a vice-president of the International. In 1931 the left-wingers almost disrupted Local 20, and Gingold resigned as its manager and went to work in a shop. In 1936 Dubinsky appointed him an organizer for the International, and soon after that he took over his Pennsylvania post.

Gingold is the reliable, efficient old-timer, thoroughly seasoned by his thirty years in the labor movement.

Harry Wander

The Nestor of the GEB is Harry Wander, manager of the Eastern Out-of-Town Department. In 1907, when the International was still in its infancy, he was already an officer of the union. He went through the Great Revolt of the cloakmakers in 1910, the conflicts and confusions of the Hourwich affair, the misery of the civil war, the resurgence of the union in NRA days—and through it all he remained a staunch right-wing trade unionist.

Wander was born in Galicia in 1879. After learning the tailoring trade in the old country he went to London in 1902, and two years later came to New York. Almost as soon as he arrived he went to work as a skirtmaker and joined Local 23. In 1907 he was a member of the local's executive board and a delegate to the Cloak Joint Board, and in 1916 he became the manager of the local. Two years later he was elected a vice-president of the International. During the civil war, when the Communists were in control of the cloakmakers, President Sigman made Wander the manager of the Union Health Center. But in 1929 Wander was back on the Cloak Joint Board as its secretary-treasurer. Next year he was put in charge of the Eastern Out-of-Town Department, which today has jurisdiction over almost 39,000 workers in a wide territory surrounding New York City.

Mellow though extremely reserved, vastly experienced as an administrator and negotiator, Harry Wander enjoys the confidence of the thousands of "NRA babies" in his district as well as of the old-timers in the International.

George Rubin

The cloak department of the Eastern Out-of-Town Department is headed by George Rubin.

George's father was a carpenter, and as a boy he learned his father's trade. In 1906, at the age of sixteen, he left Russia and settled in Philadelphia. There he became a cloak presser and joined the local pressers' union in 1909. During the Philadelphia cloakmakers' strike of 1913 he was very active on the picket line and became a popular figure among the workers. But his career in the union was interrupted by the World War, during which he served overseas. Upon his discharge from the Army in 1920, he went back to his trade and two years later became a business agent. In 1926, at the height of the civil war in the International, he was chosen manager of the Philadelphia Cloak Joint Board, the only Joint Board in the country which remained practically untouched by Communist infiltration; in fact Rubin was able to help the International financially at a time when it was fighting for its life.

In 1932 Rubin became a vice-president of the International. He took up his present job in 1936. He supervises 8500 cloakmakers in Wander's district.

Rubin's record is that of a man who came up from the picket line. And he does have a strong proletarian touch in his make-up. Honest, direct, somewhat rough though friendly in his manner, he is a typical AFL business agent who has risen to the inner circles of leadership.

Louis Levy

In charge of the International on the West Coast is Louis Levy. There is nothing of the trade union bureaucrat in Levy's make-up. A man of deep libertarian convictions, he began life as a follower of Prince Kropotkin and is to this day a philosophical anarchist who looks at the trade union movement from the point of view of mutualism, the doctrine of collective self-help. In the International he is the most prominent member of a small fellowship of anarcho-syndicalists who were the personal friends

and supporters of President Sigman, such people as Max Bluestein, Rose Pesotta, Rose Mirsky, Simon Farber and Nicholas
Kirtzman. In practical trade union politics this group has always associated itself with the progressive forces in the ILGWU
and has looked askance at the interference of outside political
parties. They were, and are, radical Gompersites.

Louis Levy was born in 1892 in the Ukrainian town of Ro-
manovka, near Kiev. His father was a tailor and taught him the
trade. At the age of twelve Louis was initiated into the labor
movement when he joined a union of tailors' apprentices in his
native province.

In 1907 the family came to Philadelphia and the boy went
to work as a cloak operator's helper. Four years later he came
to New York and joined Local 1 of the cloakmakers. During the
next few years he became very popular among the garment
workers as one of the most active rank-and-filers in the city.
He was especially energetic in promoting the movement to
amalgamate the reefer makers of Local 17 with the cloakmakers
of Local 1. As an anarcho-syndicalist Levy was a devout industrial unionist and considered it outrageous for men working in
the same shop at essentially the same trade to belong to two
different locals. But he couldn't buck the craft separatist influence of Heller and Breslaw, and in 1917 he was expelled from
the union as a "disrupter." For the next three years he tried
to make a living as a glazier but starved most of the time. But
in 1920 he got back into the union and in the same year became
a member of the executive board of Local 1. In 1923 Levy was
elected manager of the local and held the post until the Communists captured the local two years later.

During the civil war Levy was one of the most uncompro-
mising and effective opponents of the Communists. He lifted the
struggle to an intellectual level quite alien to the average union
politician. For eighteen months, while working in the shop, he
and his friends issued a weekly publication, the *Union Worker,*
in which they exposed the tactics of Communist infiltration into
organized labor in much the same spirit in which Kropotkin
polemicized against Lenin.

In 1930, when the civil war was over, Louis Levy once more became the manager of Local 1. And in 1936 his persistent effort to bring about the permanent fusion of Locals 1 and 17 was realized; Local 117 was formed with Levy as manager.

In July 1938 Levy had serious breakdown, and after his slow recovery Dubinsky sent him to the Pacific Coast as regional director. Today this region has a membership of over 8000.

Levy went to work at the age of ten and never attended school. But like most philosophical anarchists in the labor movement—of whom Gompers was the outstanding example—his outlook on life and society is thoughtful, mature and seasoned by a wide reading of social literature.

Jennie Matyas

A very interesting personality in Levy's district is Jennie Matyas. In 1910, at the age of fifteen, she joined the old Local 25 of the New York waistmakers. Thirty-three years later, in 1943, she received her A.B. cum laude from the University of California. The three decades in between were filled with every variety of union activity, occasionally interrupted by scholarships to educational institutions in America and Europe. Today she is the manager of the knit-goods workers in San Francisco, and she represents the AFL on the National Women's Advisory Committee of the War Manpower Commission.

Bernard Shane and H. D. Langer

The leading representative of the International in Canada is Bernard Shane, general organizer in Montreal.

Shane is an old-time cloakmaker who joined the union in 1909 and preceded Louis Levy as manager of Local 1 in New York. Like Levy he has always been a philosophical anarchist. After working at his trade and as an organizer in New York, Philadelphia, Chicago, St. Louis and Toronto, Shane was sent in 1934 to take charge of the Montreal market. A skillful organizer and negotiator, he was the first to unionize effectively the conservative French-Canadian garment workers.

The other important garment center in Canada is Toronto, where the leader of the ILGWU is H. D. Langer. Langer is a Canadian who joined the union in Toronto in 1918 at the age of sixteen. For the next twelve years he worked in a shop, and in 1930 he became a business agent for the local Joint Board. Today he is its manager and also the general secretary of the Canadian Co-ordinating Committee of the International. A good mixer and able citizen, Langer stands high in the labor and community life of Toronto.

Frank R. Crosswaith and Maida Springer

There are almost 10,000 Negro members in the ILGWU. Some years ago Dubinsky invited Frank R. Crosswaith, a well-known Negro labor man, to join the union staff as a general organizer. A native of the Virgin Islands, where he was born in 1892, Crosswaith came to this country in his teens and spent almost eight years in the Navy as a mess boy. Back in civil life he fell under the influence of Debs and ever since then he has been an active socialist and trade union organizer as well as an important figure in the Negro world. In 1942 Mayor La Guardia appointed him a member of the New York City Housing Authority. A powerful speaker, Crosswaith has been of great value to the International as a propagandist for democratic and anti-Communist unionism among the colored people.

A very different type of Negro leader in the International is Maida Springer. Born in Panama in 1910, she came to this country as a little girl and became a dressmaker. In 1932 she joined Local 22 of the dressmakers and from 1939–43 she served on its executive board. Since then she has been the educational director of Local 132 of the plastic and novelty workers. Reserved, extremely intelligent and thoroughly familiar with the many-sided and delicate problem of race relations, Maida Springer's influence among the colored garment workers extends far beyond her own local union.

Rose Pesotta

The only woman vice-president of the International is Miss Rose Pesotta, who likes to work as a dress operator in a shop whenever she is not busy as a union organizer. This is quite unusual for a vice-president of an American union to whom a high union post is always available. She is a philosophical anarchist with a distaste for political entanglements. A woman of energy and charm, she knows how to enlist the loyalty of young workers to the union as a great cause rather than as a mere protective agency. As an organizer she has the dramatic touch of a stage director.

Some years ago she was organizing a number of sportswear plants in Los Angeles, employing mostly young women. She picked out a dozen of the best lookers, dressed them up in stunning evening gowns, and then they all marched up and down in front of the Biltmore Hotel. They made it very clear that they were not trying to picket the hotel but to bring their case before the public. Movie stars and other fashionable folk gathered around the girls and wanted to know what it was all about. The cops couldn't very well get tough with a bevy of Dorothy Lamours; indeed they became somewhat unnecessarily chivalrous. The papers featured this photogenic demonstration and the employers soon found themselves in the position of so many Simon Legrees exploiting beautiful slave girls—and the strike was quickly settled with union recognition.

Everybody in the ILGWU was mighty proud of Sister Pesotta, even the congenital cynics among the cloakmakers, who are not easily impressed. "What other union, I ask you," an old cloakmaker friend of mine boasted, "has a Joan of Arc who can run a strike like a Gilbert and Sullivan show?"

Rose Pesotta was born in 1896 in the Ukraine. Her father was a merchant and she received a fair education in private schools. In her early teens she joined the underground revolutionary movement, organizing discussion groups among factory workers. In 1913, at the age of seventeen, she came to this country and a year later joined Local 25 of the waistmakers. In 1922 she was elected to the executive board of Local 22, formed as an offshoot of Local 25. During the next decade she held a series of important posts on various strike committees while working steadily as a dress operator. Miss Pesotta is very proud of her craftsmanship. In 1933 she was appointed a general organizer by Dubinsky, and the following year was elected a vice-president. Since then she has been mostly on the go as an organizer and strike leader, conducting campaigns in New York, Los Angeles, San Francisco, Seattle, Boston, Canada and Puerto Rico. In 1936 she was loaned to the CIO to aid in the organization of the Akron rubber workers, and in 1937 she helped organize the automobile workers in Michigan and Ontario.

But in spite of her busy career as an organizer Miss Pesotta's main interest has always been in the educational and social activities of the union. Her leadership is of the romantic-reformist variety so characteristic of many women who rise in social movements. And she has the urge to self-improvement of this type. At one time or another she has attended the Rand School of Social Science, the New School for Social Research, the Bryn Mawr School for Workers in Industry, the Wisconsin Summer School for Workers. In 1926 she graduated from Brookwood Labor College.

The diplomat has been entirely left out of Miss Pesotta's make-up. She is apt to say exactly what she thinks, let the chips fall where they may. And sometimes they fall on the path of her influence upon her colleagues.

THE INDUSTRIAL FUTURE

Today the ILGWU reaches into every section of the United States and Canada and into every branch of the women's garment trades—from Miami to Vancouver and from plastic ornaments to tailor-made coats and suits. Its income in 1943 was almost $8,300,000, of which every penny was accounted for. Such is the International empire, which dresses half the American nation. But empires, in this revolutionary age, have an uneasy time of it. The future of the women's garment trades is perplexing and uncertain; and how uncertain can be dramatically indicated by some of the questions which are worrying the International.

1. What will happen when war production ceases and thousands of former garment workers, mostly young women, now engaged in making airplanes, try to get back to making dresses?

2. What will happen when the new and highly rationalized garment factories set up during the war, often with the assistance of government funds, cease producing uniforms and parachutes and go into civilian production? Most of these plants are operating in traditionally non-union and low-wage sections of the country. How will the International meet this challenge of technical efficiency coupled with low working standards?

3. Will peace restore the prewar tendency of the garment industry to drift away from the old established and union-disciplined centers to new and sparsely unionized sections of the country? Will the bitter competition between the various markets be resumed?

4. What will happen when the greatly increased wartime purchasing power of the American woman is suddenly reduced by billions of dollars; and when, at the same time, the garment industry will have to compete for its share of the shrunken national income with renewed mass production of such household needs as vacuum cleaners, washing machines and refrigerators?

5. Will the simplification in design, accelerated by the war, continue, or will there be a reaction against functionalism and streamlining in dress?

Will the American designer be able to hold his own after the war or will Paris once more become the fashion capital of America?

6. What will be the impact on the industry of synthetic fabrics so highly developed during the war? "Wool" can be made of milk, of redwood bark, or of a compound of coal, air and water. "Silk" can be made of fiber glass or of coal, oil and salt. Synthetic rubber is used in the manufacture of corsets and brassières. In time DuPont and other such laboratories may dress the American woman in thin air.

7. What effect will scientific management have on the craft system in the union? Some modern plants in the South and Southwest are already operating on the "section system," in which the operator no longer sews the entire garment but only certain parts of it, which are then routed to the next section. A few plants are even introducing the "line system," which is an assembly line without a belt.

8. Finally, what is the future of the needle? There already exists a "sewing" machine which welds fabrics with radio short waves instead of stitching them together with needle and thread. What will happen when the needle and thread, or their descendants, can sew everything in the same plant, from panties to parachutes and from men's ties to topcoats? What are the jurisdictional storms ahead?

These questions will have to be answered, some in the immediate and others in the more remote postwar future. Unlike the United Mine Workers, which is an indivisible industrial union, the ILGWU is a closely knit federation of almost autonomous crafts. And their delicate interrelation is sensitive to the least pressure of technological or managerial development, to every change in the use of fabrics and to the slightest shift in the wind of fashion. Difficulties may develop not only between the various crafts in the International but also with the men's tailors in the Amalgamated Clothing Workers. Some factories under Amalgamated jurisdiction are already manufacturing, in more or less speak-easy secretiveness, "mannish" suits and coats for women.

The leaders of the International are uneasy. "To fight technological development and change in public habits makes no sense," Dubinsky told me. "And jurisdictional arguments will settle nothing. When the printers tried to fight the linotype machine, the machine hit back and almost wrecked their union —until they accepted it, and now they're better off than ever before. The thing to do is to meet the situation."

In 1943 the General Executive Board appointed a special subcommittee of seven vice-presidents to survey the industrial future of the women's garment workers. And the research and engineering departments of the union are already hard at work on all these problems.

CONCLUSIONS

Some years ago *Life* magazine ran a long picture story about the International, headed *A Great and Good Union Points the Way for the American Labor Movement*. Dubinsky was pleased. "That was a grand story," he said. "But we mustn't take it too seriously," he added. "After all, the ILGWU is in a consumers' and not in a basic industry, and most of our people belong to minority groups. We have never kidded ourselves that we could lead the whole of American labor. The best we can do is to lead ourselves as well as we can—and thus contribute something to the rest of the labor movement."

This business of leadership is nowadays often on the minds of the more thoughtful labor men. Of late a self-critical note, more mood than indictment, has crept into their talk. They lament "the lack of leadership" in labor, a lack for which they blame the historical moment rather than individuals. They are afraid of the increasing anti-labor propaganda. They have a vague but oppressive sense of anxiety about labor's place and power after the war. And when in this prognostic plight, they often end up with a nostalgic tribute to Samuel Gompers. Then they are apt to return to the father image of the tribe.

"If Gompers were alive today," Dubinsky told me, "a lot of things would be different. There never would have been the split between the AFL and CIO. For it was obvious from the vote in the 1935 AFL convention that in another year or two we industrial unionists would have had the majority. There was just no one with the old man's unique moral authority to prevent secession.

"It is from the split in organized labor that most of our troubles come. It opened the way for the Communists in the CIO. It was bad for labor's relations with the government. A united labor movement, with the essentially democratic traditions of the AFL, would have been a far more constructive force in our national life than two competing federations which try to use every issue, even issues on which they agree, to outmaneuver each other."

It is Dubinsky's pet theory that all labor needs, in order to play a sane and beneficent public role, is peace and unity in its own ranks. Further than that he doesn't like to think.

Dubinsky's diagnosis is only half true. I too believe that Gompers might have prevented the split in the AFL. But Du-

binsky leaves out a lot of other things Gompers would have said
and done.

Gompers, the irreconcilable enemy of the omnipotent state,
who went so far as to oppose workmen's compensation laws,
would have tried to keep labor from plunging headlong into the
New Deal. He undoubtedly would have welcomed Section 7A
of the NIRA, which permitted labor to organize freely, but it is
very doubtful whether he would have approved the corporativism
of the NRA setup. He would have fought the concentration of
power in the hands of the executive, legislation by decrees and
directives, the growth of the bureaucratic Leviathan in general.
He would have raised holy hell when Mr. Wallace proclaimed
that we have too much "Bill of Rights democracy" and not
enough of the "economic democracy" of the Soviet variety.

Matthew Woll, the intellectual spokesman of the AFL, who
was closest to Gompers, expresses the fears of our voluntaristic
trade union movement very clearly in an editorial in the February
1944 issue of the *American Photo Engraver*, the official journal
of his union.

The late Huey Long [Mr. Woll writes] once remarked with the
authority of an experienced demagogue that if Fascism ever came
to America it would come masked as anti-Fascism. The mechanism
for postwar Fascism camouflaged as anti-Fascism is here already in
the steadily proliferating federal agencies set up to mobilize our industry and manpower for war.

The psychological atmosphere in which Fascism flourishes is beginning to make itself uncomfortably evident. It is evident in the administrative arrogance which substitutes government by directive
for government by law, in an even more frequent resort to the smear
and the frame-up in lieu of honest replies to criticism or queries on
matters of public concern.

I quote Mr. Woll to indicate a growing feeling among the
traditional democrats in American labor. To be sure, the totalitarian undertows in our proliferating bureaucracy are not
fascist and may not lead to fascism. They are, however, characteristic of all Popular Front regimes—such as the immediate

prewar government in France—which provoked fascist reaction.

But Dubinsky refuses to see the dangers in this situation. And so do the other leaders of the International. Their socialist background does not predispose them to view the encroaching state with such alarm, though in the labor movement they fight all totalitarian trends with discriminating vigilance. But probably the most decisive factor in their uncritical devotion to the New Deal and the Roosevelt Administration is the immense success the ILGWU has had this last decade. It is easy for them to be enthusiastic about an Administration under which their union has grown from 40,000 to 310,000, with all the glory and power which that implies. For all his social intelligence, Dubinsky lacks that final touch which would lift his high-minded opportunism to the level of statesmanship.

Early in 1944 four Liberty ships were launched in Baltimore. They were christened the Morris Hillquit, the Meyer London, the Benjamin Schlesinger and the Morris Sigman.

The four men for whom these ships were named were among the founders, builders and guides of the organized garment workers. Their total careers spanned half a century before the New Deal. When they came to this country as young men they settled in the ghettos of New York and Chicago, went to work in the sweatshops and threw themselves into the labor movement.

Immigrants and radicals, bringing with them the best traditions of Old World libertarianism, they soon ranged themselves with our indigenous labor and radical movements, in whose struggles—and factional fights—they partook. Under their guidance, the women's garment workers fought their way through every insurgent philosophy—from the Knights of Labor to the Communists—until they finally arrived at a philosophy of right-wing democratic trade unionism which characterizes the American labor movement at its best.

The launching of the four ships dramatizes the long journey the women's tailors have made from the alien slums of our cities and the purple class struggles of the last century. Today the International is one of the most constructive unions in the country. And it is constructive precisely because its roots are so deep in the traditions of American labor. Its progressivism has grown organically out of these traditions, which it has helped to create in its long and stormy history.

In recent years the ILGWU has become part of American community life far more than at any time in its past. Before the Dubinsky administration the International restricted its outside interests almost exclusively to labor and radical causes. It was active in the defense of Tom Mooney and of Sacco and Vanzetti. It supported the Great Steel Strike of 1919 and other important union campaigns. It aided friendly laborite institutions and journals, such as the Rand School and the old socialist New York *Call*.

Today the International still aids such causes. But it also backs organizations and movements which have nothing in particular to do with organized labor. Local union officers in various parts of the country serve with business, church and social leaders on boards of philanthropic and educational institutions and are active in civic bodies of all sorts. The International is munificent in its gifts to organizations like the American Red Cross, the Federal Council of Churches of Christ in America, the Federation of Jewish Philanthropies, hospitals, orphanges, homes for the aged, refugee organizations, community chests.

In the war effort the ILGWU has surpassed itself. In the first four War Loan drives it raised a total of $85,000,000. It has contributed millions to Allied and American war relief. And its affiliates throughout this country and Canada have mobilized their people for civilian defense and war work.

The evolution of the International has been, in a very significant sense, the evolution of a small union, bounded by its own little labor and radical world, into a great institution of labor which is an integral part of the American community. This evolution has taken place in our labor movement in general. But the story of the International illumines it most dramatically because, though it is one of our oldest unions into whose making has gone every native working-class expression since late Reconstruction days, it has had to absorb wave after wave of immigrant workers and assimilate them into American life. The dialectic of this process has been the Americanization of America for three centuries.

Index

Holt, Hamilton, editor of the *Independent,* 70; president of Rollins College in Florida, 73; 285
Holzer, Louis, acquitted of murder charge, 93–94
Hoover, Herbert Clark, 203
Hourwich, Dr. Isaac A., chief clerk of cloakmakers' Joint Board, 81–88, 92, 110, 113, 121, 314, 333
Hourwich, Nicholas, son of Dr. Isaac A., 112–13
Howard, Charles P., 265
Howe, Elias, inventor of the sewing machine, 3
Hull, Cordell, 201
Hull House, in Chicago, 14
Hutcheson, William, 197, 230
Hyman, Louis, chairman of the Joint Action Committee, 126; sketch of his career, 127–30; 134–37, 141, 145–46, 249

"Immigrant unions," 23
Independent, 70, 73
Independent Cloak Pressers Union, in the IWW, 54–55, 120
Independent Labor League, dissolved, 251
Industrial Co-operative, 168
Industrial Council, 141
Industrial Relations Commission, 84
Industrial Revolution, 2
Industry Planning program of Julius Hochman, 259, 308, 311
Industry Planning through Collective Bargaining, pamphlet by Julius Hochman, 223
International Cloak Makers Union of America, 42, 44
International Clothing Workers Congress, 225
International Federation of Trade Unions, 225
International Labor Office of the League of Nations, 190
International Ladies' Garment Workers Union (ILGWU), 15 *passim;* its foundation, 23; its cultural activities, and the stage show *Pins*

and Needles, 20; receives charter from AFL, 48; its growth, 49; its donations, 98; civil war, 107 *et seq.;* effect of 1929 crash, 151; suspended from AFL, 269; its educational program, 286–94, 303–4; athletics and health, 298–300; effect of the war, 308; its engineering help, 317–18; its empire, 326–27
International Ladies Garment Workers of the World, a racket, 93
International Trade Union Educational League, 133
International Union Bank, 237
International Workingmen's Association, the First International, 29–30
Italian American Labor Council, 239, 241
IWW (Wobblies), attempt to wreck AFL, 54; 7, 27, 29, 32, 55, 112, 120, 133, 158

Jacksonian democracy, 25
Jacksonian Era cited, 2–3
Jeffersonian democracy, 25–26, 157
Jewish Daily Forward, 41, 45, 50, 63, 66, 86, 92, 102–3, 162
Jewish Federation of Labor, 37
Jews in the garment industry, 4 *et seq.*
Johnson, Carl E. (Scott), 115
Johnson, Gen. Hugh Samuel, NRA administrator, 207, 211, 244, 256
Johnson, Dr. Samuel, 83; his adage on patriotism, 281
Joint Action Committee, 126–28
Joint Board of Cloakmakers, of Chicago, 50, 75–76, 143, 328; of New York, 54 *passim;* merged with dressmakers, 124, 222–23; separated, 154; 284
Joint Board of the Dressmakers, 116; merged with cloakmakers, 124, 222–23; separated, 154; Philadelphia wins strike, 206
Joint Board of Sanitary Control, in cloakmaking industry, 67–68

Jonasson, Meyer, cloak manufacturer, 38
Julian, Mortimer, elected president of ILGWU, 56
Junior Size Creation of St. Louis dress industry, 313
Justice, official organ of ILGWU, 98, 100, 119, 123, 181–83, 288, 301, 325
Justicia, Spanish organ of ILGWU, 301

Kaplan, Benjamin, 229
Katovsky, Abraham, of the Cleveland Joint Board, 328–29, 331
Keats, John, 291
Kelley, Florence, factory inspector, 79, 87
Kellogg, Paul, editor of the *Survey*, 88
Kelly, Edward Joseph, mayor of Chicago, 328
Kibitzer, humorous journal, 234
Kid Dropper (Nathan Kaplan), gangster, 253
Kirchwey, Freda, publisher of the *Nation*, on a picket line, 77
Kirchwey, George Washington, dean of Columbia Law School, 89
Kirtzman, Nicholas, 116, 335
Kleinman, Henry, indicted but acquitted, 94
Knights of Labor, Noble Order of the, activity in the garment trades, 34–35, 284; losing ground there, 37, 39, 43; 17, 26–29, 31–32, 45–47, 156, 158, 344
Know-Nothingism, 25, 28
Koppenheim, Louis, 43
Kramer, Philip, 329–30
Krankenkasse, sick-benefit society, 180
Kreindler, Charles, 181, 306, 329–31
Kropotkin, Peter Alexeivich, 6, 236, 334–35
Kunz, Morris, 43

Labor Lyceum, 48
Labor Stage in New York, becomes

part of ILGWU, produces *Steel*, by John Wexley, 296; folds up, 298
Labor Temple, 284
Ladies' Garment Cutter, 170
Ladies Garment Worker, official organ of the ILGWU, 81, 182; renamed *Justice*, 98
Ladies Tailors of Chicago, furnish strikebreakers for cloak manufacturers, 76
Ladies Waist Makers Union Locals 12 and 25, 60
La Follette, Fola, on a picket line, 77
La Follette, Robert Marion, Jr., 318
La Guardia, Fiorello Henry, mayor of New York City, 192, 196, 297, 323
Langer, H. D., Toronto leader of ILGWU, 337
Langer, Louis, 125, 131
Lanza, "Socks," gangster, 138
Lassalle, Ferdinand, 30
Lavelle, Msgr. Michael J., 63
Lefkowitz, Samuel, indicted but acquitted, 94
Legs Diamond gang, hired by employers in ILGWU strike, 138; disappear, 140
Lehman, Herbert H., governor of New York, lends ILGWU $25,000, 151; 136, 152, 256
Leibowitz, Herman, strikebreaker killed in cloakmakers' strike, 93
Leiserson, Dr. William Morris, quoted on the task system, 10–11
Lemlich, Clara, her challenge to a mass meeting, 61–62
Lenin, Nikolai, 31–32, 82, 114, 335
Lepke (Louis Buchalter), gangster, 13, 141, 253–55
Levine, Aaron, friend of Dubinsky's, 165–66
Levy, Abraham, lawyer, 93
Levy, Louis, 116, 219, 250, 334–36
Lewis, John Llewellyn, of the United Mine Workers, 16 *passim;* organizes the CIO with help of the Communists, 33; his "Canossa,"